What Is
Political Islam?

What Is
Political Islam?

Jocelyne Cesari

LYNNE
RIENNER
PUBLISHERS

BOULDER
LONDON

Published in the United States of America in 2018 by
Lynne Rienner Publishers, Inc.
1800 30th Street, Boulder, Colorado 80301
www.rienner.com

and in the United Kingdom by
Lynne Rienner Publishers, Inc.
3 Henrietta Street, Covent Garden, London WC2E 8LU

Library of Congress Cataloging-in-Publication Data
Names: Cesari, Jocelyne, author.
Title: What is political Islam? / Jocelyne Cesari.
Description: Boulder, Colorado : Lynne Rienner Publishers, Inc., 2018. |
  Includes bibliographical references and index.
Identifiers: LCCN 2017035339 | ISBN 9781626376922 (hardcover : alk. paper)
Subjects: LCSH: Islam and politics.
Classification: LCC BP173.7 .C473 2018 | DDC 320.55/7—dc23
LC record available at https://lccn.loc.gov/2017035339

British Cataloguing in Publication Data
A Cataloguing in Publication record for this book
is available from the British Library.

Printed and bound in the United States of America

 The paper used in this publication meets the requirements
of the American National Standard for Permanence of
Paper for Printed Library Materials Z39.48-1992.

5   4   3   2   1

Contents

Acknowledgments

Thank you to the colleagues and friends who have obliged me to sharpen my ideas through multiple exchanges, conferences, and workshops: Nathan Brown, Jose Casanova, Jonathan Fox, Robert Hefner, and John Voll.

Special thanks for their institutional support to the Berkley Center for Religion, Peace, and World Affairs at Georgetown University, the Cadbury Center for the Public Understanding of Religion at the University of Birmingham, and the Prince Alwaleed Bin Talal Islamic Studies Program at Harvard University.

I would like to thank especially my two remarkable research assistants, who have worked tirelessly with me to make this book happen: Kathleen Guan and Frederick O'Loughlin. Special thanks to Waskito Jati for his invaluable feedback on the Indonesia chapter.

1

Political Islam: The Nexus of State, Religion, and Nation

In the March 2015 issue of *Atlantic Monthly*, Princeton scholar Bernard Haykel declared, "Muslims who call the Islamic State [ISIS] un-Islamic are typically . . . embarrassed and politically correct, with a cotton-candy view of their own religion 'that neglects' what their religion has historically and legally required."[1] His words were a response—albeit simplified—to multiple declarations from clerics around the world who had condemned the caliphate as un-Islamic.[2] Haykel's article drew scholars of Islam and politics into the public debate in an unprecedented way. Some agreed that ISIS is indeed Islamic, while others rejected this premise. Prominent political figures such as then secretary of state John Kerry added to the confusion by calling ISIS's leaders apostates.[3]

This controversy encapsulates two contentious questions that run through most scholarship on Islam and politics. First, is political Islam in any way decipherable from the tenets of the Islamic tradition, or is it mostly about secular actors misusing religious references? Second, is political Islam an exclusively modern political phenomenon, or is it indebted to long-standing Islamic religious commitments?

Most political scientists either dodge these questions or downplay the Islamic dimension of political Islam. They see it as a

1

multifaceted social movement and focus on its modes of recruit-ment, mobilization, and strategy.[4] They also emphasize opportunity structures such as the broader political context. For example, the growing influence of Islamic movements in the last three decades is usually attributed to the political liberalization of the 1990s.[5] Although this scholarship has provided a wealth of information on how these movements gain political ground, the question of why they are more influential, compared to other social movements or political groups across Muslim countries, remains unanswered.[6]

In this book, I take on this "why" question. Defining political Islam as a multifaceted religious nationalism, I begin with the premise that it has materialized due to the cultural and political specificities of the nation-states built on the collapse of the Ottoman Empire. Essentially, I shift the focus of the debate from professional Islamic political parties or groups to the shaping of modern political cultures.

My argument differs from the scholarly perspective dominant among religious and Islamic studies, which tends to pitch modern politics and the state as incompatible with the Islamic tradition. For example, in *The Impossible State*, Wael Hallaq argues that the "modern state is a bad fit for Muslims" due to the incompatibility and contradictions between "Islamic governance" and the "West-ern" modern state. In Hallaq's view, the European invention of a sovereign modern state goes against the "Islamic state," which is organized "organically" around God's sovereignty with sharia as the moral code. Islamic politics is therefore solely confined to "executive rulers of rotating dynasties . . . external to the embry-onic tight embrace between jurists and community." The organiz-ing principle of life is the individual Muslim's "care of the self" and adherence to the sharia.[7]

Historical reality, however, reveals a much more complicated dialectic between ideas and social contexts, rendering this incom-patibility theory difficult to hold outside the realm of normative theories.[8] In fact, political Islam is better defined as a political culture that cannot be read exclusively in light of the premodern Islamic tradition because it is the result of the Islamic tradition's dual processes of nationalization and reformation/westernization. In this respect, I contend that there is no opposition between the state and Islam, since the nation-state is the major structural element that made political Islam possible in the first place.

There is a solid scholarship describing both the nation-building processes in postcolonial Muslim countries[9] and the reformation of Islamic thinking since the nineteenth century, especially the pioneering work of Bobby Sayyid and, most recently, Nathan Brown.[10] However, at best, these two threads of knowledge do not inform each other; at worst, they conflict. In the pages that follow, I combine both threads of knowledge with the hope of overcoming the modern/traditional and secular/religious dichotomies. In discussing the doctrinal changes in Islamic thinking and how they are intertwined with the building of national identities and state institutions, I intend not to attribute all religious changes to the rise of the nation-state but to demonstrate how modern political conditions have altered religious concepts of community, law, and tradition.

It has been proven abundantly that most theories or concepts used in political science have been shaped by the Western experience and then applied to political situations in Muslim countries (or elsewhere). For this reason, the religion/politics and secular/religious divides inherited from the European and North American political experiences influence scholarly understanding of what is religious or Islamic.[11] Hence, most scholars of politics dismiss the life experiences of Muslims in various contexts as "subjective" and therefore irrelevant to "objective" knowledge. By contrast, a second thread of scholarship, mostly in anthropology and sociology, has analyzed Western cultural influence as a tool of political imperialism and focused on the religious experiences of Muslims that stand at odds with the westernized political contexts in which they take place.[12]

This book is not another attempt to objectify political Islam by dismissing the religious variable. Nor is it a project of restituting the "incommensurability" of political Islam because of its authentically Islamic dimension. While the exportation of nationalism and state is the direct outcome of the unequal relationship of power between the West and the other parts of the world, it is only one part of the story. The other part is the role of local actors in adapting and recreating these concepts. While Western concepts were indeed imposed during colonialism, they were neither totally endorsed nor entirely rejected by local elites. Furthermore, the Western state was not merely an oppressive or annihilating force in the preexisting reality. In fact, the promoters of "indigenous" tradition often readapted it willingly and sometimes in opposition to the colonial powers in order to compete with foreign political concepts. To assume that the Islamic religion and local cultures remained authentic is to understand political Islam only as a reaction of "indigenous" actors to preserve their "untouched" heritage.

Similarly, the local champions of the Western culture did not simply duplicate it. It is therefore misleading to analyze the modus operandi of Muslim "liberal" "secular" states within the parameters of the ways European or North American counterparts behave. For example, in *Formations of the Secular*, Talal Asad draws a sharp distinction between Arab nationalism and Islamism. He argues that Arab nationalism is committed to the doctrine of separating law and citizenship from religious affiliation and confining Islamism, which seeks to restore Islam to its central social position, to the private domain.[13]

In fact, as I show in this book, there was no such neat demarcation between "westernized" nationalists and "traditional" Islamist actors. Despite having opposing goals, these two groups were in continuous dialogue from the nineteenth century to the decolonization phase (at least). The effect of this cross-pollination on modern political understandings of religious terms such as *taqlid* (tradition), *ijtihad* (interpretation), and *ummah* (community) has been underestimated. Both groups, even if not in agreement, rely on these contemporary meanings.

Consider the renewed academic interest in Middle Eastern sectarianism in the wake of the Iraqi and Syrian crises. Some scholars such as Saba Mahmood and Nader Hashemi and Danny Postel see sectarianism as a reaction against the "imported" state or the Western influence on the region.[14] Others—such as Melani Cammett, Ben White, Max Weiss, or Toby Matthiesen—see it as triggered by the incomplete or failed adoption of liberal governance.[15] By addressing the legal and political conditions for sectarianists, these scholars take the role of the state seriously. Nonetheless, they neglect the changes brought by the state to preexisting religious communities and groups. As such, sectarian divides are often seen as the remnants and/or exacerbation of the *millet* system of the Ottoman Empire, when in fact they are a different beast entirely.[16] The transition from Muslim empire to nation-state marked a decisive rupture, one that drastically changed the social and cultural conditions of the *millet* system.[17]

The presence of religious communities and Islamic concepts within nation-states is due not simply to their resilience and unchanged nature. They are, in fact, unprecedented hybrid institutions, concepts, and ideas. They can be considered "vernacular modernities," not because they are "untouched" indigenous alternatives to external Western modernity but because they are syncretic responses by local actors faced with new challenges.

Therefore, it is important to take into consideration the way all actors have played a decisive role in adapting/adopting external concepts, granting them specific meanings by using indigenous terminology and in the process changing or adding new connotations to these indigenous concepts. Political Islam is not the outcome of an impossible clash between Western modernity and authentic noncolonized Islam, as it is often presented by Islamist actors and (some) scholars alike. Rather, it results from grafting the concepts of religion, nationalism, and secularism in Muslim territories. It must be understood in terms of its own cultural premises and not as a mediation of forces from elsewhere, whether it is a transfer of economic grievances, a medium for old class politics, or a vehicle for new political identities.

Hence, it is necessary to go beyond groups' interests and pay more attention to institutional projects. In this respect, political Islam derives as much from the institutional space it inhabits as from the social position of individuals who become Islamist. My investigation starts with the introduction of the concepts of nation and state, meaning the institutional architecture of social relations shared by all political actors, secular and Islamic. Consequently, the key to my argument is the assertion that a proper analysis of religious and political practice depends on a robust conceptualization of the modern nation-state.

State-centered approaches to religious mobilizations are undoubtedly significant.[18] They usually emphasize the tensions created by the self-governing power of religious groups, particularly religious institutions, in the face of state power. When it comes to Muslim countries, state actions are usually considered a key factor in the politicization of religion.[19] More generally, state-centered scholarship examines control of religious activities by the state, as well as the state's appropriation of religious symbols and functions.[20] Some sociologists, such as Colin Beck, have argued that state-building activities, specifically a regime's incorporation of religious institutions and symbolism, are the primary explanation for the variation in Islamic mobilization across the Middle East.[21]

However, while the development of state policy is crucial, cultural processes cannot be reduced to state actions.[22] As such, I prefer the Foucauldian concept of governmentality, which emphasizes the connection between techniques of the self (governing the self) and techniques of domination (governing others).[23] Governmentality refers to different procedures for regulating human behaviors; it is not limited to state actions or policies. In fact, state actions are not decipherable outside the ingrained acceptance by citizens of these techniques, or what Norbert Elias calls *habitus*. Therefore, we cannot explain policies without analyzing the sets of acquired ideas, emotions, behavioral codes, and social etiquettes that people in a given territory associate with political power and community. Under these conditions, religion becomes a significant mode of power. Analyzing the politicization of religion in general, as well as Islam in particular, means paying attention to specific governmental apparatuses and relevant bodies of knowledge.

Religious traditions, organizations, discourses, and practices are a part of governmentality even when they have relative autonomy from the state. Notably, Islam was already an institutional space before the nation-state. Through a network of sacred sites and ritual spaces, community centers, associations, schools, hospitals, courts, and charities, Islam offered a social space from which to mobilize, as well as a concrete cosmos within which to imagine and prefigure an alternative vision of the social. At the same time, Islam remained independent from the political institutions of the caliphate. With the building of the nation-state, Islamic institutions became identified with the nation. Meanwhile, state rulers simultaneously restructured them to fit the recomposition of the Islamic religion around the notions of private belief and individuality.

In sum, I argue that political Islam first emerged as a modern technique of governmentality with the adoption of the nation-state and the westernization/secularization of Islamic tradition. From this perspective, nationalism—that is, the loyalties organized through the state in the name of the political community—creates the nation, rather than the reverse.[24] Nationalism is a program for the co-constitution of the state and the territorially bounded population whose name it speaks.[25] In Roger Friedland's words, "Nationalism is not simply an ideology: it is also a set of discursive practices by which the territorial identity of a state and the cultural identity of the people whose collective representation it claims are constituted in a singular fact."[26] While nationalism offers a form of representation, it does not determine the content of the representation or the identity of the represented collective subject, whether they are civic, liberal, ethnic, and/or religious.

One may contend that my linking of political Islam with religious nationalism is hardly new. Scholars who have made this argument before have emphasized that Islamism shares with Arab nationalism a strong anti-Western sentiment that has become more influential after the decline of secular nationalism.[27] However, as I demonstrate in this book, political Islam is not simply a religious version of the national ideology, or rather, merely an ideology. More accurately, political Islam is the cultural bedrock on which both nationalist and Islamist ideologies are grounded.

In this respect, political Islam takes four main forms—coercive, hegemonic, civil, and transnational or global—which are at play today in both national and international contexts. To elaborate, first, political Islam is a technique of coercion and discipline exacted by the state on a given territory and population, creating cultural identities in which national and Islamic belongings become intertwined. In Chapter 2, I provide a conceptual history of key terms such as *ummah* (community) and *taqlid* (tradition), which are critical to the shaping of this modern political culture by "secular" and religious actors alike.

Chapter 3 presents the dominant form of religious nationalism, which I have called hegemonic in my previous research.[28]

Building on this earlier work, I focus here on Egypt and Turkey, because they usually serve as exemplary cases of secular nationalism. In both Egypt and Turkey, religious hegemony occurred because Islamic institutions and religious authorities were absorbed into the state system, which made Islam central to national identity but also up for ideological competition. Based on the findings of my previous research, in this chapter I present the correlation between religious hegemony and low levels of democracy across countries. Hegemonic Islam has a direct influence on civil liberties and human rights ranging from freedom of speech to sexual liberties. I also discuss the inclusion-moderation paradigm and argue that the insertion of Islamiç parties into political systems is not a sufficient condition for moderation. As attested by the evolution of the Justice and Development Party in Turkey since 2007, when the Islamic party reflects the majoritarian national culture and is a part of hegemonic Islam, there is less probability that it will moderate ideologically.

In Chapter 4, I discuss Indonesia and Senegal as two of the few Muslim countries not defined by hegemonic Islam (i.e., the state has not absorbed religious institutions, and religious diversity is acknowledged). In these two countries, can Islam be considered as a form of religious nationalism close to a civil religion? Robert Bellah's decisive work has described civil religion as the nonsectarian religious beliefs shared by all citizens regarding the symbols and history of their nation. The cases of Indonesia and Senegal, however, are better explained by introducing Jean-Jacques Rousseau's original take on civil religion. Rousseau analyzes civil religion as a state-centered project aimed at securing the loyalties of citizens through rituals and symbols. Thus, in this chapter I look at civil Islam as a specific combination of social and state-centered approaches to religion and show how the social dimension of civil Islam in Senegal has superseded the state-centered project, while the opposite has taken place in Indonesia.

Chapter 5 addresses radical transnational Islamic movements as the most recent expressions of political Islam. Instead of interpreting these movements as the negation of the religious nationalism described in Chapters 3 and 4, I show that they operate under the political meanings infused into religious concepts at the time of nation-building. In other words, global political Islam, especially in its radical forms, is the global dissemination and alteration of the national political cultures that see the *ummah* as a transnational imagined community. In this respect, the globalization of political Islam illustrates a broader trend, the globalization of nationalism, that underlies most international conflicts today.

Throughout the book, I present hegemonic, civil, and global political Islam as evolving categories that continuously interact and compete with each other, both nationally and internationally.

Notes

1. Wood, Graeme. "What ISIS Really Wants." *Atlantic*. March 2015. http:// www.theatlantic.com/features/archive/2015/02/what-isis-really-wants/384980.
2. One of the rare religious authorities to do so was Shaikh Ibrahim Saleh al-Hussaini, who called on other Muslim leaders to declare ISIS "infidels" at a conference hosted by al-Azhar University. The shaikh continued to say that "a Muslim who fights another Muslim is an infidel." See Ibrahim, Ayman S. "So ISIS Is Not Infidel—Are Christians?" *First Things*. December 16, 2014. https://www.firstthings.com/web-exclusives/2014/12/so-isis-is-not-infidelare -christians.
3. Kaplan, Michael. "ISIS Not Islamic? John Kerry Calls Terror Group 'Apostates.'" *International Business Times*. February 3, 2016. http://www.ibtimes .com/isis-not-islamic-john-kerry-calls-terror-group-apostates-2291791.
4. See Clark, Janine A. *Islam, Charity, and Activism: Middle-Class Networks and Social Welfare in Egypt, Jordan, and Yemen*. Bloomington: Indiana University Press, 2004; Schwedler, Jillian. *Faith in Moderation: Islamist Parties in Jordan and Yemen*. Cambridge: Cambridge University Press, 2007; Snow, David A., and Scott C. Byrd. "Ideology, Framing Processes, and Islamic Terrorist Movements." *Mobilization* 12, no. 2 (2007): 119–136.
5. Sutton, Phillip, and Stephen Vertigans. "Islamic 'New Social Movements'? Radical Islam, al-Qa'ida and Social Movement Theory." *Mobilization* 11, no. 1 (2006): 101–115.
6. Hafez, Mohammed M. *Why Muslims Rebel: Repression and Resistance in the Islamic World*. Boulder, CO: Lynne Rienner Publishers, 2003.
7. Hallaq, Wael. *The Impossible State: Islam, Politics, and Modernity's Moral Predicament*. New York: Columbia University Press, 2012, p. 272.
8. For a critique of the incompatibility theory from a legal perspective, see Emon, Anver M. "Codification and Islamic Law: The Ideology Behind a Tragic Narrative." *Middle East Law and Governance* 8 (2016): 275–309.
9. See Nasr, Vali Reza. *Islamic Leviathan: Islam and the Making of State Power*. Oxford: Oxford University Press, 2001; El-Affendi, Abdelwahab. *Who Needs an Islamic State?* London: Grey Seal, 1991.
10. For example, Esposito, John, and John Voll. *Makers of Contemporary Islam*. Oxford: Oxford University Press, 2001; for detailed bibliographical

references related to Islamic reformism, see part one. See also Sayyid, Bobby. *Islamism as Philosophy: Decolonial Horizons*. London: Bloomsbury Academic, 2017; Brown, Nathan. *Arguing Islam After the Revival of Arab Politics*. New York: Oxford University Press, 2016.

11. See Pasha, Mustapha Kamal. "Nihilism and the Otherness of Islam." *Millennium: Journal of International Studies* 42, no. 1 (2013): 177–197; Mirsepassi, Ali, and Tadd Fernee. *Islam, Democracy and Cosmopolitanism: At Home and in the World*. New York: Cambridge University Press, 2016.

12. See Asad, Talal. *Formations of the Secular: Christianity, Islam, Modernity*. Stanford, CA: Stanford University Press, 2003; Mahmood, Saba. *Politics of Piety: The Islamic Revival and the Feminist Subject*. Princeton, NJ: Princeton University Press, 2005.

13. Asad, *Formations of the Secular*.

14. See Mahmood, Saba. *Religious Difference in a Secular Age: A Minority Report*. Princeton, NJ: Princeton University Press, 2016; Hashemi, Nader, and Danny Postel. *Sectarianization: Mapping the New Politics of the Middle East*. New York: Oxford University Press, 2017.

15. See Cammett, Melani Claire. *Compassionate Communalism: Welfare and Sectarianism in Lebanon*. Ithaca, NY: Cornell University Press, 2014; White, Ben. *The Emergence of Minorities in the Middle East: The Politics of Community in French Mandate Syria*. Edinburgh: Edinburgh University Press, 2012; Weiss, Max. *In the Shadow of Sectarianism: Law, Shi'ism and the Making of Modern Lebanon*. Cambridge, MA: Harvard University Press, 2010; Matthiesen, Toby. *The Other Saudis: Shiism, Dissent and Sectarianism*. Cambridge: Cambridge University Press, 2014.

16. White, *The Emergence of Minorities*, 59.

17. The term *millet* refers to non-Muslim communities living in an Islamic state. During the Ottoman Empire, the word defined the autonomous religious communities led by separate leaders who connected their groups to the central government. See "Millet." *Encyclopaedia Britannica*. July 20, 1998. https://www.britannica.com/topic/millet-religious-group.

18. See Swanson, Guy. *Religion and Regime: A Sociological Account of the Reformation*. Ann Arbor: University of Michigan Press, 1967; Rokkan, Stein. "Dimensions of State Formation and Nation-Building: A Possible Paradigm for Research on Variations Within Europe." In *The Formation of National States in Western Europe*, ed. Charles Tilly, 562–600. Princeton, NJ: Princeton University Press, 1975.

19. Wiktorowicz, Quintan. "Civil Society as Social Control: State Power in Jordan." *Comparative Politics* 33, no. 1 (2000): 43–61.

20. See Clark, *Islam, Charity, and Activism*; Hafez, *Why Muslims Rebel*; Moaddel, Mansoor. *Jordanian Exceptionalism: A Comparative Analysis of State-Religion Relationships in Egypt, Iran, Jordan, and Syria*. New York: Palgrave MacMillan, 2002; Nasr, *Islamic Leviathan*; Starrett, Gregory. *Putting Islam to Work: Education, Politics, and Religious Transformation in Egypt*. Berkeley: University of California Press, 1998.

21. Beck, Colin J. "State Building as a Source of Islamic Political Organization." *Sociological Forum* 24, no. 2 (June 2009): 337–356.

22. See, for example, the work of Nathan Brown on the Egyptian public space: Brown, *Arguing Islam*.

23. Foucault, Michel. *The Government of Self and Others: Lectures at the Collège de France, 1982–1983*. Edited by Arnold I. Davidson. Translated by

Graham Burchell. Houndmills, Basingstoke, Hampshire, UK: Palgrave Macmillan, 2010.

24. Calhoun, Craig. *Nationalism*. Concepts Social Thought. Minneapolis: University of Minnesota Press, 1998.

25. Friedland, Roger. "Money, Sex, and God: The Erotic Logic of Religious Nationalism." *Sociological Theory* 20, no. 3 (2002): 381–425.

26. Ibid., 386.

27. Luciani, Giacomo. *The Arab State*. Berkeley: University of California Press, 1990.

28. Cesari, Jocelyne. *The Awakening of Muslim Democracy: Religion, Modernity, and the State*. New York: Cambridge University Press, 2014.

2

Muslim Nationalism and the Secular State

Nationhood rooted in religion refers to the alignment of religious collectivity, political sovereignty, and territory. One can argue that the coterminality of territoriality and religion is nothing new, as it can be found in premodern groupings such as tribes, in which territory, people, and God line up.[1] Nonetheless, religion in nationhood is different from its premodern forms because it can be used as the foundation of identity for the majority group as well as for minorities. Even in the case of secular nationalism, which operates on the distinction between the nation and religions, religious communities do not completely separate from the national culture.

For example, Britain and the Netherlands were both seen as Protestant nations until well into the nineteenth century, when Catholics were accepted as legitimate members of the nation.[2] Similarly, the nationalist Bharatiya Janata Party (BJP) in India has consistently framed the nation as an ancient Hindu civilization, diminishing the significance of Muslim and Christian groups and concealing that the contemporary state is actually a product of the imperial encounters with the British.

Specific to Muslim forms of nationalism is the territorialization of Islamic belonging, which manifested itself in ways unknown in the former Muslim empires. This territorialization went hand in hand with the elimination of religious and cultural

13

diversity, which led to a form of religious nationalism that I call hegemonic.[3] Until the nation-state, Islamic belonging did not perfectly align with the *ummah* (community). In fact, before the collapse of the Ottoman Empire, the *ummah* designated the territorial totality under the caliph's rule. This included all groups of Muslims and non-Muslims (Christians, Jews, Hindus, etc.)—a far cry from the current dominant meaning of the term *ummah* as the community of all Muslim believers.

Kemal Karpat discusses how the combined forces of capitalism, European occupation, and Ottoman reforms led to the disintegration and restructuring of social order. In particular, the rise of the urban middle classes transformed collective identifications of Muslims. Revivalist groups considered themselves as part of the universal *ummah* while still purposefully upholding their sense of ethnic and linguistic identity through folk Islam and Sufi paths (*tarikat*). As established local customs gained prominence, the Islamic faith simultaneously became more global and unifying. This change was appealing to the "transforming elites," who advocated Western ideas, as well as to the more traditionalist middle classes, albeit for different reasons.[4]

The advent of the nation-state created a congruence between Muslims of a certain denomination (for example, of the *maleki* versus the *shafi'i* school) and bounded territory.[5] This congruence tended to illegitimate all other religious groups, even when they remained present in the bounded territory (for example, the Alevis in Turkey). This territorialization of Islamic belonging went hand in hand with the elevation of certain Islamic prescriptions as rules for the new nation, such as the folding of Islamic procedures for marriage and divorce into civil law. This is a major breakaway from the modernization process in Europe, where separation of state authority from religious institutions and ideas was the crucial condition for modern citizens.

According to dominant Western narratives and imageries, the religious identity of the individual departs from the national identity and becomes increasingly privatized with the expansion of political and civic rights (even though this story does not reflect the diversity and nuances of such historical processes that took place in European and American nations). Charles Taylor has superbly demonstrated that Western secularity is the culmination of a historical progression of ideas about religion, such that "authentic" religiosity became increasingly associated with personal commitment and a conception of the world as immanent. In premodern times, immanent and transcendent axes were connected in God's project for the believers under the guidance by the Catholic Church. The nation-state broke this connection at the end of the Wars of Religion, when the king took on the regulation of "worldly" affairs (civil law, education, etc.) and relegated the church to the management of the "transcendent." This also meant that the roles of the church on the immanent axis were increasingly understood exclusively in terms of "worldly" goals and values—peace, prosperity, growth, social justice, and the like.[6]

This shift led to two major changes: first, the concept of good political order and social virtues was disconnected from Christian ethics; second, the world became divided between the immanent and the transcendent. This divide was the invention of Latin Christendom and, incidentally, Christendom's contribution to the secularization process.[7] The Western understanding of the secular builds on this separation. It affirms that the "lower," immanent or secular order is all that there is and that the "higher," transcendent order does not regulate the "lower." A believer in the transcendent is therefore expected to keep his beliefs to himself and not to let them influence the political or social practices in which he engages. This is the foundation of the distinction between private convictions and public behaviors.[8]

Because of the influence of this European history on political theories, modernization is seen as a separation between the "this-wordly" and the "otherworldly," relegating religion to faith and beliefs with no direct implication on social and political realms. In this respect, the triad of modernization-privatization-democratization has served as the gold standard for political development. For this reason, political Islam has often been read as the public return of religion and, hence, an anomaly. But we should not forget that Émile Durkheim, the founding father of sociology, emphasized that the symbolic presence of the divine is integral to the construction of the social—an insight that was lost somewhat in the modernization of Europe but has much relevance to political

Islam.[9] Durkheim's insight sheds light on the fact that Islamic symbols, concepts, and institutions have been integral to the constitution of modern political orders. From this perspective, political institutions do not merely appropriate, co-opt, or instrumentalize Islam; they redefine it as part of the new social and political order. Muslim nationalism becomes the collective identity innate to each individual, and submission to the new political system extends from this individualism. Muslim nationalism is not simply state use of Islam for political control. Rather, it is a trait of the psyche of citizens under the new political order, embodied in automatic behaviors inculcated since childhood. Such a mentality is the outcome not simply of an ideological transformation but also of a material one illustrated by the creation of new religious institutions embedded in the state apparatus.

In other words, these deep-rooted attitudes are the results of parallel political and religious reforms starting at the end of the Ottoman Empire, which occurred separately but became inextricably enmeshed. It is important to bear in mind that these changes came with the inclusion of the Muslim Empire within the Westphalian order in the nineteenth century. Until then, concepts of territory and statehood were not central to the definition of Muslim polities, as they were for European states. Additionally, territorial claims in these polities were often in a state of flux due to the movement of people and the multiplicity of ethnic loyalties. It is worth noting that I use the term *state* to refer not to just any form of political governance but specifically to the nation-state that emerged from the breakdown of Christendom at the end of the Wars of Religion and was then exported everywhere through colonialism and trade. To say it differently, there is a tendency nowadays to use the term *state* loosely to refer to political power at all times—for example, the "Ottoman state." Political power is indeed as ancient as human kind, but that does not mean that every form of political power qualifies as a state. Historically, the "nation-state" is a modern construct that concentrates and monopolizes the use of violence over a territory aligned with a population (defined by culture and/or language). This type of political power emerged in Europe and became the international norm with the collapse of empires and the decolonization processes.

Although exported, the nation-state is not simply a duplicate of European states. In fact, in most Muslim countries state leaders forged national identities through different procedures and religious and cultural choices, to the extent that it is more relevant to speak of a "state-nation" than of a "nation-state."[10] The preeminence of the state can be observed throughout all nation-building processes, but the extremely rapid changes initiated by the state elites are specific to the postcolonial countries. There was no Turkish or Pakistani nation before these countries' independence; they were literally created overnight. New identities, forged in less than two generations, irremediably altered the relation of Turks and Pakistanis to Islam.

When it comes to evaluating the postcolonial nation-states, it is often argued that some, if not most, are failed states. This diagnosis is accurate when it comes to the efficiency and legitimacy of the state institutions but much less so when it comes to national identities. In fact, the success of the postcolonial states has been in the shaping of national identities with Islam at the center. Two events set in motion the changes that led to the building of state-nations in the Ottoman Empire: the 1798 expedition of Napoleon Bonaparte in Egypt and the 1856 Treaty of Paris. The former set the parameters for the never-ending debate on Islam and modernity with the rise of the modernist-reformist movement (Salafiyya) and pan-Islamism (a political project of social cohesion based on Islamic belonging). The latter event refers to the Ottoman Empire's symbolic inclusion in the Westphalian order, when, for the first time, at the end of the Crimean War a representative of the Ottoman Empire was invited to the diplomatic negotiations. In the aftermath of this symbolic inclusion, three disparate factors contributed to the adoption in Muslim lands of the Westphalian state system in the first half of the twentieth century: the fall of imperial governments in the region; the rise of local nationalist movements in urban centers such as Cairo, Tunis, Baghdad, and Damascus; and the emergence of states with demarcated territorial boundaries that pursued their self-interest and experienced hostile territorial disputes with neighboring states. Pro-Western, liberal "civilizationalism" also became the dominant paradigm of the Ottoman modernists and reformists, despite strong internal resistance to Western imperialism. This opposition stemmed from the population's objection to the Western critique that the caliphate was not "civilized" enough to gain the loyalty of its Christian subjects. This resistance subsequently led to two different movements: pan-Islamism and pan-Arabism.

The ultimate objective of pan-Islamism was the political unity of the Muslim population under Islam rather than according to race or nationality.[11] Pan-Arabism, on the other hand, recognized the cultural and linguistic affinity among Arabs and aimed to establish a single state for a united Arab nation.[12] Despite divergent political goals, these two movements developed in close proximity in the last period of the Ottoman Empire and were both influenced by European political principles.

Starting in the mid-nineteenth century, with the rise of the Young Turk Movement, constitutionalism and parliamentarism were championed as prerequisites for imperial revival and for reconciliation with Islamic norms, such as the consideration of the concept of *shura* (consultation).[13] The Young Turks did not envision a secular regime; rather, they conceptualized sharia as the foundation for reform and freedom.[14] The pinnacle of this movement's achievements, the Ottoman constitution of 1876—modeled on the Belgian constitution of 1831—established an appointed upper house of Parliament and an elected lower house with legislative authorities. This development signified a shift toward a civic Ottoman identity but did not challenge the traditional structure of the political system. The sultan was not accountable to the elected assembly and was authorized to dissolve it and to suspend the constitution whenever he wanted, which is indeed what Abdulhamid II did in February 1878, when he was convinced that the democratic experiment weakened his position.[15]

Egypt's more prolonged and turbulent experiments with representative assemblies served as the main scene for the modernist Islamic conceptualizations of politics and therefore merit particular attention. None of the advisory institutions established in Cairo during the nineteenth century involved rulers who conceded their monopoly on decisionmaking. However, they signal the linkage between political freedom and social progress as well as the use of Islamic terms to justify Western forms of government. In September 1829, Muhammad Ali (r. 1805–1848) convened, for the first time, the Majlis al-Mushawara, an appointed consultative council that consisted of 156 members and was presided over by his son, Ibrahim. It gathered once a year to carry out its advisory role on matters of administration, education, and public works.[16] Such an institution indicated that the rulers saw certain formalized forms of public participation as a way to enhance their political standing. Ali's official bulletin, *al-Waqa'i' al-Misriyya*, compared the council to the British Parliament and the French National Assembly, while Rifa'a al-Tahtawi (1801–1873), head of Egypt's language school and of the state's translation department, invoked the term *shura* (consultation) to describe the US Congress.[17] However, it is not clear whether the terminological confusion between elected councils with legislative and supervisory authorities and an appointed council without any actual power was deliberate.

In the path opened by Ali, Sa'id Mohammed Pacha (r. 1854–1863) created an appointed state council that also remained purely advisory. After him, Isma'il Pacha (r. 1863–1879) established in November 1866 the Majlis Shura al-Nuwwab, an assembly of seventy-five delegates elected by Egypt's male population. European journalists at the time saw it as the equivalent of the French legislative bodies. Similar to its predecessors, the assembly possessed only advisory authority. Isma'il was under no obligation to accept its advice, and he alone had the authority to convene, adjourn, or dissolve it. However, to impress his European creditors with his constitutional aims, he consulted with the assembly on various matters, particularly those related to finance and infrastructure.

These political changes paralleled reformist religious thought—known as Salafiyya—although it is not proven that the modernists of the time endorsed the term.[18] Salafiyya, which refers to the Salaf (early Companions of the Prophet Muhammad), has garnered confusing meanings because of its current use by the followers of Muhammad ibn Abd al-Wahhab's doctrine, or Wahhabism, which greatly differs in its orientation and goals from the modernist-reformist movement of the nineteenth century.[19] The former rejects the teachings of the four Sunni schools of jurisprudence, or *madhahib*, and advocates the imitation of the Prophet Muhammad by emphasizing the Hadith (accounts of the words and deeds of the Prophet). The latter also rejects the consistent observance of the schools of jurisprudence but, unlike Wahhabism, encourages new interpretations.[20] The reformist-modernist movement is understood as an attempt to resist the cultural influence of the West and therefore presented as the paragon of religious authenticity in turning inward to the Islamic heritage to compete with Western cultural input. For example, the *Oxford Encyclopedia of Islam*'s entry for *Salafiyya* reads, "In its inception, however, Salafiyya did not involve direct opposition to European imperial rule over Muslims. Rather, the intellectual figures of the movement saw it as internal Islamic reform to compete with the scientific and economic leadership of the West, through education and scholarship."[21]

This kind of description, as noted by Talal Asad in the *Formations of the Secular*, often downplays the deep influence of Western cultural and political concepts on this revivalism,[22] which, I would add, irremediably changed the meanings of traditional concepts such as sharia, *taqlid* (tradition), *ummah* (community), and jihad. In colonial times, and even more so after some nations' independence, the capture of Islam by the state solidified these political connotations of traditional concepts and made them "natural" to masses and clerics alike. Even less frequently explored—but in fact most important—is the fact that this westernized Islamic thinking has irremediably changed the tenets of the Islamic tradition. Therefore, the debate about the nature of political Islam in light of medieval concepts, as seen in the dispute about the religious nature of the Islamic State (ISIS), is moot. In fact, it is misleading to think that Islamists refer to sharia or *ijtihad* in their premodern senses. Take for example the following assessment by Noah Feldman: "Political Islamists—Islamists for short—recognize that the classical legal rules, derived from the Quran, the actions of the Prophet Muhammad, need to be supplemented by further legal and administrative regulations. When they seek to incorporate Shari'a into their constitutions, they are usually asking for modern legislation informed by classical Islamic law, and also sometimes for a rule that no legislation may violate classical Islamic legal rules."[23]

No doubt there is a claim to include Islamic law in secular legal systems. But the call for Islamic law is actually not informed by classical legal rules because there is no such thing as state law in the classic tradition of Islam. Islamists are in fact operating on a westernized concept of Islamic law that they share with secular nationalists. The difference is that they want to expand the rule of this law to new domains, while secular actors are content with the status quo. For this reason, the distinction between Islamic reform and Western nationalism is not as clear-cut as political actors claim. In other words, that the former is opposed to the latter does not mean it was not influenced by it. In fact, Islamic reformism was the outcome of the importation of Western ideas into traditional concepts and methodologies. In its initial phase, as mentioned above, Islamic reformism was actually modernist and pro-Western. In itself, it was neither good nor bad. Its anti-Western shift occurred later, at the time of decolonization and under the yolk of the authoritarian nation-states.

Under these conditions, political Islam is the outcome of never-ending interactions between intellectual, theological debates and institutional changes. For the sake of analysis, the following chapters will successively present both, although in reality the two processes were not so distinct.

The Orientalization of Islamic Thinking

Salafiyya was the direct outcome of encounters with European intellectual and political concepts. Consequently, new meanings were infused into terms such as *ijtihad* (interpretation) and *taqlid* (tradition). I refer to this transformation as *orientalization* because the new meanings were shaped by the Western perception of Islamic civilization. No doubt such a qualification is bold, even provocative. Specifically, it means that the Muslim reformers took at face value the Western parameters for evaluating Islam (for example, tradition versus change and progress) and promoted reforms of Islam based on these Western meanings. While the modernists aimed at adopting the Western concepts, the reformists strove mainly to change the tenets of the Islamic tradition in order to compete with Western intellectual input. In their transformation efforts, they implicitly adopted the Western perception or critique of Islam.

The Egyptian Rifa'a al-Tahtawi's critique of the tradition exemplifies this orientalization of Islamic thinking.[24] After returning from a state-sponsored mission in France, al-Tahtawi faced the challenge of explaining important Western institutions to a Muslim audience that was both uninformed and suspicious. He believed that Europeans had benefited from Islamic civilization in the past and that his visit to Paris was an opportunity to regain this influential role. In his view, France and Egypt had taken opposite directions: the French had not "pursued the religious path," and the Muslims had strayed away from the path of science and philosophy.[25] Referring to the Hadith "Wisdom is the stray sheep of the believer who must seize it wherever he finds it," al-Tahtawi argued for the adoption of certain Western innovations, but with Islamic underpinnings.[26] Using conventional means of reviewing prevailing opinions while interpreting them in the light of the European concept of social progress, al-Tahtawi's critique of Islamic juridical discourse actually reinforced the major trope of oriental discourse about the stagnation of Islamic thinking.[27]

Indira Gesink discusses al-Tahtawi's analysis of Jalal al-Din al-Suyuti's (1445–1505) classical legal writings—specifically, the defining features of a *mujtahid* (interpreter).[28] Al-Suyuti distinguished between independent *mujtahidin* (interpreters), who were confined to existing frameworks, and unrestricted *mujtahidin*, such as the founders of the *madhahib* (traditional schools of jurisprudence), who designed interpretative frameworks for other jurists. Although al-Tahtawi explained how different scholars and *madhahib* ranked the *mujtahidin*, he nevertheless neglected to distinguish between the independent and unrestricted ones.[29] This omission may appear negligible but is one among many of the seemingly insignificant changes leading to the flattening of hierarchies of scholars, paving the way to the "democratization" of *ijtihad* that allowed modern Islamists with no theological background to provide religious interpretations.

Taqlid *Opposed to Progress* and Ijtihad *as a Tool for Social Change*

In the same vein, Gesink explores how al-Tahtawi perceived *taqlid* (tradition) as a principle and mind-set opposed to progress.

In his critical take on tradition, the rules of *madhahib* contained all the legal answers, innovation was dangerous "because it departed from inherited truths,"[30] and "the highest point of civilization was a Golden Age of the distant past."[31]

In favor of al-Tahtawi's position, it can be argued that the compendium of decisions by the founders of the four schools and their immediate followers (*ummahat*) indeed restricted the latitude of majority or minority opinions within each school; their decisions had moved *taqlid* toward traditionalism in the sense that anything found in the *ummahat* was untouchable. References to these commentaries became especially important in later juridical debates. The less a contemporary scholar could challenge a rule, the more practicable the rule was in a court of law or as a guideline for Muslim behavior. By the late Middle Ages, this process had come so far that compendia of *mukhtasarat* (summary of legal rules) for each school were produced. They were simple statements of "what our school says" about each topic and situation to aid the judge. Thus, these *mukhtasarat* probably come closest to our idea of a law code in Islamic law, and in many instances, the judges would use them as such, basing their rulings on them in the same manner that a European judge would base his on the single reference to his country's legal code.

Yet, al-Tahtawi downplayed other aspects of the decision process. First, the authority of the *mukhtasarat* was informal, and judges did not have to base their judgments on them. They could look for and find other sources within their schools; in difficult cases they could ignore these compendia and go directly to a mufti or other higher authority. Second, the formulations of these compendia did not stop legal developments in the school. On the contrary, the reformulation and sophistication of the legal rules continued—albeit in a more circumscribed form—through fatwas, legal opinions given by recognized scholars. Such fatwas would have to conform to the consensus of the schools but could redefine this consensus to fit what the mufti wanted to say.

In his criticism, al-Tahtawi claimed that *taqlid* was more than juridical practice and in fact was a cause of social stagnation. He saw it as a worldview fundamentally opposed to progress.[32] Al-Tahtawi's solution to the problem of *taqlid* was to reopen the gate of *ijtihad* by reexamining and reinterpreting the Quran and Hadith.[33] In his articles published in *Rawdat al-madaris*, he argued that a human being's "natural goal" is to be educated through *ijtihad*.[34] While some ulemas claimed the gate of *ijtihad* was closed, al-Tahtawi argued in his twenty-four-page supplement, *al-Qawl al-sadid fi al-ijtihad wa al-tajdid* (Forthright speech on *ijtihad* and renewal), that the practice of *ijtihad* had not actually ceased and was beneficial to faith.[35] Al-Tahtawi reasoned that the Prophet had not apprehended everything new as harmful; an innovation was only harmful if God had explicitly forbidden it. Restrictions against scientific study, according to him, had stemmed from the wrong interpretation of a prophetic saying in which Mohammad had noted that a man could ensure continuance of his actions after his death by leaving one of three things: alms, an upright son, or "knowledge by which one benefits" (*ilm yuntafa'u bihi*). Al-Tahtawi claimed that the third legacy had been misunderstood to include only spiritual benefits from religious knowledge and that the phrase "beneficial knowledge" (*ilm al-nafi*) in no way omitted materially beneficial knowledge—that is, vocational and applied sciences.[36]

Similarly, al-Tahtawi thought it necessary to revive *ijtihad* in order to "renew religion" because "there may be discovered in the words of Prophecy that which would not have occurred to the Companions [of the Prophet]."[37] In his view, *ijtihad* was more than a method for legal derivation. He considered it as a means to social change. Therefore scholars should use it to legitimize new fields of inquiry such as scientific knowledge, rendering it necessary for progress.[38]

To summarize, *taqlid* became associated with a stagnant way of thinking that was unable to provide response to the new social circumstances, while *ijtihad* became the prerogative of any scholar of Islam who intended to have an influence on these new social circumstances. Limits imposed by the procedures and rules of each school were therefore no longer acceptable. Both new meanings orientalize Islamic tradition in the sense that they contribute to the "*imaginaire* or imaginary" of Islam in need of revitalization through Western input.

Jamaal al-Din al-Afghani
and the Influence of Protestant Reform

Jamaal al-Din al-Afghani (1838–1897) and al-Tahtawi shared the same negative view of *taqlid*.[39] The former said that Islam needed a Martin Luther and that the Protestant model of advancement was natural for Islam, as Islam was

> almost unique among religions in censuring belief without proof, rebuking those who follow suppositions, reproaching those who act randomly in the darkness of ignorance, and chiding them for their conduct. This religion demands that the pious seek proof [for their beliefs] in the sources of their religion. . . . Its lessons articulate that happiness results from reason and insight, and that wretchedness and error accompany ignorance, neglect of reason, and the snuffing of insight's light.[40]

Al-Afghani taught that the Protestant Reformation held the "secrets of successful revitalization" and that Luther's revival, which was based on application of human reason to religious sources, saved the decline of Christian European society, which had previously submitted to church authority.[41] Citing François Guizot, he wrote,

> One of the most significant causes influencing Europe in its path to civilization was the appearance of a sect in this country that said: we have the right to investigate the sources of our beliefs, and demand proof for them. . . . And when this sect gained power and its ideas spread, the minds of the Europeans were freed from the malady of ignorance and stupidity, and they were stimulated into an intellectual circuit and returned to [the study of] scientific subjects and worked hard to acquire the elements of civilization.[42]

Al-Afghani's activism is a relevant example of the Western influence on Islamic thinking, which casts reformism in a positive light in contrast with "tradition" and sees modernization in opposition to the conservatism of traditional thinking. To stimulate a new and enlightened public opinion, al-Afghani began to spearhead a movement to develop newspapers critical of and shedding light on corrupt government and foreign activities, which kept

Egypt's Muslims behind.[43] In 1877, he ran a journalism school in an effort to harmonize science and religion.[44] He mentored disciples interested in Sufism—among them Muhammad Abduh.[45] He also gave speeches to the masses and educated elites in patriotic and scientific ideas, sparking the Urabi movement.[46] Furthermore, he led an Arab masonic group called the Eastern Star lodge.[47] Finally, al-Afghani was in Paris from 1882 to 1884, where he organized the revolutionary society Jamiyat al Uwat al-Wuthqa (firmest bond) to combat imperialism.[48] We hence see a pattern emerging: the Muslim scholar who is also an activist and takes advantage of the media resources of his time. This pattern repeated itself later on in the cassettes of Shaikh Kishk, the videos of Osama bin Laden, and the use of social media by ISIS.[49]

The Western influence on al-Afghani does not mean that he supported or was supported by Western powers of the time. In fact, while Egyptian masses were fond of al-Afghani, foreign diplomats disliked his opposition to imperialism.[50] Due to his praise of philosophy and his indulgence for unbelief, al-Afghani also entered into conflicts with the ulemas of his era. For example, in a public lecture at the University of Dar al Funun in Istanbul, he compared philosophy to prophecy and praised the former, raising the ire of the ulemas and causing his expulsion from the city.[51]

Al-Afghani endorsed the inputs of previous reformist thinkers, such as the idea of individual responsibility within the traditional notion of *ijtihad* and the association of religious thinking with external principles and social issues. He also added a more activist dimension to the movement by reaching out to a broader audience and making the fight against Western political imperialism an important element of his legitimacy. In one of his pamphlets, *The True Causes of Man's Happiness and Distress*, al-Afghani draws similarities between patriotism and religious faith, therefore opening the path for interplay among nationalism, Islam, and pan-Islamism, which underlies until now all expressions of political Islam.[52]

The Social Reforms of Muhammad Abduh

Following the paths of al-Tahtawi and al-Afghani, Muhammad Abduh (1845–1905) continued the denigration of traditional modes of acquiring and producing Islamic knowledge.[53] As grand mufti of Egypt from 1899 to 1905, he often ignored points of law in favor of equity, justice, and social welfare.[54] He envisioned freeing the Egyptian people from bondage to tradition and helping them adapt Islam to the requirements of modern civilization.[55]

Abduh applied these ideas to the interpretation of law and religious practices. One example is his controversial *Transvaal Fatawas* (1903), which addressed the religious practices of a Muslim minority within a Christian society. In one ruling, Abduh glossed over the restriction that prohibits eating improperly slaughtered animals and declared that eating animals killed by Christians was permissible. Abduh emphasized the Quran verses permitting Muslims to eat the same foods as Jews and Christians, such as Sura 5:5: "The food of the People of the Book is lawful for you and your food is lawful for them." He thought that requiring Transvaal Muslims to eat meat prepared only by Muslims might isolate them from their Christian neighbors. All throughout this ruling, he emphasized issues of intent, unity, and peaceful coexistence over minor, potentially divisive details.[56]

In this respect, he was very adamant that whoever made a legal decision on the basis of the literal meaning of the text only, without understanding the *rwh al-Shari'a* (the spirit of the law), was not a *faqih* (jurisconsult).[57] He promoted the legal maxim *Inna al-'ibrata bi al-maqsid wa al-ma'ani la bi alfaz wa al-mabani* (the moral is in the intentions and meanings, not in articulations and basis), which is the foundation of the existing discussion on Islamic reform known as *maqasid al-Shari'a*, endorsed nowadays by Muslim Brothers in different locations.[58] Abduh emphasized the concept of *tammadun* (i.e., the totality of perfection "whether literary, material, sensual or metaphysical") as equivalent to the eighteenth-century European concept of civilization.[59] He believed Islam was the ideal religion, as its teachings harmonize with reason and emphasize *aql*, man's capacity to understand, comprehend, think about, and appreciate Allah's creatures.[60] In his view, although reason and religious revelation fulfil different functions as separate paths to truth, they do not contradict each other.

Nonetheless, Abduh understood that Europeans progressed intellectually due to freedom of thought. Although he believed

Muslims should not imitate the Europeans, he was also convinced that they could learn from them by using reason and *ijtihad*.[61] In an 1898 essay, *Risalat al-tawhid* (Message on unity), he advocates for political freedom, the emancipation of women, and the need to anchor law in political freedom and public opinion.[62] He also suggests that the ideals and values commonly associated with European progress are in fact universal human ideals, which Islam embodies best.[63] All religions originally exhibited these universal ideals (*wijdan al-sadiq*), but non-Muslims lost them over time. The revelation of Islam reintroduced these ideals, which were appropriated by Europeans during the Crusades and inspired the Reformation. Abduh therefore believed that European humanitarian values were originally Islamic.[64] In his aspiration to reform Egypt, he emphasized the need to free Islamic thinking from *taqlid*, which was blind imitation of the past, in order to evaluate new facts liberally and apply them to solutions relevant to contemporary times.[65] In his view, tradition and imitation are almost synonymous, which is a trope of contemporary Islamist and secular thinking. In Abduh's view, implementation of religious duties requires civil administration rather than mere obedience to an unjust head of state.[66] He believed that a rigid vision of religion can easily lead to government despotism and misuse of power. Authority should be based on people's wishes, with religion serving as a "rational guide" in the people's interests.[67] Civil power in Islam should rest on the *ummah*, the only source of legitimacy for a ruler. In this respect, an educated citizenry that knows the difference between the beneficial and the harmful, between order and disorder, is key to just and fair ruling.[68] Without civilian knowledge of moral distinctions, the ruler would be unable to "establish stability for his authority, and all the reforms he imagined for them and for himself, which he put into the principles of his government, would be like straw on the water of drawings in the air."[69] In other words, Abduh emphasized that the role of religious leaders is not to counsel the prince or implement his politics but to strengthen the moral features of local communities.

Abduh also noted that Islam does not recognize a so-called religious authority, as Muslim believers can access the Quran as well as the Hadith without human mediation. A mufti, *qadi* (judge), or shaikh therefore has no religious authority beyond guidance and should not claim any all-encompassing authority.[70] Abduh also remarked that "according to the Shari'a, nobody held the authority to control individual belief."[71] Islam is the religion, while sharia is the methodology of life.[72] Sharia is "more specific in meaning than religion," as different messengers can change laws, but religion is absolute.[73]

Following al-Afghani, Abduh practiced pragmatism, choosing to be guided by whichever school of law was the best fit for a particular pressing issue—a practice eventually known as *talfiq* and used in existing civil state law.[74] Instead of following the specific rules of a particular *madhab,* Abduh adhered to the principle that *al-maslahah al-mursalah* (public interest) took precedence over every other consideration.[75] *Fiqh* (Islamic jurisprudence) is the practical knowledge of the sharia, or the "science of the laws of Islam." Juristic consensus (*ijma*), analogical deduction (*qiyas*), juristic preference (*istihsan*), and public interest are all methods to solve problems according to the general principles of the sharia using human reason, particularly when the *fuqaha* (legal scholars) cannot directly interpret the Quran or Hadith.[76]

Abduh was aware that these interpretations required *ijtihad* as well as scientific modes of reasoning.[77] He believed that if Muslims were unable to secure their beliefs via proofs, they would be very vulnerable to rational or atheist objections to their faith. Abduh suggested that ulemas with knowledge should also undertake their own *ijtihad* in accordance with contemporary issues, such as the problems of divorce and polygamy.[78] The ulemas must be in the "vanguard of the acquisition of sciences." Their moral influence over the masses would allow them to "incite the people to learn what they need to protect their religion."[79]

Abduh also applied his interpretation of progress (*tammadun*) to reform Islamic education. Although he had internalized European ideals, he was against overt anglicization and attempted to create a "hybridized framework" for authentic Islamic revolution of thought.[80] The purpose of education in Egypt would be like the purpose of education in Europe: to produce moral individuals with internalized civil norms. However, the internalized norms would be of Islamic morality rather than the "outright imitation of

European customs." The curriculum would supply a community identity emphasizing the unity and pride of Islam, in addition to the means for material success.[81]

From 1880 to 1882, Abduh was the editor in chief of the government journal *al-Waqa'i al-Misriyya* and used his power to make educational reform one of the publication's chief concerns. Abduh saw the reform of the university of al-Azhar as the greatest service for Islam.[82] He criticized its lack of organized curriculum, regular registration, attendance policies, student assessment, and moral supervision.[83] He spearheaded the creation of an administrative council, advocating for changes in curriculum and textbook use.[84] Abduh believed the ministry should come to accept that Egyptians required openness to new ideas to progress—an openness best learned in a European-model school system.[85] He admired Herbert Spencer's *On Education*, from which he adopted the ideas of utility, active learning, sciences related to indirect self-preservation, and practical education. Abduh was also inspired by Leo Tolstoy, who advocated the importance of religious morality for individual happiness and a high-functioning society.[86] In 1892, he established the Muslim Benevolent Society, which founded seven schools for 766 poor children and provided an experimental field in national education.[87]

It is worth noting that the resistance to this reformist movement was both theological and political. Abduh received pushback from the clerics at al-Azhar, who refused to see *ijtihad* as a way to educate and strengthen the national community. They worried that the new *ijtihad* advocated by Abduh required critical examination of *madhahib* rulings and therefore critique of ulemas, which could lead to "religious anarchy by destroying trust in the religious law."[88] The practice of unrestrained *ijtihad*, in their view, could result in further divisions in the religious community and ultimately in "chaos for lay believers."[89]

Some of these clerics, such as Shaikh Abd al-Rahman al-Sharbini, accused Abduh of "secularizing the Islamic institution."[90] Gesink details how, when the first edition of his *Risalat al-tawhid* was released in 1898, rumors spread that it contained heresies such as denials of God's unity and affirmations of atheism.[91] Abduh was accused of "shortcomings of character" and "denying the existence of God and His unity."[92] Furthermore, when he provided financial support to al-Azhar students excelling in geography and arithmetic but not in Islamic subjects, his critics believed he swayed students to leave religious studies for more profitable subjects, "encouraging materialism and the slow death of the Shari'a."[93] There was also criticism against Abduh's *Transvaal Fatawas*, mentioned earlier.[94] To his peers, Abduh's comments insulted their intelligence and moral authority. One al-Azhari shaikh went as far as to censure *Al-Manar*, a journal in which Abduh regularly published articles critical of the ulemas. The shaikh said, "*Al-Manar* is a harmful paper that treats the ulama with scorn and refuses to acknowledge the saints. I do not even like to see it, and thanks to God, I have never read it at all."[95]

Abduh's promotion by Khedive Abbas Hilma to al Azhar Administrative Council in 1895, irritated many ulemas who believed he lacked moral fiber as well as the legal training necessary for the revival of *ijtihad*.[96] The al-Azhari shaikh al-Babghallo al-Misri distributed handwritten leaflets to smear Abduh's reputation. One had a drawing of Abduh holding the waist of a naked European woman while a dog pawed his leg, making him ritually impure.[97] Additionally, critics of Abduh believed his abandonment of tradition threatened the prestige of conventionally accepted norms and opened the door to corrosive political influence. Shaikh Muhammad Ilish, the Moroccan chief mufti of the al-Maliki school of thought and Abduh's professor, believed that internal division endangered the Islamic community and that Abduh's proposals, which aimed to improve society, would actually deteriorate it. Furthermore, Abduh's political critics, among them journalists with a nationalist agenda, as well as Khedive Abbas Hilmi II, depicted him as a "tool of imperialists," "factor of invasive European culture," and "colonial agent," among other pejoratives.[98]

From 1897 to 1905, Abduh's critics engaged in an ad hominem campaign to discredit his reforms by associating them with social Darwinism and the British occupiers.[99] These attacks increased after his August 1903 visit to England, where he asked to meet Herbert Spencer to discuss education.[100] These condemnations were weaved astutely into the nationalist discourse on resistance to imperialism.[101]

Abduh channeled the ideological notions of al-Tahtawi and al-Afghani, such as the value of science and progress and the utility of religious principles for social advancement, into education. He therefore turned Islamic methodology into a tool for social transformation. It was nevertheless the responsibility of the state rulers, not the ulemas, to dramatically change the traditional education system and hence the tradition itself, a turn of events that Abduh did not anticipate.

The Westernization of Education and Sharia

Institutional transformations wrought by the colonial powers and actively endorsed by the local elites paralleled the secularizing trend in Islamic thinking. The most significant changes took place in the domain of education and the application of sharia.

Westernization of Religious Transmission and Adoption of Western Concepts of Knowledge and Education

Encounters with the French and the British deeply transformed the traditional mode of religious transmission at all levels, from the university to the elementary school. *Halqa*, or a circle of study around a shaikh specialized in an area of law, characterized traditional Islamic teaching, which entailed reading texts out loud and engaging in a dialectical process of discussion, through personal connections between the shaikh and students. Dialogue, revision, and repetition were standard techniques of instruction. There were no formal examinations, but teachers observed the progress of each student through discussions. Emphasis was placed on memorizing the Quran as well as portions of the Hadith. These schools or madrasas produced ulemas and managed their personnel. As such, they were linked organically to medieval local communities and operated independently of the central political power.

As a consequence of encounters with Europe, this traditional mode of educational transmission gradually gave way to the Lancaster model, that is, a rules-based system intended to maximize efficiency in classrooms. In this system, all aspects of classroom behavior and lesson progress are written rules. Orders, such as "face front" and "show slates," are written on boards along the walls to test students. Knowledge is disseminated through written language and top-down authority.[102] The key difference between *halqa* and the Lancaster mode of education is the nature of communication: while the Lancaster system is implicitly coercive, the *halqa* model is contractual.

The seed of change came from the creation of new schools that taught knowledge imported from Europe. In 1847, Muhammad Ali created national military schools in Cairo based on the Western model.[103] Consequently, Gesink remarks, many students completed their studies quickly at al-Azhar and then moved on to military schools. These schools compelled al-Azhar reformers, such as Abduh, to call for greater access to scientific education and broader training in religious schools.[104] As a result, the secular/religious divide, previously unheard of, became a key feature of the education system.

An enthusiastic admirer of the Lancaster method, Shaikh Muhammad al-Ahma al-Zawahiri, a graduate of al-Azhar, published a comprehensive critique of religious education called *Al-Ilm wa al-ulama wa al-nizam al-talim* (Knowledge, scholars, and the system of instruction) in 1904.[105] He argued that shaikhs and religious students displayed "poor morality" and thereby lost the public's respect. Al-Zawahiri's solution was to use utilitarian techniques by regularizing admissions, dividing studies into *wasa'il* (means) and *maqasid* (ends), and holding shaikhs accountable for supervising students' behavior as well as the introduction of new subjects.[106]

Al-Azhar faculty opposed the reforms and managed to rally the support of Ahmad Shafiq Pasha, the khedive's secretary at the time.[107] Consequently, a comprehensive reform package called the Internal Reorganization Code, or New Order, was issued in 1908. The New Order stopped the reforms initiated by Abduh but did not go back to the *halqa* mode of transmission either. It completely reorganized the school by enacting efficiency-based pedagogies and bureaucratic procedures.[108] Internal Organizational Plan No. 1, known as *Al-la'iha al-dakhiliyya*, divided al-Azhar's curriculum into three levels: elementary, secondary, and higher. Achievement was assessed through yearly written and oral examinations in the three mandatory areas of religious subjects, Arabic language, and mathematical sciences. Practical and vocational skills, such as the workings of Egypt's various court systems, were emphasized.[109] This New Order raised internal objections but was finally accepted by the clerics. This is how the head of the reform committee described their final surrender: "The committee reviewed the law and after long discussions, it agreed on the project. I feared that some of the ulama would grumble, especially the reactionaries among them [*al-raja'iyin*], so I requested that the committee decide that there was nothing in the code that contradicted the principles of the Islamic religion, and that was done."[110]

The change was profound: Azharis now faced the dilemma of assessment via standardized exams. This "compulsion to teach to the test" was distinctively modern.[111] Similar transformation at the elementary levels of transmission echoed these changes in the high institutions of learning.

Reform of All Levels of Islamic Education

While educational changes brought by the interactions with Europe occurred in the late Ottoman period and beyond, assumptions about their inevitability obscure important nuances and an array of alternative possibilities, such as a more pronounced role for Islam.[112] Late-nineteenth and early-twentieth-century educational reforms in the Ottoman Empire were driven and shaped by competition from missionary enterprises—most of which were Christian—and raised simultaneous admiration and hostility toward the European model. This acculturation resulted in a mix of different schools: military and civilian, foreign and domestic, public and private. Before encounters with Europe, there were no curricula or rules for the conduct of classes. The madrasa was "an education institution alongside the mosque, the sufi convent, and the private home or shop."[113] For a madrasa to have a curriculum signaled the force behind the modern Western model.[114]

There was an unprecedented growth in new types of schooling among both state and missionary schools. *Mektebs* (Quran schools) themselves were divided into "traditional" and "modern" and used two different textbooks (known respectively as "old ABC" and "Ottoman ABC").[115] In his analysis of Ottoman biographies, Benjamin Fortna describes the case of one student, Tevfik Saglam, who attended two *mektebs*: in the first he learned the traditional text in Arabic; in the second, which was closer to home, he studied the "modern" textbook. Tevfik Saglam himself used the word "modern." These different textbooks were symptomatic of the state's efforts to reshape schools through the introduction of a new curriculum. Little is known regarding the process of commissioning such texts, but it appears that beginning in the 1850s, several Ottoman writers were tasked with producing them. New texts appeared along with curricular changes, resulting in the difference reported by Saglam.[116]

Nonetheless, the ultimate aim of the *mekteb*, as a religious institution, was to teach the Quran. In Fortna's account, another student, Hamid Ziya, recalled, "Here we studied the Quran; I have no recollection of anything else being taught." Other subjects were secondary and only included to support religious instruction. To know the whole Quran by heart was the "ultimate aim."[117] Surprisingly, there was sizable overlap between *mektebs* and "modern" state schools in terms of pedagogical and disciplinary methods. Even when students switched to state schools, they valued the *mekteb* in retrospect, as the material covered in religious institutions prepared them for "secular" schools.[118] The addition of religiously based texts, such as Cevdet Pasa's *Kisas-i enbiya* (Stories of the prophets), to the late-Ottoman state curriculum after the 1880s further blurred the differences between *mektebs* and state schools.[119] These parallels suggest that it may be more helpful to think of the variety of schooling options in the late Ottoman Empire as forming a unified system rather than as sharply divided between religious and secular.[120]

Similarly, both British administrators and Muslim reformers undertook several efforts to reform madrasas in India during the colonial period. These initiatives fueled competing visions of the madrasa as well as of the status of Islam in society.[121] Colonial officials sought to tap into the familiar and that which they considered self-evident, such as the divide between secular and religious. Yet, as Muhammad Zaman discusses, they routinely found themselves in situations without obvious distinctions between the two in India's education systems.[122] This lack of clarity made the Indians appear "inferior" in the eyes of the British rulers and much in need of "enlightened governance and liberating reform."[123] In their efforts to reform, it was therefore crucial for the British to distinguish between the religious and the nonreligious, the personal and the public.[124] After the revolt of 1857, however, a policy of religious neutrality called for exclusion from the general curriculum of all formal instruction in religion.[125] In June 1858, the first director of public instruction in Punjab remarked, "I ordered all village schools to be removed from the precincts of mosques and other buildings of a religious character. I then ordered that the schools should be closed rather than held in such buildings. . . . I [also] directed the disuse of all books of a religious character in the schools."

While madrasas fell into the category of religious institutions, the government continued to administer or financially support many of them. Nonetheless, British officials still favored secular education and continuously evoked the familiar distinctions between religious and secular learning in their analyses of the madrasas. One of them remarked, "Thus indigenous religious schools . . . [are] entitled to a grant from the Government . . . so long as they teach secular subjects in a satisfactory manner."[126] Furthermore, the British established the criterion of "useful instruction" in education in the spirit of English utilitarianism. Commenting on the allocation of funds by the East India Company for advancing education in India, James Mill wrote, "The great end should not have been to teach Hindoo learning, or Mahomedan learning, but useful learning. . . . In professing, on the other hand, to establish Seminaries for the purpose of teaching mere Hindoo, or mere Mahomedan literature, you bound yourself to teach a great deal of what was frivolous, not a little of what was purely mischievous, and a small remainder deal indeed in which utility was in any way concerned."[127] British initiatives at reform were limited to the madrasas they supported financially or established themselves, such as the Calcutta Madrasa founded by Warren Hastings in 1781. The emphasis on "useful learning" left little room for religion in general, let alone instruction in virtues and modes of spiritual salvation.

This policy stimulated multiple reformist movements similar to those in Egypt. For example, the Deobandi movement[128] created the first madrasa to emulate the British style of education. Ironically, the Taliban, oft-presented as the paragon of anti-Western authentic Islamic movements, emanates from this reformist movement. Madrasas everywhere on the Indian subcontinent began to have "a set curriculum, with separate classes for students of different levels, an academic year, annual examinations, and networks of affiliated madrasas."[129] They started to devote extensive time to teaching "ancillary sciences," such as syntax, and "rational sciences," or logic, rather than "purely religious sciences," such as the Quran, law, and Hadith. Observing these changes, Shibli Numani lamented, "There is not even one purely religious madrasa in the whole of India, no institution worthy of being considered the 'madrasa' in terms of its all-embracing concern [with the religious sciences] and its grandeur."[130]

Finally, the British emphasized moral instruction—which they saw as lacking in Indian education systems—through literature, which, along with training in practical "useful" skills, began to replace formal instruction in religion in government schools. They sought to foster a generation of ulemas in greater touch with their people and with an intimate knowledge of Arabic, which many colonial officials regarded as one of the "classical languages of India."[131]

As a result of these reforms, the secular/religious divide became and remains the lens for classifying institutions of education, even if the content of the religious curriculum has been secularized. Interestingly, the opposite transformation took place in Western-style schools, where Islamic references increasingly shaped secular curricula, as attested by the development of law schools in Egypt.

Introduction of "Secular" Law Schools in Egypt

Languages were an important part of legal studies in the 1860s and 1870s. Deciding in 1881 that Turkish was no longer practical, Victor Vidal, founder and dean of the Khedivial Law School, increased instruction in Arabic to the detriment of Turkish. The development of technical Arabic vocabulary to express French legal concepts ensued. Other reforms took place, especially the creation of a curriculum consisting of two years of preparatory work and three years of legal education. This curriculum provided instruction in sharia, Franco-Egyptian law, Roman law, and translation.[132]

As a result of these reforms, on the brink of independence, there were six schools of higher education in Egypt for legal training and academia. Three of them emphasized the teaching of the Franco-Egyptian legal system, preparing Egyptians in civil, administrative, criminal, and constitutional law, as well as for the sharia courts of family law.[133] Professors at these schools were mainly trained in Europe. The three other schools—al-Azhar, Dar al-Ulum, and the Shari'a College—specialized in sharia scholarship and court training. Compared to the first three, they were deemed "conservative" because they upheld Islamic legal principles.[134]

When the British occupied Egypt in 1883, they offered the continuity of French law as a "palliative in exchange for having unilaterally occupied a territory that both powers had been managing jointly."[135] When the Native Courts (*al-mahakim al-ahliyyah*) were established (see below), it took five years for the Khedivial Law School to revise its curriculum to prepare students for work as advocates, judges, and clerks in these new courts. The curriculum was taught in French except in those areas dealing with sharia court laws, and the faculty of the school, dominated by European teachers, focused on the Franco-Egyptian codes.[136] A license in French or Egyptian law from this school would eventually become the "best ticket" to a career in the Native Courts. But in the mid-1880s, the government still mainly appointed to Native Courts judges who had worked in the *nizamiyyah* courts.[137]

At the same time, leading faculty members of Dar al-Ulum and the Shari'a College, such as Ahmad Abu al-Fath (1866–1946) and Abd al-Wahhab Khallaf (1888–1956), taught sharia at the Khedivial Law School, which allowed more conservative scholars of Islamic law to influence academic discourse on the subject at an institution where European legal tradition dominated.[138] They held degrees from sharia schools and wore the cloak and turban.

In fact, these sharia scholars were considered reformists at the time, as they were influenced by European law and worked collaboratively with scholars of Franco-Egyptian law. Nonetheless, they were still concerned with showing that the sharia was on the same level as Franco-Egyptian law with regard to applicability and modernity.[139]

Between 1875 and 1930, Islamic legal education in Egypt primarily covered Egyptian academic heritage, Hanafi law, and Arabic texts.[140] Only in the years following Egypt's independence in 1923 did Islamic legal scholarship become open to other influences, such as the legal literature of other Arab and Muslim countries. This spurred a movement of comparative Islamic-European legal research at the Cairo University Law Faculty.[141] Islamic legal revivalists also called for the development of substantive law in highly salient matters such as murder and usury.[142] The early revivalists praised the European's "easy-to-use" reference books.[143] The convenience of a legal system offering "single, uniform, and final answers to single questions" was particularly attractive. Thus, Islamic legal revivalists advocated for the writing of Islamic law books modeled on the Dalloz series and European mechanisms of appeal and civil procedure.[144] This trend had five major ideological tenets:

1. Admiration for European advancements in juridical science, including a reverence for the codification of European customary and Roman law
2. Depiction of Franco-Egyptian laws as foreign and unsuited to Egyptian society
3. Presentation of sharia as relevant and comprehensive for the present era and belief that the jurisdiction of Islamic law should include all civil, criminal, procedural, constitutional, and other legal matters, not just family law
4. Promotion of Islamic positive laws to replace Egypt's Franco-Egyptian laws through reorganization, homologation, and codification
5. Islamization of the current legal system by jurists, who were particularly competent to compare European and Islamic laws and codify modern laws in courts[145]

To adapt sharia to fit modern conditions, these Islamic reformists advanced the principle of *takhayyur* and *talfiq* (change and aggregation).[146] In cases where the use of *talfiq* was not sufficient, they promoted the reopening of *ijtihad*, freeing themselves from the procedural limits of tradition as advocated by al-Tahtawi a century before. Finally, the doctrine of *siyasa shariyya* (governmental implementation of Muslim law by decree) would allow the enforcement of government legislation over sharia courts through the legislative preparation of a comprehensive collection of laws.[147] This single collection would clearly present laws and allow courts and private individuals to know the exact rule applicable to a particular legal issue. In "Islamic Jurisprudence and Legislation" in the *Shari'a Lawyers Journal*, Muhibb al-Din al-Khatib[148] sums up most of the conceptual and methodological changes in Islamic law of that period that directly shape today's political Islam: appeal of synthetic codes, dismissal of the premodern tradition, and exaltation of political sovereignty over Islamic law.

> If the precious treasure of Islamic jurisprudence had come upon the modern Europeans, and had they counted it as part of what they had inherited from their Roman and Greek ancestors, then by now it would have been published in reference encyclopedias, in every language of the world, and organized to the utmost degree. In the European system there is no such thing as a law that cannot be easily found by referring to an encyclopedia of reference. [In order to accomplish the project of codification,] all of their various law schools agreed on a single law for each problem. Their laws contain sophisticated ideas, rules, and opinions. After a long period of comprehensive research, the Europeans masterfully distilled thirteen centuries of jurisprudence to its essences. As for us, we have not thought about doing anything like that. . . . Our researchers are forced to read sixty volumes just to attain a result that could be accomplished in fifteen minutes if they were able to work in a single reference book, or had we thought to write a reference encyclopedia of fiqh along the models of Carpentier, Dalloz, and Benedict.
>
> In addition to the Islamic nation having perpetrated disgraces in the technical organization of Islamic legal thought, our

Islamic governments have adopted foreign laws like the French and Swiss civil codes. . . . [W]hat does that law have to do with the Shari'ah, with which the Muslims are well acquainted, and which has embodied their spirit for fourteen centuries?

As for the men of the Shari'ah, who know the encyclopedias of Western law in foreign languages, and who are amazed by the precision of their formation . . . who will earn for himself a page of eternal glory and present himself for such work in the field of Shari'ah, appointing alongside of him bands of brothers and colleagues? For if we had a uniform reference encyclopedia of Islamic jurisprudence that brought together all the schools (madhahib) and rules, and that pointed to the rules reliably and precisely, that would smooth the way for extending our academic knowledge of Islamic doctrine (fiqh) to the legislative sphere when the opportunity arises. We could then move beyond our shameful position before God and mankind.[149]

This Islamic legal theory, adopted by reformists from the 1930s through the 1950s, profoundly influenced how jurists wrote the legal codes and academic doctrine in civil, criminal, procedural, constitutional, and other areas of law. Islamic legal thinking was therefore a decisive thrust toward the codification of sharia as well as its establishment as state law.

Sharia as State Law

As pointed out by scholars of Islam, sharia has never been collected and specified in a particular law book. It is best understood as a shared opinion of the community of scholars, based on a literature that is extensive but not necessarily coherent or authorized by any single body.

As an uncodified procedure, sharia stands in sharp contrast with most existing legal systems, where the law is written down in what is called a law code and validated by a specific body. It developed independently and often in opposition to the political power. The legal scholars (*fuqaha*) were in theory—and, especially in the early period, also in practice—educated and recruited quite autonomously from the rulers. In fact, they may well be considered the most representative social institution in the early Islamic period. Certainly, if we look for a dichotomy between state apparatuses and society, the scholars belonged in the latter category.

Under colonial power and later nation-state rule, sharia was transformed into a technique of governmentality in most Muslim territories. During the early decades of British rule in India, this transformation was most troublesome to Muslims. Law was defined by the colonial power as "the law of religious communities" (with Muslims subject to Muslim law, Hindus subject to Hindu law) and in the process codified and frozen. Sharia became Anglo-Muhammadan law, in which core issues such as law of evidence and interpretation of offense were British imports rather than Islamic. In this context fatwas, or religious rulings, took on a new legitimacy.[150] While traditionally issued by judges, they were now given to believers directly by a court official: the mufti. As a consequence, believers became a "vehicle for disseminating ever more detailed guidance on everyday life behaviors, including in the purview decisions about customary practices that had been of little concern to the state, but were of great importance to Muslims seeking to preserve an authentic expression of their religion under alien rule."[151] Similarly, sharia in Egypt was increasingly advocated as a comprehensive resource for the development of positive laws enforced by the state. At the same time, its domain of application was significantly reduced. By 1876, the application of sharia was restricted solely to personal status.[152] Yet even in personal law, the procedures adopted in courts, as well as the content of the law, marked a stark break with traditional sharia.[153] The Egyptian legal reforms of the nineteenth century resulted in the introduction of a Western civil code system as the basis for the country's entire national legal structure.[154] Sharia was therefore replaced by governmental enactments in the form of codes and statutes modeled after Western laws.[155]

The Mixed Courts system (*al-mahakim al-mukhtaltah*), established in 1875 to solve conflicts between Egyptians and foreigners, was later complemented by Native Courts. In both courts, the codes of laws were modeled on the Napoleonic code, even in domains of law still based on Islamic precepts such as civil law and family law.[156] The Mixed Courts system was the latest manifestation of "capitulations laws," which had affected foreigners in the Ottoman Empire for years. The Native Courts system emerged from the Mixed Courts system.[157] The latter judged civil and commercial cases between foreigners of different nationalities.[158] The former were "the courts for Egyptians," adjudicating all civil and commercial cases when no foreigners were involved.

Both European and Egyptian political figures saw the creation of the Native Courts in 1883 as part of an ongoing reform process that started in the 1860s with Ottoman-style *nizamiyyah* courts, which had already annexed portions of the jurisdiction of traditional sharia courts.[159] Egyptian political leaders saw the Native Courts as a way to escape Ottoman rule and assumed that they would eventually subsume Mixed Courts and bring all civil and criminal cases under the jurisdiction of Egyptian judges. The Native Courts were desirable as a tool for both "phasing out extraterritorial jurisdiction" and justifying calls for Egyptian independence from European political control.[160]

While Mixed Courts are often thought to have been imposed by European power, in fact local elites established them. Mixed Courts were first dominated by Europeans and North Americans, with French being the principle language used (though both English and French were official languages). They were a "prestige forum of legal practice" for both European and Egyptian law professionals, with Egyptians increasingly appearing as lawyers and judges in the later years.[161] Counterintuitively, the Native Courts involved a greater degree of direct European responsibility since they were created under direct occupation from 1883 to 1884.[162] Unlike the Mixed Courts, the Native Courts were dominated by Egyptians, and the operating language was Arabic, though from the 1880s and 1890s, the benches and bar association did include Europeans strategically placed as "quality-control supervisors" representing British personnel. Each appellate court had at least one European judge, thus ensuring European control over the jurisprudence of Egyptian courts.[163] Both court systems were modeled after French courts, with a two-tiered, hierarchal organization for appeals (small claims, first instance) and several judges on each bench. The Mixed Courts persisted until their jurisdiction was folded into the Native Courts in 1935, which were thereafter known as National Courts (*al-mahakim al-wataniyyah*).

Though discussed since the 1870s, these changes in the court system were catalyzed by the British occupation. Many Egyptians operating the Egyptian government after 1882 were the same ones who had contributed before 1882 to the creation of the Mixed Courts system in cooperation with Europeans.[164] It took only two years for the Egyptian rulers to put the Native Courts in operation across the country. This involved employing a relatively small number of judges and clerks, most of whom were white-collar workers in need of jobs. Even unemployed Azhari graduates found judgeships in the courts during the 1880s.[165]

After independence in 1923, legal reform in Egypt focused on modernizing sharia law (i.e., personal law). The Egyptian approach to family law was "piecemeal" compared to the Ottoman Law of Family Rights.[166] The postindependence codification was seen as an "innovative step towards the emancipation of women."[167] Law No. 25 (1920) specifically concerned husbands who did not financially support their spouses. The family law codes of the 1920s allowed wives to free themselves from marriage on the grounds of nonsupport and marital difficulties causing harm. This enhanced their security, as husbands could no longer exercise their right of unilateral divorce (*talaq*). In 1949, a newly reformed civil code took effect; it was described as "comparative law, Egyptian Civil Law, and the Shari'a," with "comparative law" referring to French, German, Polish, and Russian codes. Though the sharia was utilized, the code provisions were often built on other sources and then connected to an applicable sharia rule only at the end.[168]

During the same period, new forms of Islamic legal writing (as discussed above) were developed as a result of the demand by Egyptians for the revival and reapplication of Islamic law.[169] This was in direct response to Egypt's previous adoption of European laws, which many saw as an affront to Egypt's autonomy.[170] As pointed out earlier, French and British legal methodology deeply influenced this Islamic legal revivalism. Additionally, Western inspiration came in handy when rules were not in conflict with sharia requirements, as well as when Islamic jurisprudence lacked legal provisions for specific cases. The promulgation of sharia jurisdiction through governmental enactments and *siyasa shariyya* allowed for the use of rules of Western legal inspiration. Yet this resulted in the so-called Islamic legislation to be found in the form of Western codes and statutes, with content derived from Islamic jurisprudence. Such legislation is not purely Islamic, as not all the legal rules contained within it derive from the sharia.[171]

Outside the case of Egypt, "Western" legal rules continue to be an important part of Islamic legislation, with the unintended outcome of secularizing traditional sharia. The degree to which Muslim governments have contributed to this secularization shows in the extensive codification and enactment of Islamic pre-scriptions in areas such as criminal law, which were hitherto far removed from the initial goals of the modernist-reformists.

While traditional sharia sources mention forbidden and oblig-atory acts, they specify no penalties. According to the *taazir* doc-trine, when an offense is mentioned in the Quran or Hadith with no specific punishment attached to it, the punishment of a partic-ular offense—taking into account its nature, the amount of harm inflicted, and the social and legal circumstances of both the offender and the victim—was at the discretion of the judge. There were no attempts to codify these offenses and punishments. As noted by Butti al-Muhairi in his case study of the current United Arab Emirates (UAE) legal system, adoption of Islamization poli-cies by the postcolonial state, along with a unified legal system, led to governmental enactments for criminal law rules concerning *taazir*.[172] Governmental enactments therefore became the only true sources of *taazir* law. Codification of the *taazir* in a penal code implied that government intervention was necessary for the enforcement of any *taazir* legal rule provided by the sharia. The UAE's federal legislature therefore contrastingly stresses "secular, human elements" (in this case, governmental enactment) as the development of Islamic criminal law.[173] It acknowledges that law is "the product of the state," a premise deeply in conflict with tra-ditional precepts of Islam.

To sum up, the transfer of religious authority from the inde-pendent clerics to the state, along with the transformation of sharia into state law, pervades all Islamist agendas today and is inherited from the institutional and intellectual changes analyzed above. Most interestingly, these changes have been enacted by secular rulers and penetrate also secular political thinking in Muslim countries, although neither secularists nor Islamists would agree with such an assessment.

Whither the Tradition?

The point of this overview of the codification process is not to conclude that sharia is incompatible with the modern state. On the contrary, it aims to show how Islamic concepts and methodologies can be flexibly adapted to the state system. This modern sharia has supplanted traditional modes of interpretation to the point that the premodern version does not inform discussions among religious authorities today. In other words, the codified sharia is not limited to state administration. It is now part and parcel of the teachings and transmission of the tradition. Today's Islamists do not relate to their classical tradition by translating it into their modern predicaments. They engage instead with the modern and politicized versions of sharia, through *taqlid* and *ijtihad*, which came from the dual process of ideational and institutional changes brought by imperial encounters and the building of the nation-state. As such, while comparing sharia to its "authentic" premodern version is a worthwhile academic exercise, it does not shed light on the nature of political Islam.

In fact, the classical tradition is not even systematically taught in sharia faculties today. Monique Cardinal has reviewed the course material and curricula at five sharia faculties, including al-Azhar, and shows that the classical tradition is not thoroughly taught. As discussed above, students at the sharia faculty of al-Azhar undergo courses in all legal domains, which prepares them to compete alongside law students at other Egyptian law schools while looking for jobs. Moreover, according to Cardinal's research, the time designated for teaching Islamic legal theory has decreased due to the introduction of Western positive law (*al-qanun*).

At al-Azhar, Islamic legal theory is taught in four half-year courses to undergraduates in the Al-Shari'a al-Islamiyya program and in five semesters to its undergraduates in the Al-Shari'a wa'lqanun program.[174] The teaching of Islamic legal theory at al-Azhar is divided into *al-dars al-mawdui* (teaching of subjects) and *al-dars al-nassi* (teaching of textual rulings). In the *mawdui* class, the professor goes through the subject matter and then reads excerpts from classical texts. The goal is to encourage students to read the classics efficiently. The professor also offers his own manual, which is a more simplified version of the classics, as a way to help students understand the gist of the assigned classical texts. Students are tested on both texts, but "the balance weighs in the favor of the professor's manual."[175] Professors adopted these modern textbooks as early as 1946, and they have become prevalent since then.

Cardinal discusses in detail Muhammad al-Khudari's *Usul al-fiqh*, published in 1911 and known as the "first modern legal theory textbook."[176] Al-Khudari initially wrote *Usul al-fiqh* by examining classical treaties. However, he soon realized that his students at the School of Judges in Cairo were not well read in the shorter and longer sources of Islamic legal theory. This prompted him to transform his book into a textbook. Other authors, such as Abd al-Wahhab Khallaf, a professor at the Faculty of Law at Cairo University, published a manual that aimed to make the Islamic legal theory practical and "to clothe the Islamic legal tradition in Western garb." He set out to prove that Islamic legal theory is as modern as the Western legal tradition. He included "the substantive law of the new codes and its legal terminology into the textbook."[177] Similarly, Ali Hasaballah, Muhammad Abu Zahra, Zaki al-Din Sha'ban, and Muhammad Shalabi argued that Islamic legal theory and substantive law "had been displaced by Western-imported law and practices."[178]

Cardinal analyzes thirty-three textbooks used across different Muslim countries to teach Islamic legal theory. She shows that only two of the books, *Nihayat al-sul 'ala minhaj al-wusul* and *Sharh al-talwih 'ala al-tawdih*, rely on classical sources[179] and are used at al-Azhar.[180] Nevertheless, these two books, along with the rest of those that she examines, are basically summaries (*mukhtasarat*) that encourage memorization of "the basic principles of a discipline and then its commentary (*sharh*) or supercommentary (*hashiya*) to understand them."[181]

Ultimately the sharia referenced today by secular state as well as Islamic actors is a modern construct resulting from the hybridization of the education system and state policies analyzed above. This politicized conception of sharia entails three main and somewhat contradictory dimensions:

1. Sharia is implemented by state rulers, not ulemas.
2. It is divinely inspired.
3. It concerns primarily family law and sometimes criminal law.

These three features are the basis of contentious politics, pitting secularists and Islamists against each other. On one hand, secular actors do not want an expansion of sharia to criminal law or other legal domains; nor do they contest the existence of sharia-based state law in family matters or the role of the state in regulating sharia law. On the other hand, Islamists consider sharia divinely inspired but envision its implementation by the state. A brief incursion into the existing positions of Islamists and clerics illustrates this shared conception.

Sharia as State Law by Islamists and Ulemas

The conception of sharia by traditional clerics often overlaps with the more political approach, although the clerics reveal some discomfort and oscillate between references to the premodern version while working within the parameters of the modern one.

Take, for example, the positions of Yusuf al-Qaradawi in *Madkhal li dirasat al-Shari'a al-Islamiya* (1993), as analyzed by Haifaa Khalafallah:[182]

> Qaradawi equates Shari'a with fiqh. Despite doctrinal evidence that he himself brings forth in various places in the book, Qaradawi attacks the rejection of fiqh by many orthodox groups as "incorrect, for fiqh is without doubt a Shari'a science because it is a discipline based on divine revelation." He further declares, "one cannot make the distinction between fiqh and Shari'a as simply being a difference between fiqh as manmade and Shari'a as of divine origin."[183]
>
> . . . Qaradawi discusses the Qur'an's usage of the term "Shari'a" and its root verb "shara'a": Qaradawi's standard linguistic examination reveals that, in neither its Quranic nor literal sense, does the word Shari'a refer to a specific [act] or set of laws. How then, one might ask, might the Quranic presentation of the word have been altered to denote later concepts? Qaradawi ignores this question altogether.[184]

Regarding sharia as divinely sanctioned, Khalafallah writes,

> Despite Qaradawi's mention that fiqh is, among other things, a product of human reasoning, human consensus, and even prevailing customs, Qaradawi makes no clear distinction between that which is divinely sanctioned and that which is of human provenance. . . . Using this ambiguity, Qaradawi presents a number of fiqh constructs that developed over time as the constituent elements of Shari'a from which the actual rules are to be derived. This ambiguity allows him to introduce the constructs of sunna and ijma [consensus of religious authorities] as absolute concepts and not subjects of inquiry.[185]

Meanwhile, if we look at political actors advocating for sharia and an Islamic state, we see an even clearer adoption of the modern, state-centered sharia. For example, according to the platform of the Justice and Development Party in Morocco,[186]

> A just state is founded based on justice that articulates and interprets justly in its ruling. It stands for the designation of a just ruler, who was chosen by the ummah based on satisfaction and consensus. The origin of justice comprises the sovereignty of justice, the shura, and a just ruling. A state would not attain justice until it follows a Shari'a that rules with fairness and righteousness. That way God will support its victory. A state that rules with virtue and condemns vice . . . are two main basis to building a just state: A divine Shari'a and an ummah that supports divine victory.[187]

Furthermore, consider the declaration of an Islamic constitution[188] by the Egyptian Muslim brotherhood:[189]

3 :

تستمد شرعية السلطة من
إقامتها لشرع الله
رضى الأمة بها.
ولها حق الطاعة، وحق النصرة، فضلاً عن حراسة الوجدان ما أطاعت الله
ورسوله.

Shari'a derives its power from God's law. The nation is satisfied with this. That which obeys Allah and his messenger has the right of obedience, the right of conquest, as well as to guard its conscience.

ة 1 :

الإسلام دين الدولة، وعقيدته مصونة، وشريعته واجبة، ومشروعيّته هي العليا فوق كل النصوص، ومصدره الأ ساسي الوحي: قرآناً وسنة، وكل ما يخالفه رد وباطل.

Islam is the religion of the state, its creed is inviolable, its law is an obligation, its legitimacy is the highest of all the texts, and it is the basic source of revelation: the Quran and the sunnah, and all that violates this answer is false.

ة 10 :

أحكام الشريعة تطبق تطبيقاً إقليمياً داخل الدولة، وتطبيقاً شخصياً على المسلمين خارجها. ولأهل الكتاب عقيدتهم وشعائرهم وأحكام الأسرة الخاصة بـهم.

Sharia is applied within the state and applied personally by Muslims abroad. The People of the Book share their religious practices and rituals and rules of their own families.

On the Ikhwan Web (the Muslim Brotherhood's official English-language website), in *The Principles of the Muslim Brotherhood*,[190] one can read,

A significant part of the Shari'ah tenets consists of rules and principles. Hence judges would exert their intellectual energy to deduce rulings for individual sub-cases with no need to have general laws promulgated by the rulers.

The comprehensive Islamic system remained the dominant one in the Islamic States. This does not mean that the application was perfectly sound or that no wrongs or sins were perpetrated by rulers. In fact, many of the texts have been abandoned or incorrectly interpreted.

The following assessment is a puzzling analysis of the deprivation of sharia as state law by the colonial power, when in fact the opposite occurred:

The first consequence of such [Western] invasion has been the exclusion of the Islamic Shari'ah from being the constitution and law that rules the state and the basic system of society. Egypt was occupied [by Britain] in September 1883, [and] hardly a year after the invasion, the so-called 'national courts' were established.

The call of the Muslim Brotherhood was based on two key pillars:

1. The introduction of the Islamic Shari'ah as the basis controlling the affairs of state and society.
2. Work to achieve unification among the Islamic countries and states, mainly among the Arab states, and liberating them from foreign imperialism.

The Western media also talk too much about the term 'Political Islam' or the groups of political Islam. . . . In fact, the aim behind this misrepresentation is to bring back to mind the history of religious or church governments in the Western countries. This is major fallacy and a serious manipulation of the tenets of Islam and of the truth about the ends of many Islamic groups and movements with the Muslim Brotherhood at their head.

As an exception to this dominant apprehension of sharia as state law, Islamist actors in Tunisia have refused such associations since the Jasmine Revolution of 2011. Rachid Ghannouchi, the founder of the Ennahda party in Tunisia, has declared,

The implementation of Shari'a is not part of our platform; our priorities are instituting democratic organization including freedom for all citizens without discrimination. We believe that Islamic legislations should not be imposed, as they are based on conviction and faith. There's no compulsion in religion. Freedom is given to all in their chosen lifestyle. It should also be noted that a part of the Tunisian civil law is derived from Shari'a and so is the Code of Personal Status. Islamic sciences are still taught in the Tunisian educational system and the Ministry of Religious Affairs is responsible of monitoring mosques. All what is mentioned indicates that the state did not disconnect from Islam, it is actually paying attention to it.[191]

Finally, one could object to my argument about the decline of the Islamic tradition by saying that such changes, from premodern to modern conceptions of sharia, are signs that the tradition is in fact still alive. But the transformations of sharia into state law, the debasement of the ulemas, and the negative connotation of *taqlid* are not indicators of a living tradition. They are, in fact, signs that tradition has become traditionalism, a perception shared today by both Islamist and secular actors across Muslim countries. Traditionalism entails fixing the teachings of the tradition in the past and making them irrelevant to the challenges of the present. It is one thing to reject blind imitation of the past and entirely another to dismiss the methodology that allows new interpretations at the core of any living tradition in the present. As astutely pointed out by Alasdair MacIntyre, when tradition is contrasted with reason and its stability is seen as an obstacle to change, the tradition is dying or already dead.[192] Ossification sets in when the people in a group begin arguing endlessly over definitions and attempt to codify implicitly established but imprecise elements of the tradition.

An example of this ossification appears in an open letter to Abu Bakr al-Baghdadi, the leader of ISIS, written by an impressive group of Sunni clerics around the world. They argue against ISIS as follows:

1. It is forbidden in Islam to issue fatwas without all the necessary learning requirements. Even then fatwas must follow Islamic legal theory as defined in the Classical texts. It is also forbidden to cite a portion of a verse from the Quran—or part of a verse—to derive a ruling without looking at everything that the Quran and Hadith teach related to that matter. In other words, there are strict subjective and objective prerequisites for fatwas, and one cannot "cherry-pick" Quranic verses for legal arguments without considering the entire Quran and Hadith.

2. It is forbidden in Islam to issue legal rulings about anything without mastery of the Arabic language.

3. It is forbidden in Islam to oversimplify sharia matters and ignore established Islamic sciences.

4. It is permissible in Islam [for scholars] to differ on any matter, except those fundamentals of religion that all Muslims must know.

5. It is forbidden in Islam to ignore the reality of contemporary times when deriving legal rulings.

6. It is forbidden in Islam to kill the innocent.

7. It is forbidden in Islam to kill emissaries, ambassadors, and diplomats; hence it is forbidden to kill journalists and aid workers.

8. Jihad in Islam is defensive war. It is not permissible without the right cause, the right purpose and without the right rules of conduct.

9. It is forbidden in Islam to declare people non-Muslim unless he (or she) openly declares disbelief.

10. It is forbidden in Islam to harm or mistreat—in any way—Christians or any "People of the Scripture."

11. It is obligatory to consider Yazidis as People of the Scripture.

12. The re-introduction of slavery is forbidden in Islam. It was abolished by universal consensus.

13. It is forbidden in Islam to force people to convert.

14. It is forbidden in Islam to deny women their rights.

15. It is forbidden in Islam to deny children their rights.

16. It is forbidden in Islam to enact legal punishments (*hudud*) without following the correct procedures that ensure justice and mercy.

17. It is forbidden in Islam to torture people.

18. It is forbidden in Islam to disfigure the dead.

19. It is forbidden in Islam to attribute evil acts to God.

20. It is forbidden in Islam to destroy the graves and shrines of Prophets and Companions.

21. Armed insurrection is forbidden in Islam for any reason other than clear disbelief by the ruler and not allowing people to pray.

22. It is forbidden in Islam to declare a caliphate without consensus from all Muslims. Loyalty to one's nation is permissible in Islam.
23. After the death of the Prophet, Islam does not require anyone to emigrate anywhere.

This list, far from making a strong argument in favor of the Islamic tradition, actually reinforces traditionalism by confining Islamic thinking to a "do and don't" list. In other words, citing terms or topics discussed in the past or asserting what the tradition says does not make it alive. What makes a tradition alive is the use of the methods transmitted from past scholars to make sense of the present. In this regard, we can conclude that today neither the established clerics nor the Islamists operate within the traditional framework.

Notes

1. Hudson, Charles. *The Southeastern Indians*. Knoxville: University of Tennessee Press, 1976.
2. Van der Veer, Peter, and Hartmut Lehmann. *Nation and Religion: Perspectives on Europe and Asia*. Princeton, NJ: Princeton University Press, 1999.
3. Cesari, Jocelyne. *The Awakening of Muslim Democracy: Religion, Modernity, and the State*. New York: Cambridge University Press, 2014.
4. Karpat, Kemal H. *The Politicization of Islam: Reconstructing Identity, State, Faith, and Community in the Late Ottoman State*. New York: Oxford University Press, 2001.
5. Within the Islamic tradition, there are four schools of jurisprudence—Hanafi, Shafi'i, Maliki, and Hanbali—all named for their respective founders. In the ninth and tenth centuries, these schools were consolidated and separated from the caliphal political power.
6. Taylor, Charles. *The Secular Age*. Cambridge, MA: Harvard University Press, 2007.
7. Ibid.
8. Ibid.
9. It is on this insight from Émile Durkheim that Robert Bellah built his concept of civil religion for American society.
10. Alfred Stepan, Juan Linz, and Yogandra Yadav generalized the use of the term *state-nation* in their edited volume. See Stepan, Alfred C., Juan J. Linz, and Yogandra Yadav. *Crafting State-Nations: India and Other Multinational Democracies*. Baltimore: Johns Hopkins University Press, 2011.
11. Lee, Dwight E. "The Origins of Pan-Islamism." *American Historical Review* 47, no. 2 (1942): 278–287.

12. Reiser, Stewart. "Pan-Arabism Revisited." *Middle East Journal* 37, no. 2 (1983): 218–233.

13. With the Young Ottoman movement (1865), a contemporary form of political ideology first emerged in the Islamic Middle East, almost completely through civil bureaucracy. Led by Namik Kemal, the movement emphasized the need for activism and critique of the Tanzimat to solve the empire's problems. It ultimately led to the promulgation of the constitution in 1876. For more information, refer to Findley, Carter Vaughn. "The Advent of Ideology in the Islamic Middle East (Part II)." *Studia Islamica* 56 (1982): 147–180.

14. Riedler, Florian. *Opposition and Legitimacy in the Ottoman Empire: Conspiracies and Political Cultures.* Abingdon, UK: Routledge, 2011, pp. 26–41; Hanioğlu, M. Şükrü. *A Brief History of the Late Ottoman Empire.* Princeton, NJ: Princeton University Press, 2010, pp. 103–104.

15. For an evaluation of the Ottoman constitution and parliament, see Devereux, Robert. *The First Ottoman Constitutional Period: A Study of the Midhat Constitution and Parliament.* Baltimore: Johns Hopkins University Press, 1964; Brown, Nathan J., and Adel Omar Sharif. "Inscribing the Islamic Shari'a in Arab Constitutional Law." In *Islamic Law and the Challenges of Modernity*, ed. Yvonne Yazbeck Haddad and Barbara Freyer Stowasser. Walnut Creek, CA: Altamira, 2004, pp. 59–60; Shaw, Stanford J., and Ezel Kural. *History of the Ottoman Empire and Modern Turkey.* Cambridge: Cambridge University Press, 1976, pp. 174–189, 213–214.

16. Landau, Jacob M. *Parliaments and Parties in Egypt.* Tel-Aviv: Israel Publishing House, 1953, p. 7.

17. Ayalon, Ami. *Language and Change in the Arab Middle East: The Evolution of Modern Political Discourse.* New York: Oxford University Press, 1987, pp. 110–126.

18. Lauzière, Henri. *The Making of Salafism: Islamic Reform in the Twentieth Century.* New York: Columbia University Press, 2016.

19. Muhammad bin 'Abd al-Wahhab (1703–1792) was born in 'Uyaynah, a village in the region of Najd. He took his first religious education from his father, Shaikh 'Abd al-Wahhab, who was a prominent judge and religious scholar of the time. Afterward, bin 'Abd al-Wahhab embarked on a new educational path in Al-Madinah al-Munawwarah and Basra in Iraq, where he was taught by a number of Islamic scholars (*ulama*). He returned to his village and began his own preaching with the goal to purify Islam from traditional schools of jurisprudence and from any practices associated with superstitious beliefs. He was known to coerce people to accept his interpretations of Islamic prescriptions. After being expelled from his village for his extreme views and conduct in 1744, he was received by Muhammad bin Saud in his settlement. Together, they aimed to expand the al-Saud political influence by creating an army and coercing people into following the Wahhabi doctrine. All who converted were expected to join the army and perform jihad for the cause, including those who converted out of fear. See Algar, Hamid. *Wahhabism: A Critical Essay.* North Aledon, NJ: Islamic Publications International, 2002.

20. Scholars such as Khaled Abu El Fadl have noted that with the international religious influence of the Saudi kingdom, Wahhabism and Salafism have become synonymous, hence erasing the initial modernist connotations of the term *Salaf.* See Fadl, Khaled Abou El. *The Great Theft: Wrestling Islam from the Extremists.* New York: HarperSanFrancisco, 2007.

21. For the whole debate on the impossibility of the Islamic state and the nature of political Islam, see the *Salafiyya* entry in Martin, Richard C., ed. *Encyclopedia of Islam and the Muslim World*. Farmington Hills: Gale, Cengage Learning, 2016.

22. Asad, Talal. *Formations of the Secular: Christianity, Islam, Modernity*. Stanford, CA: Stanford University Press, 2003.

23 Feldman, Noah. "A Lesson for Newt Gingrich: What Shari'a Is (and Isn't)." *New York Times*. July 17, 2016. https://www.nytimes.com/2016/07/17 /opinion/sunday/a-lesson-for-newt-gingrich-what-shariah-is-and-isnt.html.

24. Rifa'a al-Tahtawi (1801–1873) was an Egyptian religious scholar trained at al-Azhar in Islamic disciplines. He was mentored by a Shaikh Hasan al-'Atta, who supported Muhammad Ali's reform program. He was exposed to European ideas as a religious teacher in Ali's first student mission in Paris, after which he helped develop a new education system in Egypt that encouraged language instruction and the integration of European and Islamic ideas. See "Tahtawi, Rifaa al-." In *The Oxford Dictionary of Islam*, ed. John L. Esposito. Oxford Islamic Studies Online. Accessed July 20, 2016. http://www.oxfordislamicstudies .com/article/opr/t125/e2310.

25. Al-Ṭahṭāwī, Rifāʿah, and Daniel L. Newman. *An Imam in Paris: Account of a Stay in France by an Egyptian Cleric, 1826–1831*. London: Saqi, 2004.

26. Husry, Khaldun Sati. *Origins of Modern Arab Political Thought*. Delmar, NY: Caravan Books, 1980.

27. Gesink, Indira. *Islamic Reform and Conservatism: Al-Azhar and the Evolution of Modern Sunni Islam*. New York: I. B. Tauris, 2014, p. 67.

28. Al-Suyuti was an Egyptian scholar, intellectual, and teacher. He was deeply involved with the political and religious conflicts of his time, and his work mostly focuses on Islamic sciences. Some of his books deal with Quranic exegesis, including his famous *Mastery in the Sciences of the Qurʾān*. *Al-muẓhir fī ʿulūm al-lughah wa anwāʿihā* (The luminous work concerning the sciences of language and its subfields) is a well-known linguistic encyclopedia by al-Suyuti that covers "the history of the Arabic language, phonetics, semantics, and morphology." See "Al-Suyuti." *Encyclopaedia Britannica*. May 16, 2007. https:// www.britannica.com/biography/al-Suyuti.

29. Jalal al-Din al-Suyuti, whose ranking al-Tahtawi summarized, separated between the independent *mujahidun*, such as the founders of the Sunni law who "devised the hermeneutical structures other jurists used to derive judgment," and the unrestricted *mujahidun*, who derived rulings from within the present hermeneutics, such as himself. By ignoring this distinction, al-Tahtawi could more easily state that his contemporaries did acknowledge the *mujahidun* who belong to the first rank.

30. Gesink, *Islamic Reform*, 66.

31. Ibid., 66.

32. Ibid., 67.

33. Ibid., 66–67.

34. Ibid., 68.

35. See al-Tahtawi, Rifa'a. *al-Qawl al-sadid fi al-ijtihad wa al-tajdid*. Cairo: Matba'at wadi al-neel, 1867; Gesink, *Islamic Reform*, 68.

36. Gesink, *Islamic Reform*, 68.

37. Ibid.

38. Ibid., 71.

39. Jamaal al-Din al-Afghani was a political activist best known for spearheading the pan-Islamic movement. He lived in Cairo from 1871 to 1879 and, along with Islamic scholar Muhammad Abduh, modernized the interpretation and teaching of the Islamic tradition. He ran a Free Mason society and encouraged his students to be politically active and to publish in newspapers. He also advocated anti-imperialism against the British, writing in Arabic to be more accessible to audiences. Many of al-Afghani's followers would go on to become leaders in Egyptian politics. For more information, see "Afghani, Jamal al-Din al-." In *The Islamic World: Past and Present*, ed. John L. Esposito. Oxford Islamic Studies Online. Accessed July 20, 2016. http://www.oxfordislamic studies.com/article/opr/t243/e8.

40. Gesink, *Islamic Reform*, 73.

41. Ibid.

42. Ibid.

43. Bin Salamon, Ahmad. *Reform of Al-Azhar in the 20th Century*. Diss., New York University, 1980, 65.

44. Ibid., 66, 67.

45. Ibid., 68.

46. The Urabi movement was a protest led by Ahmad Urabi (1841–1911), who was dissatisfied with Egypt's educated class, as well as with the ethnic discrimination within the Egyptian military. For more information, see "Urabi Revolution." Histories of the Modern Middle East. Accessed January 2, 2017. http://laits.utexas.edu/modern_me/egypt/2/urabi; Salamon, *Reform of Al-Azhar*, 69–71.

47. Ibid., 68.

48. Ibid., 71.

49. Abdal Hamid Kishk (1933–1996), a graduate of Al-Azhar, was a preacher and activist known for his sermons about the social and political conditions of Egypt and his opposition to the state. Dissemination of his speeches on cassette contributed to his extreme popularity in the 1970s.

50. Salamon, *Reform of Al-Azhar*, 69.

51. Keddie, N. R. *Sayyid Jamāl ad-Dīn "al-Afghānī": A Political Biography*. Berkeley: University of California Press, 1972.

52. See Keddie, N. R. "Afgani, Jamal-al-din." *Encyclopaedia Iranica*. Accessed December 25, 2016. http://www.iranicaonline.org/articles/afgani-jamal -al-din, I/5, 481–486.

53. Abduh was a disciple of al-Afghani, accompanying him on a trip to Paris from 1882 to 1884 to write articles for Jam'iyat al'Uwat al-Wuthqa on topics such as British imperialism, the French colonies, and the Ottomans. Before that, during al-Afghani's stay in Egypt, Abduh contributed several articles to *al-Ahram* and other newspapers that chronicled al-Afghani's rising impact. In 1888, Abduh returned from exile and was appointed judge in the Court of First Instance, making him the only shaikh among European judges. In 1891, he became a counsellor at the Court of Appeals in Cairo, and in 1899 he was appointed grand mufti of Egypt, the highest state authority on the interpretation of Islamic law. For more information, see "Abduh, Muhammad." In *The Oxford Dictionary of Islam*, ed. John L. Esposito. Oxford Islamic Studies Online. Accessed July 20, 2016. http://www.oxfordislamicstudies.com/article/opr/t125 /e15.

54. Salamon, *Reform of Al-Azhar*, 73, 74.

55. Taizir, Aswita. *Muhammad Abduh and the Reformation of Islamic Law.* PhD diss., McGill University, 12.

56. Gesink, *Islamic Reform*, 189.

57. Taizir, *Muhammad Abduh*, 27.

58. See ibid., 28; Masud, Muhammad Khalid. *Shari'a Today: Essays on Contemporary Issues and Debates in Muslim Societies.* Islamabad: National Book Foundation, Iqbal International Institute for Research and Dialogue, 2013.

59. Gesink, *Islamic Reform*, 79.

60. Taizir, *Muhammad Abduh*, 17.

61. Ibid., 21.

62. Amarah, Muhammed. *Risalat al-tawhid lil Imam Muhammad Abduh.* Cairo: Dar al-Shoruq, 1994.

63. Gesink, *Islamic Reform*, 169.

64. Ibid., 169.

65. Taizir, *Muhammad Abduh*, 46.

66. Salamon, *Reform of Al-Azhar*, 77.

67. Ibid., 75–76.

68. Gesink, *Islamic Reform*, 168.

69. Ibid., 168.

70. Salamon, *Reform of Al-Azhar*, 76.

71. Taizir, *Muhammad Abduh*, 56.

72. *Sharia*, in its traditional sense, means "way" or "path." It was the methodology used by ulemas or scholars of Islam to produce meaningful interpretations.

73. Taizir, *Muhammad Abduh*, 21.

74. *Talfiq* is a legal term that describes the process of deriving rules from different schools of Islamic law. For more information, see "Talfiq." Oxford Islamic Studies Online. Accessed August 16, 2017. http://www.oxfordislamicstudies.com /article/opr/t125/e2323. See also Taizir, *Muhammad Abduh*, 17.

75. Ibid., 61.

76. Ibid., 26.

77. Gesink, *Islamic Reform*, 170.

78. Abduh issued two fatwas: one in favor of monogamy in opposition to polygamy and one against monopoly by the husband of the divorce procedure (*talaq*). Both rulings derived from his direct interpretation of the Quranic verses. Taizir, *Muhammad Abduh*, 43.

79. Gesink, *Islamic Reform*, 78.

80. Ibid., 166.

81. Ibid., 80.

82. Salamon, *Reform of Al-Azhar*, 81.

83. Gesink, *Islamic Reform*, 168.

84. Salamon, *Reform of Al-Azhar*, 80.

85. Gesink, *Islamic Reform*, 82.

86. Ibid., 168.

87. Salamon, *Reform of Al-Azhar*, 75.

88. Gesink, *Islamic Reform*, 174.

89. Ibid., 174.

90. Shaikh Abd al-Rahman al-Sharbini was a *shafi'i* jurist and the president of al-Azhar in 1905. Although in favor of reforming al-Azhar, he was against incorporating modern sciences into the curriculum. He was concerned that the students would neglect Arabic and Islamic studies and instead focus on modern sciences.

See الشيخ الشربيني وبداية عهد الضعف في تاريخ الأزهر (Shaykh al Sharbini and the beginning of Al Azhar decline). Accessed August 30, 2017. http://www.Islamist-movements.com /26653. See also Salamon, *Reform of Al-Azhar*, 81.

91. Gesink, *Islamic Reform*, 170.

92. Ibid., 171.

93. Ibid., 182–183.

94. Ibid., 189.

95. Ibid., 167.

96. Ibid., 169.

97. Ibid., 190.

98. Ibid., 165.

99. Ibid., 169. There is some evidence that Abduh became aware of the theory of evolution and its implications in the 1880s; contrary to the ad hominem campaign against him, however, his observations never accumulated into a coherent opinion on its legitimacy (or lack thereof). He acknowledged the Quran's ambiguity regarding the origin of man as proof of "authentic revelation." Most remarkably, in 1896, he alluded to a rejection of the theory of natural selection in *Risalat al-tawhid* but did not address it specifically. He argued that the Quran addresses the origin of man in a fashion that can "neither be rejected by Jews, nor by contemporary scientists who had presented proofs against the belief."

100. Ibid., 191.

101. Ibid., 169; Shavit, Uriya. *Scientific and Political Freedom in Islam*. London: Routledge, 2017, p. 124.

102. Gesink, *Islamic Reform*, 22.

103. Muhammad Ali (also known as Mehmed Ali) was the Ottoman sultan's viceroy in Egypt. He initiated the modernization of Egyptian society during the French occupation between 1798 and 1801. Facing hostility from the Ottoman sultan, he attempted to strengthen his position by implementing changes such as improving the agricultural and irrigation systems and rearranging the administrative system to better control economic development. See Rivlin, Helen Anne B. "Muhammad 'Ali." *Encyclopaedia Britannica*. March 6, 2013. https://www.britannica.com/biography/Muhammad-Ali-pasha-and-viceroy-of-Egypt.

104. Gesink, *Islamic Reform*, 22.

105. Ibid., 206.

106. Ibid., 207.

107. Ahmad Shafiq Pasha was an Ottoman grand vizier. He introduced Western political components into the established system, including political institutions, a constitution, and a parliament. He believed that education, not revolution, is key to change. He was exiled in 1877 after he led a coup d'état to overthrow Sultan Abdulaziz. For more, see "Midhat Pasha, Ahmad Shafiq." Oxford Islamic Studies Online. Accessed January 2, 2017. http://www.oxfordislamicstudies.com/article /opr/t125/e1508.

108. Gesink, *Islamic Reform*, 197.

109. Ibid., 214.

110. Ibid., 212.

111. Ibid., 215.

112. Fortna, Benjamin C. "Education and Autobiography at the End of the Ottoman Empire." *Die Welt Des Islams*, n.s., 41, no. 1 (2001): 1–31.

113. Bulliet, Richard W. "The Shaikh Al-Islām and the Evolution of Islamic Society." *Studia Islamica* 35 (1972): 53–67, 65.

114. Zaman, Muhammad Qasim. "Religious Education and the Rhetoric of Reform: The Madrasa in British India and Pakistan." *Comparative Studies in Society and History* 41, no. 2 (1999): 294–323.
115. Fortna, "Education and Autobiography," 17.
116. Ibid., 17.
117. Ibid., 21.
118. Ibid., 18.
119. Ibid., 19.
120. Ibid.
121. Metcalf, Barbara Daly. *Islamic Revival in British India: Deoband, 1860–1900.* Princeton, NJ: Princeton University Press, 1982.
122. Zaman, "Religious Education," 296.
123. Ibid., 296.
124. Ibid.
125. Ibid., 297.
126. Ibid.
127. Ibid., 301.
128. The movement to reform traditional Islamic thinking emerged in 1867 from the Dar Al Ulum Deoband created by Shah Waliullah Delawi (1703–1762).
129. Ibid., 304.
130. Ibid., 306.
131. See Zaman, "Religious Education," 308; Metcalf, *Islamic Revival*, 46.
132. Wood, Leonard G. H. *Reception of European Law, Origins of Islamic Legal Revivalism, and Foundations of Transformations in Islamic Legal Thought in Egypt, 1875–1960.* PhD diss., Harvard University, 2011, p. 304.
133. First, the Khedivial Law School, which would eventually become the Law Faculty of Cairo University, issued a license in Egyptian law. Second, the École de droit français du Caire issued a license in French Law. The third school was King Farouk University, which also issued an Egyptian law license modeled after the Khedivial Law School. Ibid., 32.
134. Ibid., 33.
135. Ibid., 56.
136. Ibid., 88.
137. *Nizamiyyah* courts were an Ottoman institution introduced in Egypt in the 1860s. Unlike the sharia courts, they operated under the direct authority of the sultan bureaucracy and dealt with civil and criminal laws.
138. Dar al-Ulum University, established in 1872, accepted al-Azhar students, and memorization was its learning method. It offered subjects from both religious and secular education. It is now part of the faculty of Cairo University. See "Dar al-Ulum." Oxford Islamic Studies Online. Accessed January 2, 2017. http://www.oxfordislamicstudies.com/article/opr/t125/e498.
139. Wood, *Reception of European Law*, 37.
140. Ibid., 21.
141. Ibid., 22.
142. Ibid., 515.
143. Ibid., 510.
144. Ibid., 515.
145. Ibid., 142–143.
146. Al-Muhairi, Butti Sultan Butti Ali. "Islamisation and Modernisation Within the UAE Penal Law: Shari'a in the Modern Era." *Arab Law Quarterly* 11, no. 1 (1996): 34–49.

147. *Siyasa shariyya* is "Muslim law as expressed in regulatory decisions or policy of government." See "Siyasa Shar'iyya Definition." *Duhaime's Law Dictionary*. Accessed January 2, 2017. http://www.duhaime.org/LegalDictionary/S/SiyasaShariyya.aspx.

148. Muhibb al-Din al-Khatib (1886–1969) was an Egyptian activist and journalist. See Rizvi, Sayyid Muhammad. *Muhibb al-Din al-Khatib: A Portrait of a Salafi-Arabist (1886–1969)*. Master's thesis, Simon Fraser University, 1991.

149. Quoted by Wood, *Reception of European Law*, 143–145.

150. Metcalf, *Islamic Revival*, 49.

151. Ibid., 48–50.

152. Al-Muhairi, "Islamisation and Modernisation," 36.

153. Ibid., 38.

154. Debs, Richard A., Frank E. Vogel, and Al-Sayyid Ridwan. "The Development of a National Legal System." In *Islamic Law and Civil Code: The Law of Property in Egypt*. Columbia: Columbia University Press, 2010.

155. Al-Muhairi, "Islamisation and Modernisation," 34.

156. Debs, "The Development of a National Legal System," 102.

157. Wood, *Reception of European Law*, 71.

158. Ibid., 46.

159. Ibid., 73.

160. Ibid., 74.

161. Ibid., 48.

162. Ibid., 47.

163. Al-Muhairi, "Islamisation and Modernisation," 38.

164. Wood, *Reception of European Law*, 73.

165. Ibid., 76.

166. Cuno, Kenneth M. "Reorganization of the Sharia Courts of Egypt: How Legal Modernization Set Back Women's Rights in the Nineteenth Century." *Journal of the Ottoman and Turkish Studies Association* 2, no. 1 (2015): 93.

167. Ibid., 106.

168. Debs, "The Development of a National Legal System," 115.

169. Wood, *Reception of European Law*, 12.

170. Ibid., 13.

171. Al-Muhairi, "Islamisation and Modernisation," 39–40.

172. Al-Muhairi, Butti Sultan Butti Ali. "The Incompatibility of the Penal Code with Shari'a." *Arab Law Quarterly* 12, no. 3 (1997): 307–329, 309.

173. Ibid., 311.

174. Cardinal, Monique. "Islamic Legal Theory Curriculum: Are the Classics Taught Today?" *Islamic Law and Society* 12, no. 2 (2005): 229.

175. Ibid., 233.

176. Ibid., 243.

177. Ibid., 257.

178. Ibid.

179. Ibid., 243.

180. Ibid., 242.

181. Ibid.

182. Khalafallah, Haifaa G. *Rethinking Islamic Law: The Genesis and Evolution in the Islamic Legal Method and Structures*. Ann Arbor, MI: ProQuest, 1999.

183. Ibid., 22.

184. Ibid., 21.

185. Ibid., 25.

186. The Islamist Justice and Development Party stands for conservative democracy. Since 2011, it has led the executive branch of the government. Abdelilah Benkirane, who was elected as the party's leader in 2008, was appointed prime minister of Morocco in 2011. The party's platform focuses on internal reforms and political developments, including education reform and enhancing the cultural regional context.

187. "Al 'Adl Wa Al Ihsane, الدولة العادلة (State and Justice)." Aljamaa.net. January 20, 2012. http://www.aljamaa.net/ar/document/51883.shtml.

188. Jarisha, Ali. "I'lan dustor Islami (Proclamation of an Islamic constitution)." Al Mansura, Dar al- Wafa lil tibaa wa- l-Nashr wa-l-Tauzi, 1985.

189. Ibid.

190. "The Principles of the Muslim Brotherhood." Ikhwan Web. February 1, 2010. http://www.ikhwanweb.com/article.php?id=813.

191. Rachid Ghannouchi was exiled to London after falsification of the legislative elections in 1989 under Zine El Abidine Ben Ali and returned to Tunisia after the Jasmine Revolution in January 2011. He assigned himself the task of forming a coalition government between the Ennahda and secular parties upon his return. Translation from the author. Al-Ghannouchi, Rachid. "Ennahda Program Does Not Include Sharia." *Al-Majalla*. October 3, 2011. http://arb .majalla.com/2011/10/article55227372/ راشد-الغنوشي-ليس-في-برنامج-النهضة-تطبي.

192. MacIntyre, Alasdair C. *After Virtue: A Study in Moral Theory*. Notre Dame, IN: University of Notre Dame Press, 1984.

3

Hegemonic Islam

Nation building in Muslim countries resulted in a decisive reorganization of the society-state-religion nexus, unknown in premodern times because the caliphates did not subordinate Islamic institutions and clerics to political power. Furthermore, according to most scholars, divisions of labor and hierarchies between temporal and spiritual authorities were fairly well established by the tenth century.[1] While "official" ulemas certainly worked on behalf of political rulers and provided religious justification for their policies in medieval times, back then religious authorities and institutions were financially and organizationally independent of the political apparatus.

The caliphs also acknowledged the cultural and religious diversity of the population, although this did not translate into egalitarian legal and political status for people of all religions and ethnicities. The *ummah,* or community, defined as the sum of the territories and populations under caliphate rule, hence encompassed an extensive distribution of ethnic, cultural, and linguistic groups, including Muslims, Christians, Jews, Zoroastrians, Bahais, and Druzes. Even though the caliphate represented the original community, which follows the message of the Prophet Mohammad, in reality, transformed by geography, it evolved historically into a sort of secular dynasty overseeing multiple ethnic and religious groups.[2]

This tension between the ideal (of a community following the model of the Prophet) and the political reality was apparent in the distinction between the sharia and *syar* forged by the jurist consulates. Whereas sharia referred to the laws applying to Muslims, *syar* designated the laws applying to non-Muslims living under caliphate rule or to relations between the caliphate and non-Muslims at the international level.[3] Nonetheless, the modern vision of the *ummah* is removed from this imperial definition, the consensus among contemporary Muslim scholars being that the *ummah* is a spiritual, nonterritorial community distinguished by the shared beliefs of its members. The *ummah* is therefore seen as a type of citizenship that all Muslims possess independently of their territorial location.[4] For example, cleric Yusuf al-Qaradawi has declared, "I believe in the unity of the Muslim Nation with all its groups, sects and doctrines, since the entire ummah believes in one Book and one Messenger, and faces one *qiblah* [the direction that Muslims take when praying in order to face Kabah]."[5]

As the Ottoman Empire collapsed, the emergence of the state as the central political institution went hand in hand with the homogenization of the populations inhabiting the new nation's territory. That is why nation-building systematically omitted and sometimes eradicated particular ethnic, religious, and linguistic groups in order to create one nation defined by one religion and one language. This homogenization process also led to a politicized narrative of religion (i.e., political Islam).

The particularity does not lie in the fact that the nation-state redefined the rules of engagement between religion and politics, which happened everywhere.[6] The architects of all new nation-states must determine the degree to which to sacrifice the "core" collective identity of the country in exchange for the imported institutions and technologies necessary to strengthen the state both militarily and economically.[7] Specific to Muslim states is the construction of Islam as a political culture. The emergence of new political norms tied to nationalism resulted in state narratives that either referenced Islamic terminology or were diversely articulated within an Islamic framework. Both pan-Islamism and pan-Arabism contributed to the broad appeal of nationalist discourse.[8]

Islamic references and norms served to "localize" the nation-building process and legitimize state actors and policies. The outcome of such localization was the redefinition of Islam within the new state institutions.

The adoption of exterior norms in local contexts involved both grafting and pruning, two tactics often employed by local actors to legitimize external norms by associating them with pre-existing ones. Under these circumstances, proponents of new norms had to construct and carefully articulate linkages, because they were not always intuitive or natural to the masses. In Muslim countries, pruning and grafting of Islam onto state institutions and national identities primarily took place through three mechanisms: nationalization of Islamic institutions and clerics, incorporation of Islam into secular laws, and integration of Islam into public education systems. I have called the outcome of these three processes hegemonic Islam.[9]

It is important to note the differences between a dominant religion, an established religion, and a hegemonic religion. A religion is dominant when it is the religion of the majority of a given country. In such cases, the dominant religion continues to impart historical and cultural references that are considered "natural" and "legitimate." Religious symbols and rituals become embedded in the public culture and country. Examples of such dominant religions include Protestantism in the United States and Catholicism in France and Poland. An established religion is one recognized by law as the religion of the country and sometimes financially supported by the state (e.g., the Evangelical Lutheran Church in Denmark). The existence of an established church is usually compatible with the recognition of religious minorities. A religion becomes hegemonic, however, when the state grants a certain religious group exclusive legal or political rights denied to members of other religions, such as teaching religious education in public schools or funding places of worship. In other words, religious hegemony refers to legal and political privileges granted to members of a specific religion, which in most but not all cases is the dominant one.

The state's regulation of religion may assume several forms. For example, legal neutrality is on one end of the spectrum, with legal privilege on the other. There are many nuances between the two. Legal neutrality, as understood and codified in most secular democracies, entails recognition and legal protection of all religions. Separation of religion and state is not a necessary prerequisite for legal neutrality, which can be implemented even when there is state accommodation of religions (as in most European democracies) or interference of the state with religions, such as the regulation of religious practices or special tax regimes for religious groups. Additionally, legal neutrality does not mean that the law is always neutral. Frequently, the dominant religious group serves as an implicit standard for legal work concerning other religious groups.[10]

Legal privilege occurs not only when one religion is implicitly or explicitly defined as the religion of the state or the nation but also when it is granted financial resources and/or legal rights denied to all other religious groups.[11] In other words, legal privilege is reflected in the following features:

- The constitution of the country officially recognizes one religion.
- Religious foundations, learning institutions, and clerics are nationalized.
- The legal system includes some provisions of religious law.
- State schools teach the recognized religious doctrine.

The unexpected and often unseen consequences of legal privilege are state restrictions and controls on the activities of the official religion, usually involving

- a ministry of religious affairs and administration to manage the official religion
- government regulation of the use of religious symbols and activities
- state laws and policies limiting religious freedoms
- penalties for defamation of the official religion
- government interference with worship

State regulation also involves tacit or explicit discrimination against religious groups not accorded official status, such as the following:

- Minority groups do not receive government funds or resources for education, religious programs, or maintenance of property or organizations.
- Domestic or foreign religious groups are forbidden to proselytize.
- Conversion from the official religion to another, if not fully forbidden, is severely restricted.

The government is hostile toward religious minorities or may adhere to a policy of nonintervention in the case of harassment or persecution of these groups.[12] In the majority of Muslim countries, legal and political rights generally accrue to adherents of the dominant Islamic orientation (e.g., Sunni, Shiite), but not to members of other religious groups (Muslim or otherwise). More infrequently, privilege is accorded to a religious minority, such as the Sunni in Bahrain and Iraq (pre-2003). Moreover, hegemonic religion is not specific to Muslim countries and can describe Buddhism in Sri Lanka today and, to a certain extent, the Orthodox Church in Greece.[13] Meanwhile, Indonesia and Senegal are the only exceptions in the Muslim world in their attempts to create a regime of legal neutrality. In this form of religious nationalism, Islam is more than a component of national identity; it is part and parcel of state institutions that regulate everybody, even citizens who are not or do not want to identify as Muslims.

The Nationalization of Religion

Prior to the modern state, Islamic institutions were the main providers of services, from education to legal counseling, for local communities. The central political power did not exert tight control over the endowments and actions of the clerics. In contrast, Islamic institutions were included within the state system during the nation-building phase. This was done through what Ali Dessouki calls the "four methods of subordination": (1) the elimination of financially independent religious institutions, (2) the structural reorganization of religious institutions, (3) the integration of sharia courts into the National Courts, and (4) the integration of religious education into national education.[14] As such, clerics became civil servants, and religious endowments (*awqaf*) and religious schools (madrasas) came under state control.[15]

The nationalization of religious institutions and the inscription of Islam into national narratives are two main features of nation-building that have shaped the very nature of political Islam.

Absorption of Islam into State Institutions

In Egypt, structural changes started under Mehemet Ali and culminated with Gamal Abdel Nasser's 1952 reforms, which put all Islamic foundations under the control of the new Ministry of Endowments (Wizaret al-Auqaf).[16] This transfer gave the ministry control over mosques, as well as over clerics and religious institutions.[17] Similarly, the Law 103 of 1961 gave the state control over the appointment of the grand shaikh at al-Azhar, previously nominated by his peers in the ulema hierarchy. As such, the position became symbolic and lost any actual authoritative legitimacy.[18] Furthermore, three government-appointed experts, along with representatives from the Ministries of Endowments, Education, Justice, and Treasury, were integrated into the High Council of al-Azhar, which oversaw the university curriculum.[19] Under Anwar Sadat, all preachers at private mosques were required to have a license supported by the Ministry of Endowments, while preaching licenses were required for all imams at state mosques.

Up to the present, all state rulers have used al-Azhar to further their political goals. For example, Nasser solicited legal opinions (fatwas) to legitimize his socialist ideology on the basis of Islam. Similarly, Sadat used fatwas to justify political acts, such as the peace treaty with Israel and the *infitah* (economic liberalization) policy. Not surprisingly, when Muslim Brotherhood leader Mohamed Morsi became the first democratically elected president of Egypt in 2011, he relied on al-Azhar to counter the Salafi opposition to his regime.[20] When General Abdel Fattah el-Sisi overthrew him in 2013, al-Azhar shaikh Ahmed el-Tayeb, along with Coptic archbishop Pope Theodorus II and Salafi al-Nur party leader Younis Makhyoun, endorsed the new head of state.[21] Publicly, al-Azhar has openly supported Sisi and his violent repression of Muslim Brotherhood supporters, whom Shaikh Ali Gomaa, a senior al-Azhar cleric and former grand mufti, has called "putrid people" and "riffraff."[22]

Since becoming president, Sisi has made several attempts to reform al-Azhar to conform the institution to his policies. For example, in 2014 he gave an address on the Prophet Muhammad's birthday, calling for religious revolution against extremism and blaming al-Azhar for rekindling extremist religious rhetoric.[23] In an interview given to *Al-Monitor* in June 2015, Abdul Hai Azab, then president of al-Azhar, discussed the changes aimed to "correct Islamic concepts to keep the students from following those seeking to recruit them to serve the purposes of terrorism."[24] These changes include curriculum reform, to comply with Sisi's recommendation to remove militancy concepts, such as the *jizya* tax (required from non-Muslims who live under Islamic political rule). In July 2014, several textbooks used at al-Azhar were confiscated and fifteen members of the faculty dismissed after the university warned that "any student or faculty member who incites, supports or joins in protests that disrupt learning or promote rioting or vandalism will be expelled or fired."[25] Abbas Shuman, al-Azhar deputy head, explained that the banned books include passages describing the spoils of war and slavery, outdated topics relevant to the Muslim conquests.[26] These policies illustrate two major features of political Islam: first, the state regulates Islamic orthodoxy; second, the tradition is deemed outdated and must be authoritatively corrected.

Although Turkey is often presented as the most "secular" Muslim country, its state-engineered Islam exemplifies hegemonic religion. After the creation of Turkey, the appointment of laymen to positions previously held by clerics, as well as the integration of clerics into the state's administrative structure, deeply transformed Islamic institutions. In 1925, all religious movements and titles, such as shaikh, dervish, occultist, magician, and mausoleum guard, were abolished.[27] Furthermore, the office of the *şeyhülislam*—the mufti at the head of the Ottoman religious hierarchy—was closed.[28] Religious property and all other Islamic institutions were nationalized under the Ministry of Religious Affairs and Pious Foundations. Madrasas were shut down, and religious schools were integrated into national schools.[29] In 1930, religious education was removed from the curriculum. In 1997, eight years of education became compulsory for children, effectively delaying their entry into religious schools and therefore only offering standard high school education as an option.[30] All of these measures simultaneously legitimized state control of religion while minimizing religious influence in politics.[31] Islam was deprived of its previous impact in the public sphere.

The creation of the Diyanet, or Ministry of Religious Affairs, cemented the institutional fusion of the state and Sunni Islam, which discriminates against people who belong to non-Sunni groups such as Alevis and Shiites.[32] The chairman of Ehli Beyt (Shia) Scholars Association, Kadir Akaras, told *Al-Monitor*, "Most Shiite branches in Turkey maintain an independent standing from the directorate because it is against our belief to be under the guidance of any state authority."[33] The Turkish state neither recognizes non-Sunnis' places for gathering and worship officially nor offers subsidies, although members of the Alevi group have frequently requested and sought recognition.

While subduing Islam domestically, the Diyanet also maintained its relevance to migrants spread across Europe. As early as 1994, it introduced a directorate in its Foreign Affairs Department to manage religious affairs in Eurasia. This directorate is in charge of funding the construction and restoration of mosques and of managing the religious education of Muslim students and leaders in that region.[34] In 1995, the Diyanet's achievements were displayed during the first annual convention of the Eurasian Islamic Council (EIC), which encourages cooperation among Turkish Muslims abroad.[35] At this meeting, representatives from the Russian Federation complained about the lack of higher Islamic education institutions as well as teachers and imams. This request prompted the Diyanet to assign students from Turkey to existing theological faculties in Eurasia.[36] Furthermore, during the seventh convocation in 2009, a decision was made to publish classics and textbooks of Islamic knowledge to counter Wahhabi influences in Eurasia.[37] As noted by Senol Korkut, "the various problems noted in the first three EICs during the 1990s had largely been resolved by the seventh EIC."[38]

Since the 1990s, the Diyanet has built twenty-seven mosques, restored six, and paid for the internal and external decoration of many others.[39] It plans to build mosques in Tbilisi and Batumi (Georgia), Vilnius (Lithuania), and Tirana (Albania). In relation to education, the Diyanet has built Islamic schools, including three theological high schools in Bulgaria and a theology faculty in Kyrgyzstan. It has also provided scholarships to study Islam in Turkey. As many as 819 students have participated in Quran courses, "with 80 students coming from Mongolia, five from Kosovo, ten from the Crimea, and 139 from Georgia."[40] Over one hundred students from Eurasia were also registered at Imam Hatip high schools. Similarly, the Diyanet publishes Islamic literature in various Eurasian languages, including Russian, Romanian, Azeri, Mongolian, Tartar, and more. In 2008, it sent 1 million copies of religious publications and 50,000 religious calendars to Eurasia.[41]

The failed 2016 coup against the regime of Recep Tayyip Erdoğan perfectly illustrated the status of Islam in the state system. On July 15, Erdoğan and Diyanet head Mehemet Gormez issued orders to all imams of the Turkish Republic to rally citizens to denounce the military coup. Sala prayers—traditionally read at mosques to announce funerals, as well as during the Ottoman era to announce difficult times during the wars—were read overnight. Muharrem Ince, an opposition parliamentarian in the Republican People's Party, tweeted in response, "The call to prayer is not just a call to pray, but it is also a sign of our freedom, independence and our claim to this land. Same is true with the sala prayer. But I cannot stand it anymore that the mosques have become the backyard of a political party."[42]

National History and Islam

By integrating Islam into the public education system, the state posits itself as the trustworthy protector of Islamic heritage and religious guidance.[43] The onset of a state-run education system introduced the idea that national identity and Muslim identity are two sides of the same coin. In Gregory Starrett's terms, "functionalization of religion" occurs when the socialization of religion into the national education system allows the state to effectively exert social control and determine what constitutes "good social behavior" (*âdâb ijtimâ'îya*) by "good" citizens.[44] Textbooks framing the Muslim *ummah* as a source of religious knowledge have propagated the state's version of Islam rather than the *ummah*'s version.

My previous review of textbooks of varying Islamic clout in Egypt, Turkey, Pakistan, Iraq, and Tunisia reveals three shared characterizations of Islam within national narratives:

1. The blurring of intra- and interreligious diversity
2. The cultivation of national "uniqueness" by presenting Islamic history and civilization through the national lens
3. The presentation of the nation and Islam as under continuous attack by Western powers and their allies[45]

Monist Islam and homogenous national collectivity. Only the state-endorsed version of Islam is taught in public schools. As such, Islamic sectarian minorities are forced to take Islamic education classes that do not teach their specific creeds. In Egypt, Islam is the state religion, and according to Article 19 of the constitution, "Religious education shall be a principal subject in the courses of general education."[46] The schools teach the Sunni Islamic tradition, which makes no distinction between Shia, Sufism, and other branches, leaving students "with the impression that Sunni Islam is the only and correct version of Islam in existence."[47] Source materials use the Quran, Hadith, biographies of prominent Muslims, and sharia. Correct Islamic dress and behavior are taught along with the proper recitation of the Quran.[48] Public education in Egypt therefore constructs a national identity rooted in the values of Sunni Islam. Textbooks emphasize "loving the homeland which God bestowed on us. . . . Our noble religion commands us to develop it, to work for its glory and to defend its land and people."[49]

In Turkey, Islam is promoted as Turkish and disconnected from its Middle Eastern history and context. In national history, Islam is "oblivious to existing sectarian or minority differences, and serves as a locus of identity for Turkish nationalism."[50] This "Turkification of Islam"—or, in Hakan Yavuz's phrasing, its "internal secularization"—has adjusted the Islamic past to the boundaries of the new nation and portrayed it as a mainly Turkish feature alongside the Turkish language.[51]

Consequently, religious values and practices were "reformulated and presented in a way that functionalized Islam."[52] In other words, under the Kemalist regimes, Islamic values were promoted for their usefulness in a secular society and as divine legitimization of the official ideology of the secular state. Islam is therefore homogenized to allow the state to enforce its vision of a Turkish Sunni society.[53] Textbooks conflate Turkishness and Islam by presenting all Muslim scholars as Turkish and neglecting to mention sectarian divisions within Islam or to acknowledge religious minorities.

Under Erdoğan, the Turkish education system has become even more Islamized. This is in line with his mission of raising pious generations and anchoring Turkish identity in an Islamic narrative. Reforms begun in February 2012 included the introduction of entrance examinations in all high schools except Imam Hatip (religious) schools. As such, religious schools became a "selective option" in the education system, forcing students to choose between vocational and religious schools. Forty thousand students automatically had to enroll in Imam Hatip schools, including Alevi and Armenian students. Additionally, the reforms also expanded the religious content of regular academic high schools by continuing to feature only aspects of Sunni Islam. Students are now required to memorize long lists of Quranic verses, and the compulsory religious classes have been extended by one to two hours a week.[54] In May 2015, President Erdoğan's son, Bilal, announced that the number of students enrolled in Imam Hatip schools had reached 1 million, a major increase in comparison to when the Justice and Development Party (AKP) was first elected in 2002. Only 65,000 were enrolled in 2002 and 658,000 in 2013.[55]

The reforms also introduced electives on the Quran and the life of the Prophet Muhammad, which further increased the weekly number of hours for religious education. At the same time, the number of overall school hours per week was shortened, and the hours designated for different subjects were either reduced or eliminated. Svante E. Cornell notes, "In theory, these classes are elective; in practice, they may not be."[56] Additionally, in 2014, the government modified a law that augments its control over the selection of school principals, who happen to be responsible for choosing the classes offered.[57] Furthermore, the reforms of 2012 increased the influence of the Diyanet, which now operates these courses on its own.[58]

This leveling of intrareligious diversity goes hand in hand with the omission of interreligious plurality. In Egypt, Christian Coptic history is either underrepresented or completely omitted, although it plays a significant role in the nation's past.[59] As a consequence, there is no acknowledgment of religious conflict, preventing attention to discrimination against religious minorities that could effectively undermine national unity.[60] Western Christianity is also portrayed as an "essentially non-religious culture, which is primarily a military and economic rival, against which Oriental Christians and Muslims have had to defend by way of 'national unity' since the dawn of civilization."[61] Anti-Jewish sentiments have also been consistently pervasive in the curriculum. One particular textbook portrays Jews as "religiously and humanly racist and their racism and animosity go beyond Islam and Muslims to all other people and religions. They have no loyalty to whatever nation they live in and have no respect to its covenants and laws. Jews of yesterday are the Jews of today and tomorrow."[62] Such a perception, very common in anti-Semitic discourse across countries, has gained traction in modern Muslim countries because of the Israeli-Palestinian conflict and is shared by all political actors, religious and secular alike.

Similarly the creation of the "other" implies that the "us" is the state-propagated Turkish Sunni identity. This creation makes no reference to the multilingual and multireligious aspects of Ottoman history. As James A. Toronto and Muhammad S. Eissa note, even after the 2000 textbook reform, which emphasized religious tolerance in Turkish national history, there remain inherent contradictions "in promoting tolerance and respect for other religions and at the same time including material that instills an exclusivist, triumphalist attitude by emphasizing the pre-eminence of the Muslim community."[63]

In Turkish schools, Islam continues to be taught as a superior and most complete religion, as does the concept that whoever does not accept Islam and chooses another religion will "lose" and have a difficult time in the afterlife.[64] Muslim students are therefore still urged to unite against the political enemies of the *ummah* despite superficial instructions to respect non-Muslims. In this respect, political meaning takes precedence as the state redefines Islam as a modern religion adjusted to national identity.

Islam as the defining feature of national uniqueness. There have been two phases of religious educational text reform in Egypt. The first phase, under Nasser and Sadat, had a pan-Arabic focus, with 72 percent of religious education content emphasizing sociopolitical issues. These texts called for Egyptian youth to identify as Arabs "above all and to apply their Arabism and their sense of identity toward the Muslim ummah."[65] For example: "O God! Bring to us unity! O God! Re-unite the Arabs in one nation. When that happens . . . they will form the most powerful, the richest, the most knowledgeable and the most important of nations!"[66]

In contrast with the pan-Arabic phase, national education under Hosni Mubarak (1981–2011) emphasized Egyptian nationalism. Islam was described as a central feature of the *watan* (nation). For example, a first-year primary textbook said that Allah saved the *watan* from the Ashab al-Feel (People of the Elephant), ending with a poem encouraging students as follows: "And you, Muslim student, have to love your homeland (*watan*) and defend it if it is attacked by any aggressor / Because you live in it and eat from its food / And drink from the water of its blessed Nile."[67]

A tenth-grade textbook described Egypt's role in Islamic civilization in the following terms:[68]

الشعب المصري من أشد شعوب الدنيا تدينا، كما جعله هذا الضمير الديني يخشى عذاب الآخرة، فيراعي الله في عملة وسلوكه.

The Egyptian people are one of the most religious/pious people in the world. Such religious consciousness makes them fearful of the punishment of the hereafter. Hence, God considers their work and behavior.

فلا عجب أن يكون لمصر مع الإسلام شأن عظيم، فمصر صاحبة هذه الشخصية الدينية المتميزة قد حققت في اختلاف الأزمنة معاني نعتمد عليها في فهم حياتها الإسلامية، فقد تحلت بالصفات التالية:

It's no wonder that Egypt has great significance to Islam. Egypt possesses its distinguished religious persona through which it achieved meaningful actions that help us understand Islamic life throughout different times. It has demonstrated the following qualities:

١ ثبات التدين وعدم تذبذبه، والتأني في تقبل العقيدة التي تتفق مع القيم الدينية في التراث الحضاري المصري.
٢ تعمق روح الدين وعمق الاعتقاد، فلا يقف المصري عند مظاهر التدين بل يغوص في جوهر الدين ويجعله يرسخ في ضميره.
٣ التضحية في سبيل العقيدة التي تقبلها المصري بهوادة واعتدال ورسوخ، وقد رأينا كيف قدمت المسيحية أول شهدائها، كذلك فعلت بعد إسلامها، فقدمت من الشهداء على مر تاريخ الإسلام الكثير.

1. The stability of religiosity and not slumping. Taking the time to accept the dogma that overlaps with the religious values in the Egyptian heritage.
2. Deepening the spirit of religion and the depth of belief. An Egyptian does not stop at the manifestations of religiosity. He delves into the essence of religion and makes it rooted in his conscience.
3. Sacrificing in the path of creed that the Egyptian has accepted with righteousness and calm, and accepting martyrdom throughout Islamic history.

اذا جاء الفتح الإسلامي، تاني المصريون في النظر إلى الإسلام حتى اقتنعوا به، وأقبل معظمهم على اعتناقه، مصر تلقت الإسلام تلقيا مبكر الوقت، واضح المساهمة، كما تدل عن عمق تأثير مصر في حياة الإسلام عقيدة وعلما دينيا. مما يميز حياة الاسلام في مصر عن حياة غيرها، وغذي التفكير الإسلامي بعناصر غير خافية، نشير هنا الى أهمها وهو التصوف الإسلامي، إذ كانت مصر ذات تأثير واضح في بث النشاط الروحي الصوفي للمسلمين، وفي إمداده بغير قليل من العناصر الدينية والفلسفية جميعا. و بمشاركتها بعمق في هذا التصوف وتطوره، ومن المصريين الذين كان لهم مساهمة كبرى في التصوف والفلسفة الاسلامية.

Egypt received Islam in an early time, with clarity in its participation, which also indicates the depth of Egypt in Islamic life

and its sciences and religiosity. What distinguishes the Islamic
life in Egypt from the rest is its transparency in Islamic intel-
lectualism. We point here to the most significant aspect, Islamic
Sufism. Egypt has a major and clear influence in transmitting
the Sufi activity to the Muslims along with the religious and
philosophical components.

نود أن نقف قليلا أمام دور مصر الخطير في الدفاع عن دار الإسلام، بدفع العدوان ورد كيد المعتدين،
وحماية دار الإسلام والمحافظة على الثقافة الإسلامية.

We would like to withstand Egypt's role in defending dar al-
Islam by repelling the enemies and predators, protecting dar
al-Islam and preserving the Islamic culture.

كان لمصر دور هام في إطار الدولة الاسلامية بحكم وزنها الحضاري ومواردها. وكان لها أثر كبير في
الأحداث السياسية التي وقعت في الدول الإسلامية منذ أيام الخليفة علي بن أبي طالب حتى نهاية الدولة
العباسية.

Egypt has an important role in the frame of the Islamic state, given
the significance of its civilizations and resources. It had a great
role in the political events that took place in the Islamic states
since Caliph Ali bin abi Talib until the end of the Abbasid dynasty.

Under Sisi, national history has remained a powerful ideological tool. Sisi destroyed the thousands of textbooks printed during Morsi's rule to replace those from the Mubarak era.[69] As
Kamal Mougheeth notes in an article for the *Washington Post*,
"It's like the [January 25, 2011] revolution didn't happen. There
are figures in the regime who had a problem with the revolution
and are trying to attack any symbols of the revolution."[70] Government textbooks mention the January revolution in only a few
paragraphs, omitting the roles of the activists who launched the
rebellion and denigrating the role of moderate Islamists. The roots
of the revolution and the police abuses that occurred are also neglected. In 2015, even the slightest reference to revolution—such
as in Shakespeare's *Antony and Cleopatra*—was removed from
the twelfth-grade syllabus.

The political use of Islamic history is also very blatant in the
revival of the Ottoman heritage by Erdoğan. Ishaan Tharoor, in an
article in the *Washington Post*, shares that the National Education

Council, run by pro-Erdoğan members, voted in December 2014 to add Ottoman Turkish as a compulsory class in high schools. The vote provoked a massive backlash from secular groups, leading Erdoğan's prime minister to have the class offered as an elective instead. Nonetheless, "Erdogan has stuck to his guns, and rounded on his critics," remarking in a speech in Ankara, "There are those who do not want this to be taught. This is a great danger. Whether they like it or not, the Ottoman language will be learnt and taught in this country."[71] He continued, "They say, 'Will we teach children how to read gravestones?' But a history and a civilization is lying on those gravestones. Can there be a bigger weakness than not knowing this? This [breakaway from the Ottoman alphabet] was equal to the severing of our jugular veins."

Similarly, the figure of Sultan Abdulhamid II (1876–1909) has been revived as a paragon of Turkish national identity.[72] The great sultan has been "Turkey's Islamist alternative to Ataturk as a source of historical inspiration."[73] Interestingly, that Abdulhamid was an authoritarian figure appeals to Erdoğan's supporters. In their views, Erdoğan is an authoritarian leader, and "Turkey is facing lethal threats, and a strong leader must guide the nation without caring what his liberal or foreign critics say."[74]

A pro-government monthly magazine, *Derin Tarih*, recently published a cover story titled "Abdulhamid's Resistance: The Resurrection of New Turkey," featuring images of Abdulhamid II and Erdoğan side by side. It presents Erdoğan as a leader who is reproducing the sultan's legacy and facing similar challenges. "Their foreign policy strategies, health and education services, their struggles with foreign powers and the schemes planned against them" are supposedly alike.[75]

Islam under attack. The underlying master narrative that permeates history textbooks in Egypt and Turkey, among other countries, is the portrayal of Muslims as beset by existential, cultural, and spiritual struggles.[76] This provides a foundation for nationalism by enforcing a mythohistorical memory of assault upon the Muslim community by various enemies. Islam is characterized as the religion of the oppressed, emphasizing the hardships of the Prophet Mohammad and establishing continuity between past and present threats to the national community.[77] Past, present, and potential enemies include the United States in the West and the Zionists in Israel.

Textbook discussions of *al-walâya wa al-barâ'a* (loyalty and enmity) and jihad further reinforce this master narrative. Jihad is invoked as a defensive mechanism of national identity that strives "for one's own self, or for social justice, or any righteous cause, or under certain conditions, such as an armed struggle or just war."[78] As such, the historiography presented in textbooks allows the national rulers to decisively magnify "historical events in order to highlight the glory and greatness of Muslims. . . . This method aims at reviving religious and national feelings in the hearts of Muslim children in order to make them feel proud of their glorious past and to sow hope in their souls that one day they will be able to restore this glory and take their revenge on the West."[79]

Similarly, in Turkey, social studies and history textbooks imply that all states surrounding the country, along with certain groups within its society, are hostile toward Turks.[80] This creates an implicit need for constant vigilance against "others among us," or religious minorities, and "others among them," such as Christians.

Sharia as the Law of the Land

The Ottoman constitution of 1876 was the model for the development of newly independent states in the Middle East and North Africa. Consequently, two provisions only implicit in the Ottoman constitution—the proclamation of Islam as the state religion and that the head of state should be Muslim—became explicit.[81] In countries that constitutionally declare Islam the official religion, such as Egypt, sharia is implicitly or explicitly stated as a source of law.[82] The codification and reduction of sharia inherited from the colonial period led to the prevalence of Islamic prescriptions in civil legal systems.

In Egypt, Islamic provisions did not constrain legislation to a strictly Islamic framework and therefore had little effect on constitutional and political practice. Yet, most significantly, personal-status law remained under Islamic jurisprudence, specifically the Hanafi school, which had previously been official under the Ottoman Empire.[83] Although the code of personal law is called "civil," it refers to sharia as a legal basis for not just Muslims but also for corresponding religious principles for non-Muslim communities. When two persons of different religions, or undeclared religions, wish to marry, the general law in Egypt, which is the Muslim Personal Status Law, is applied de facto. Unsurprisingly, interreligious marriages are extremely rare since there is no secular civil law.[84]

This does not mean that the law is fixed. Legal reforms are implemented within the hybrid Islamic legal framework.[85] For example, the 1920 and 1929 civil laws expanded the grounds on which a woman could initiate divorce: personal harm, failure of the husband to provide maintenance, absence of the husband, the husband's imprisonment, and serious or incurable defect or disease (all causes acknowledged in the Islamic tradition). In 2000, the *Khul'* law was implemented to allow a woman to obtain a divorce without her husband's consent, under the condition that she returned the dowry.[86] Nonetheless, Salafist and other conservative Muslim groups have still found ways to challenge the *Khul'* law on religious and legal grounds, despite Islamic jurisprudence allowing it. In 2002, an amendment of the Personal Status Law (El-Khole' Article) was brought before the Supreme Constitutional Court, though the amendment was eventually ruled constitutional. Nonetheless, the resurgence of the *Khul'* law in 2000, decades after the 1929 reforms based on *talfiq* (selection and aggregation of different legal principles), reveals the malleability of the Islamic framework and how it has often readjusted under political pressures.[87]

The rise of sharia-based state law has had significant influence on Islamic orthodoxy by transforming what used to be personal religious faults into criminal political acts. Take for example the rise of apostasy and blasphemy cases within nation-states. It is worth noticing that the vast majority of Muslim countries—

with the exception of Pakistan, Saudi Arabia, and Iran—have formally removed the penal aspects of apostasy. However, civil punishments are enacted in most countries (with the notable exceptions of Senegal and, since 2014, Tunisia, where the new constitution does not explicitly prohibit blasphemy). Apostasy and blasphemy are defined as an offense, felony, or crime, depending on the specific state legislation. The severity of the punishment can range from fines, to time in jail, or death.

The Quran refers to apostasy in several verses but neither mentions nor implies its punishment in this world. The only declared punishment is in the afterlife, which makes "apostasy and unbelief a matter between God and the concerned individuals."[88] Sura 2:256 states, "There's no compulsion in religion." Similarly, Sura 18:29 says, "Let him who will believe and let him who will disbelieve." The two verses imply that involvement in religion is a matter of personal choice and conscience rather than a communal duty to impose and preserve one's faith. Sura 2:217 discusses the punishment of the apostate in the hereafter as is described: "But those of who turn back on their faith and die disbelieving will have wasted their deeds in this world and the next. They are inmates of Hell, and there shall abide forever."

In this respect, trials for apostasy were rare in Islamic history because they required eyewitnesses to public acts. For this reason, they took place only if the act disrupted social order.[89] In other words, a private/public distinction conditioned the punishment for apostasy on its public dimension and not on the believer's sin. Under sharia-based state law, this distinction between public and private dissolves, turning punishment into both a legal and a spiritual sanction.

Additionally, in classical Islamic jurisprudence, apostasy is distinct from blasphemy, a difference somewhat lost in existing legal state systems. *Sabb* (blasphemy) involves all that is "insulting" to God and the Prophet, along with religious figures such as the twelve Shiite imams for the Shiite jurists. Apostasy concerns all acts by Muslims of denying God and his Prophet.[90] Today, most legal systems combine both. The Egyptian penal code describes punishment for blasphemy as follows:

Detention for a period of not less than six months and not exceeding five years, or paying a fine of not less than five hundred pounds and not exceeding one thousand pounds shall be the penalty inflicted on whoever exploits and uses the religion in advocating and propagating by talk or in writing, or by any other method, extremist thoughts with the aim of instigating sedition and division or disdaining and contempting any of the heavenly religions or the sects belonging thereto, or prejudicing national unity or social peace.[91]

Due to the amalgamation of apostasy and blasphemy, atheism is punished under the above clause of the penal code.[92] In January 2015, twenty-one-year-old student Karim al-Banna was sentenced to three years in prison after announcing on Facebook that he was an atheist. His father testified against him. Al-Banna had previously filed a harassment complaint with the police against his neighbors, but "instead of protecting him, the police accused him of insulting Islam."[93] Al-Banna was arrested with a group of people at an establishment known as the "atheists café." The police then closed the coffee shop down, and a local administrator told a news website that it was "known as a place for Satan worship, rituals and dances."

In December 2014, the Egyptian Justice Ministry released a survey claiming that Egypt was home to 866 atheists, the highest number of any country in the Middle East.[94] "Atheists are one of Egypt's least-protected minorities, although the constitution ostensibly guarantees freedom of belief and expression," remarks Sarah Leah Whiston, the Middle East and North Africa director of Human Rights Watch. In June 2014, Karam Saber was sentenced to five years in jail for publishing his short story collection *Where Is God?* In 2011, a group of people from Beni Sueif had filed a legal complaint claiming Saber's work promoted atheism and contradicted religious teachings.[95]

Furthermore, the traditional distinction between Muslims and non-Muslims in cases of apostasy and blasphemy is also blurred. In 2013, Roman Murad Saad, a Copt, was sentenced to one year in prison for ridiculing the Quran. In late February 2016, three Christian teenagers made a short cell phone video mocking the

Islamic State (ISIS), which was interpreted as insulting Islam. In the video, the young boys portray ISIS members who pray and slit throats. They were jailed for five years for breaking the defamation of religions law. Back in 2014, another Christian, Michael Munir Beshay, was sentenced to one year in prison and fined 1,000 Egyptian pounds for blasphemy against Islam. An ex-Muslim who converted to Christianity, Bishoy Armia Boulous, remains imprisoned for a number of blasphemy-related charges.

Rulers also use the blasphemy law to stifle freedom of speech. For example, poet Fatima Naoot, who has been critical of the return of authoritarianism since 2013, was sentenced in 2015 to three years in prison for criticizing on Facebook the slaughter of animals at Eid al-Adha.[96] She references the Quranic narrative of Prophet Abraham's dream, in which God tells him to sacrifice his son to test his faith. "Millions of innocent creatures will be driven to the most horrible massacre committed by humans for ten-and-a-half centuries," says Naoot.[97] "A massacre which is repeated every year because of the nightmare of a righteous man about his good son." Naoot later wrote on a local news website that she respects all religions.

Only 100 out of a total of 596 Egyptian members of Parliament (MPs) supported a May 2016 bill to repeal the law against blasphemy, which reveals the implicit political support for the moral role granted to the state through such laws.[98]

It is also worth mentioning that even if not a penal offense, apostasy can influence the civil status of a person declared apostate.[99] For example, the Muslim Personal Status Law is applied to family matters in Egypt.[100] While such a provision seems nondiscriminatory toward other religions, it does not protect the convert from the family law consequences of conversion,[101] leading to the apostate's exclusion from inheritance. Furthermore, in some matters, personal aspects mainly found in family law can also affect civil law. For example, the Court of Cassation in Egypt declares that an apostate will lose child custody, will be denied inheritance, and may not enter a new marriage. The apostate's marriage is considered void (*batil*) because separation (*tafriq*) is legally mandated.[102] In addition to the family law consequences of conversion, there is also legislation against proselytizing by non-Muslims. In Egypt, there is no legal ban on proselytizing, but the government restricts attempts to proselytize among Muslims as well as prosecutes acts under alleged offence of blasphemy laws.[103]

The case of Kamilia Shehata Zakher is particularly reflective of the civil consequences of modern apostasy. Zakher, the wife of a Coptic bishop, disappeared from her home for a few days in July 2010. Many Coptic activists speculated that she had been kidnapped and forced to convert to Islam or had run away to convert of her own free will. A large-scale uproar demanded disclosure of her whereabouts. Ultimately, Egyptian authorities claimed that she had left home following a quarrel with her husband, and the heads of the Coptic Church determined that she had never converted to Islam at all and was home safe and sound.

Nonetheless, the event infuriated Islamists and jihadists. A member of the jihadi forum Shumukh al-Islam calling himself "Asim al-Jaddawi" urged Bedouins to kidnap and kill Christian tourists in Sinai to retaliate for Zakher's alleged forced return to the Coptic Church. Mauritanian cleric Abu al-Mundhi issued a September 1, 2010, fatwa allowing the killing of Egyptian Copts.[104] Additionally, al-Qaeda claimed responsibility for an October 31, 2010, attack on a church in Baghdad and claimed that Zakher's supposed abduction and subsequent detention by the Copts had triggered the event. The Coptic Church had forty-eight hours to free "the Muslim women incarcerated in Egyptian convents," or the group would target Christians in Egypt and elsewhere.[105] Additionally, large demonstrations erupted in Egypt in December 2004 over allegations that Wafaa Constantine, wife of a Coptic priest, had converted to Islam and subsequently been imprisoned by the Coptic Church.

In stark contrast to Egypt, Turkey eliminated Islamic provisions from family law in the 1930s, and the influence of sharia on national law has since become residual.[106] However, in the case of freedom of speech and blasphemy, Turkey's stance is comparable to Egypt's: insults against religion are inscribed in the penal code.[107] As in Egypt, since 2011, insults against religion and against the regime have started to blur. In the last ten years, "Turkey has consistently imprisoned more journalists than any other country."[108] The arrest and detention of Turkish thinkers, academics, and artists has become a common topic of discussion across news outlets and social media networks. In 2012, Erdoğan stated during his visit to Bosnia, "There should be international legal regulations against attacks on what people deem sacred, on religion."[109] Furthermore, he stated that Turkish legislators would act against blasphemous statements, and the world would view Turkey as the prime example on this matter. In an attempt to defend his stance on blasphemy, Erdoğan explained, "Freedom of thought and belief ends where the freedom of thought and belief of others start. You can say anything about your thoughts and beliefs, but you will have to stop when you are at the border of others' freedoms."[110]

Erdoğan's hardline stance against blasphemy was evident in the case of writer Sevan Nisanyan, who was convicted for his remarks against Islam. According to Turkey's semiofficial Anatolian Agency, Nisanyan "openly denigrated the religious values held by a certain portion of the population."[111] The agency also clarified that Nisanyan's prison term had been extended from nine months to one year and forty-five days, since the press was the main outlet through which the writer expressed himself. Furthermore, before Nisanyan's case, pianist Fazil Say was convicted of blasphemy after mocking Islamic practices on Twitter. He received a suspended sentence of ten months in prison, which he would only have to serve if he repeated the same or a similar crime within the next five years, according to his lawyer, Meltem Akyol. More recently, after the failed coup in July 2016, many writers, academics, and other prominent figures have been imprisoned under emergency regulations.

To sum up, hegemonic Islam is a form of political culture characterized by three main features also found in Islamic movements and exacerbated since the building of the caliphate by ISIS. First, the correspondence between belonging to Islam and belonging to the political community is taken for granted whether it is the nation, the *ummah*, or the caliphate. Second, the religious differences among Muslims, as well as between Muslims and other religious groups, are obliterated to build a homogenous Muslim nation. Third, the state takes on and expands the moral power of religious authorities by becoming the arbiter of the personal behaviors of believer-citizens. I have argued that this particular political culture, rather than Islam per se, could explain the democratic deficit of Muslim countries.

Hegemonic Islam and Democracy

There is an abundant literature on Islam's influence (or lack thereof) on the democratic flaws of the majority of Muslim countries. In my previous research, I have demonstrated that the fusion of nation-state with Islam, which defines hegemonic Islam, can be associated with low levels of democracy. Additionally, hegemonic Islam can also explain the limits of the inclusion-moderation paradigm.

State-Islam Fusion and Its Consequences for Democracy

Aiming to provide a general assessment of the influence of hegemonic Islam on democracy, I worked with Jonathan Fox on the Religion and State (RAS) project to operationalize this particular political culture.[112] This task involved identifying the state traits particularly associated with the hegemonic status of religion:

1. Privileged state funding or support for one religion (nationalization of institutions, clerics, and places of worship of one religion)
2. Insertion of the doctrine of that religion into the public school curriculum to the exclusion of other religions
3. Moralization of law and public policies based on the prescriptions of the hegemonic religion (inscription of religious prescriptions into the legal system [restrictions on freedom of speech and expression, notably apostasy and blasphemy, and prohibition of proselytism for all religions but the hegemonic one], as well as restrictions on women's rights [marriage/divorce/abortion] based on the prescriptions of that religion)

While democracy can accommodate some forms of state involvement in religion, granting hegemonic status to one religion can challenge democratic life or the transition to democracy. We transformed these dimensions into three variables, which allowed us to work with the RAS data. These variables are discussed in the research design section below. Overall our survey shows that these traits are associated with lower levels of democracy.

Research design. This study relies primarily on the Religion and State Round 2 (RAS2) data set, focusing on the 2008 data. The RAS2 data set includes 177 countries with data coded yearly from 1990 to 2008. The data are based on country reports using a wide range of sources, including (1) governmental and multigovernment organization reports from sources such as the US State Department, the United Nations, and the European Union; (2) reports by human rights groups including Human Rights Watch, Amnesty International, and Forum 18; (3) media sources primarily from the LexisNexis database; and (4) academic articles and books.[113]

To operationalize the concept of hegemonic religion, we created three independent variables using the information in the RAS country reports described above as well as from existing RAS variables. The first measures whether religious education is hegemonic. Specifically it measures whether a country supplies religious education in public schools exclusively in the majority religion. For the purposes of this variable, religious education refers to the teaching of religion in approximately the same manner as clergy would teach religion to believers.[114]

The second measures whether the government finances a single religion exclusively. While RAS2 has eleven variables measuring government financing of religion, they all measure finance in general and do not address whether it is for multiple religions or a single religion. The RAS country reports include this information, but the RAS project created no variable measuring this aspect of religious financing. Accordingly, we use the RAS country reports to code a variable as 1 if the government finances a single religion exclusively and as 0 otherwise.[115]

The third focuses on the presence of religiously hegemonic laws. The RAS2 data set has information on a number of religious laws. The variable for this study was coded based on whether the following policies were present in a country according to existing variables in the RAS2 data set:

1. Personal status defined by religion or clergy
2. Automatic civil recognition of marriages performed by clergy of at least some religions, even in the absence of a state license
3. Restrictions on interfaith marriages
4. Restrictions on intimate interactions between unmarried heterosexual couples
5. Laws specifically against homosexuality or engaging in intimate homosexual interactions
6. Prohibitive restrictions on abortion[116]

The variable ranges between 0 and 6 based on the number of these policies present in a country.[117]

This study performs two sets of tests using these variables. The first examines the frequency of these religious hegemony variables controlling for world region, majority religion, and democracy. For the purposes of this test, the laws variable is coded as 0 if no laws are present and 1 if one or more of the six laws are present. The measure for democracy used in this study is taken from the polity data set. The measure ranges from –10 (the most autocratic states) to 10 (the most democratic states) based on institutional factors, including the regulation, openness, and competitiveness of executive recruitment, constraints on the executive, and the regulation and competitiveness of political participation.[118] This establishes whether hegemonic religion is present in a wide variety of types of states.

Finally, we use ordinary least squares (OLS) regressions to test whether the three hegemonic religion variables impact democracy. We use three dependent variables for democracy. The first is the polity measure noted above, which focuses on *institutional democracy*. As the concept of liberal democracy also includes human rights and freedoms, we also include two variables from the CIRI (Cingranelli-Richards)-Human Rights Data Project. The *physical integrity index* measures torture, extrajudicial killing, political imprisonment, and disappearance. It ranges from 0 (no government respect for these rights) to 8 (full respect). The CIRI's *empowerment index* measures the following rights: foreign movement, domestic movement, freedom of speech, freedom of assembly and association, workers' rights, electoral self-determination, and freedom of religion.[119] Since this study's independent variables measure phenomena related to religious freedom, we removed religious freedom from the CIRI's empowerment index, so the version we use measures all of the listed freedoms except religious freedom. The resulting measure ranges from 0 (no government respect for these rights) to 13 (full respect).

The study tests five models for each dependent variable. The first three use each of the three religious hegemony variables as separate measures. The fourth uses all three of these measures in the same test. The fifth measures how many of the religious hegemony factors are present and ranges from 0 to 3.

We use several other control variables, which are based on previous studies of religion and democracy using an earlier version of the RAS data set.[120] First, the study uses the polity variable for the tests involving the CIRI measures. Second, it controls for the country's majority religion. Specifically, dummy variables are used for whether the country has a Muslim-majority or a Christian-majority. Controlling for Muslim-majority states has additional utility because the religious hegemony theory was developed based on practices in Muslim-majority states. This allows us to test whether the link between religious hegemony and autocracy is present in non-Muslim-majority states. While the RAS data set has more specific variables for religious majorities, these more general variables are used for several reasons. Among Muslim states, only three have non-Sunni majorities. The most common non-Muslim, non-Christian-majority states are Buddhist-majority states, of which there are eight, too few for meaningful results in multivariate analysis. It is possible to break Christian-majority states into separate variables for Catholic, Orthodox, and other-majority states. However, in tests not presented here, this resulted in no meaningful differences in the results for the hegemony variables. Finally, adding independent variables would create a ratio of independent variables to cases, which is low for this type of multivariate analysis. We control for religious diversity using a Herfindahl index, which runs between 0 and 1, with the most diverse countries scoring a 1.[121] Finally, the study controls for per capita gross domestic product (GDP) (UN Statistical Division) and a country's population size,[122] both of which are generally linked with democracy.

While all regimes, including democracies, can accommodate one hegemonic trait, hegemonic status granted to one religion, meaning the combination of two or three of these traits, is more likely to be linked to authoritarian regimes, independently of the religion.

Results. Table 3.1 shows the frequency of religious hegemony, controlling for multiple factors. Overall, while no single factor is present in a majority of countries, 58.2 percent of countries have at least one of the three religiously hegemonic traits included in this study. Religious hegemony is not distributed evenly among any of the control variables. Among world regions it is least present in the former Soviet bloc countries and Western democracies but present in all Middle Eastern states.

The question then is, What hegemonic traits are more often associated with democratic regimes? The most frequent hegemonic trait in democracies is the inclusion of religious prescriptions in civil law, with antiabortion laws being the most common. Looking only at the thirty-four most democratic states (where the polity variable is 10, its highest score), among the six types of religious laws we track, restrictions on abortion are the most common and are present in eleven of these states. Marriages performed by clergy are automatically recognized without a state license in nine of these democracies. Personal status is determined by religious law in Greece and Israel. Israel effectively restricts interfaith marriage, as nonreligious marriages are not possible in the country, though interfaith marriages performed in other countries are recognized by Israel's interior ministry. As of 2008, only Mauritius criminalizes sodomy based on an 1838 law, but it does not specifically ban homosexuality. None of these democracies ban premarital sex.

Table 3.1 Hegemonic Criteria Controlling for World Region, Majority Religion, and Democracy (in percentages)

	Number of Criteria				Specific Criteria		
	0	1	2	3	Education	Finance	Laws
All Countries	41.8	36.7	9.0	12.4	20.9	23.7	47.5
By Region							
West	59.3	33.3	7.4	0.0	11.1	11.1	25.9
Former Soviet bloc	78.6	17.9	3.6	0.0	7.1	17.9	0.0
Asia	41.4	31.0	13.8	13.8	20.7	24.1	55.2
Middle East	0.0	10.0	20.0	70.0	75.0	90.0	95.0
Sub-Saharan Africa	30.4	56.5	6.5	6.5	10.9	10.9	67.4
Latin America	37.0	51.9	7.4	3.7	22.2	14.8	40.7
By Majority Religion							
Christian, all	50.0	42.9	6.1	1.0	12.2	10.1	35.7
Christian, Catholic	54.5	36.4	6.9	2.3	13.6	11.4	31.8
Christian, Orthodox	53.8	30.8	15.4	0.0	15.4	30.8	15.4
Christian, Other	43.9	53.7	2.4	0.0	9.8	2.4	46.3
Muslim	17.0	25.5	14.9	42.6	46.8	61.7	74.5
Other	53.1	34.4	9.4	3.1	9.4	9.4	43.8
By Polity Index (Democracy)							
Polity = 10 (most democratic)	55.9	35.3	8.8	0.0	11.8	11.8	29.4
Polity = 7 to 9	50.0	45.8	2.1	2.1	8.3	10.4	37.5
Polity = –6 to 6	29.3	41.4	12.1	17.2	24.1	29.3	63.8
Polity = –10 to –7 (most autocratic)	29.2	12.5	12.5	45.8	54.2	62.5	58.3

Thus, inclusion of religion into the legal system can exist in democracies as long as the state does not restrict the practice of minority religions. While some of these laws enact religious dogma or give preference to the majority religion, few of them significantly restrict minority religions. This demonstrates that in many of these states the right to regulate civil law on religious grounds is granted to certain minority religions. For example, in Israel, Jewish, Christian, and Muslim clergy all control personal status issues for their communities. In other words, if equality of treatment is respected, the presence of elements of religious law within the legal system is compatible with democracy. It would be incompatible with democracy if the legal prescriptions of the hegemonic religion were imposed on all religious groups (e.g., Sunni prescriptions on non-Sunni Muslim groups in Pakistan).

Conversely, it seems that funding of only one religion by a state that erects this religion as hegemon is more often associated with autocratic regimes and more often combined with hegemonic traits in education and law. Tables 3.2, 3.3, and 3.4 analyze the relationship between religious hegemony and democracy, controlling for several other factors. The results are largely consistent across dependent variables and confirm the prediction that religious hegemony is associated with autocracy. Models 1 through 3 test each of the hegemony variables individually. Education is a significant predictor for only the institutional democracy variable. Finance is a significant predictor of the empowerment index and institutional democracy. The laws variable is a significant predictor of the physical integrity and empowerment indexes. Thus all of the dependent variables are influenced by at least one of the hegemony variables, but none of these dependent variables are influenced by all of them.

In model 4, none of the three hegemony variables tested together are significant predictors of any of the dependent variables. Finally, in model 5 the number of hegemonic traits variable is a significant predictor of all three dependent variables. Thus, overall, there is clear evidence that hegemony has a significant negative influence on democracy.

The control variables also produce some relevant results. The dummy variable for Muslim-majority states is not significant at the 0.5 level in any of the tests. Christian states are more democratic in three of the models with the empowerment index as the dependent variable and in all models with institutional democracy as the dependent variable. The other control variables are consistent with previous studies showing that institutional democracies more often respect human rights and that more economically developed countries tend to be more democratic. The results for population size are inconsistent with more populous countries having more institutional democracy but lower respect for human rights and freedoms. The results for religious diversity are not statistically significant.

Table 3.2 Multiple Regressions Predicting Physical Integrity

	Model 1		Model 2		Model 3		Model 4		Model 5	
Christian-Majority	-.019	.795	-.025	.733	-.029	.696	-.023	.750	-.021	.769
Muslim-Majority	.100	.194	.128	.102	.139	.077	.149	.058	.142	.069
Religious Diversity	.101	.086	.071	.243	.108	.055	.080	.193	.077	.187
Polity	.278	.000	.265	.000	.278	.000	.261	.000	.254	.000
Log-Population	-.530	.000	-.525	.000	-.528	.000	-.526	.000	-.529	.000
Log-per-Capita GDP	.384	.000	.393	.000	.375	.000	.373	.000	.382	.000
Hegemonic: Education	—	—	—	—	—	—	.002	.971	—	—
Hegemonic: Finance	—	—	-.126	.056	—	—	-.107	.127	—	—
Hegemonic: Laws	-.049	.412	—	—	-.125	.030	-.100	.065	—	—
Hegemonic: Number of Traits	—		—		—		—		-.153	.016
Df	176		176		176		176		176	
Adj R-squared	.563		.571		.575		.574		.576	

Table 3.3 Multiple Regressions Predicting Empowerment

	Model 1		Model 2		Model 3		Model 4		Model 5	
Christian-Majority	.146	.045	.138	.056	.132	.065	.141	.051	.143	.046
Muslim-Majority	-.040	.595	-.015	.844	.011	.880	.005	.953	.001	.994
Religious Diversity	-.087	.129	-.111	.063	-.067	.218	-.113	.061	-.102	.071
Polity	.543	.000	.542	.000	.555	.000	.526	.000	.530	.000
Log-Population	-.227	.000	-.219	.000	-.223	.000	-.222	.000	-.224	.000
Log-per-Capita GDP	.126	.020	.129	.017	.108	.039	.122	.027	.116	.028
Hegemonic: Education	—	—	—	—	—	—	-.062	.308	—	—
Hegemonic: Finance	—	—	-.154	.018	—	—	-.115	.094	—	—
Hegemonic: Laws	-.111	.056	—	—	-.185	.001	-.073	.172	—	—
Hegemonic: Number of Traits	—		—		—		—		-.182	.004
Df	176		176		176		176		176	
Adj R-squared	.586		.590		.603		.593		.597	

Table 3.4 Multiple Regressions Predicting Institutional Democracy

	Model 1		Model 2		Model 3		Model 4		Model 5	
Christian-Majority	.312	.000	.307	.001	.325	.000	.299	.001	.310	.001
Muslim-Majority	-.158	.090	-.137	.154	-.179	.072	-.118	.221	-.119	.217
Religious Diversity	-.052	.471	-.067	.373	.012	.868	-.090	.232	-.048	.509
Polity	—		—		—		—		—	
Log-Population	.132	.037	.150	.019	.148	.023	.136	.031	.140	.027
Log-per-Capita GDP	.189	.004	.184	.006	.158	.020	.197	.004	.160	.015
Hegemonic: Education	-.252	.000	-.240	.003	—		-.199	.009	—	
Hegemonic: Finance	—		—		—		-.151	.078	—	
Hegemonic: Laws	—		—		-.095	.192	-.010	.884	—	
Hegemonic: Number of Traits	—		—		—		—		-.257	.001
Df	176		176		176		176		176	
Adj R-squared	.351		.337		.308		.356		.345	

In sum, while other factors remain significant predictors of the democratic level of any given country, a certain type of state-religion relation that I call *hegemonic* has a negative influence on democracy. At the same time, if democracies can have hegemonic traits, then it is not the number of hegemonic rules, but their content and how they are implemented, that matters the most. This introduces a contextualized and sociological approach to the role of religion in politics that cannot be apprehended solely at the institutional level. As such, the social legitimacy of religious practices, behaviors, discourses, and actors is crucial. This social legitimacy entails all forms of social visibility of religion, such as political debates based on religious claims (abortion, contraception, blasphemy, dress code, environment, welfare, political rights), social activism by religious groups, and the presence of religious symbols in public discourses. In this aspect, social legitimacy is closely related to the private/public divide specific to each political culture. In the case of hegemony, the religion associated with the state is often homothetic with the frontiers of the public space. The hegemonic religion is a public religion in the sense that it defines and occupies all the public space, while all other religions are at best relegated to the private sphere and at worst discriminated against or repressed.

Consequently, each country is defined by a unique combination of institutional interactions and social legitimacies that cannot be captured solely through statistical analysis. For example, twenty-seven out of thirty-eight countries with two or three hegemonic traits are Muslim and nondemocratic, but such a situation cannot be explained by the so-called exceptionalism of Islam. In fact, the hegemonic status of some trends of Islam, established during the nation-building processes, also characterizes non-Muslim countries such as Bhutan or Cambodia. Hence, Muslim countries that do not experience hegemonic forms of Islam, such as Senegal, Indonesia, and Lebanon, happen to be more democratic. Introducing these two levels of religion's interactions with state and society sheds light on a more complex and contextualized approach to religion and politics that is, simply put, the separation of religion from political institutions in public life. Rather, what is distinctive are the specific meanings and practices ascribed to "religion," "ethics," "politics," and, indeed, "public" and the manner in which one's personal identifications (and thus commitments) are meant to shift along these lines. In other words, the institutional and social dynamic between religion and state creates a field of struggle and competition between political and religious actors both nationally and internationally. Relevant research therefore should focus on these fields and on the distribution of symbolic and material capital between different national and international actors.

My approach shifts the perspective from a polarized state-religion situation to complex sets of interactions between the two entities, such as adaptation, cooperation, and competition. It considers state-religion relations, particularly the construction of a hegemonic religion, which is an impediment to democracy. In other words, no religion is antidemocratic per se, but certain forms of state-religion interaction, such as restricting or privileging particular religious groups, are less often found in democracies.

More generally, this survey spotlights the influence of state institutions in the political development process, an emergent topic within the vast body of literature on democratization.[123] This reshaping of state institutions toward more democratic structures has several aspects: establishment of a strong and independent judiciary, protection of civil liberties, and legal and political guarantees of the rule of law. In some respects, this finding echoes recent work that emphasizes that the state, especially in non-Western contexts, is a prerequisite for nation-building and remains key to the management of democratization, contrary to the common wisdom that a sense of national community is the key ingredient of the state-building enterprise.[124]

The Limits of the Inclusion-Moderation Paradigm

According to the paradigm known as inclusion-moderation, including Islamic parties in the political system instead of ostracizing or repressing them leads to a greater ideological tolerance of Islamist leaders vis-à-vis multipartisan systems and elections.[125] Scholars have also focused on behavioral moderation, especially pragmatism in the parties' platforms and search for alliances with other political forces.[126] Factors that usually incite greater moderation are strategic incentive, political learning, institutional constraints, political culture, organizational mechanisms, and cooperative alliance and its different degrees.

The most recent contributions to this approach, such as those in *Islamist Parties and Political Normalization in the Muslim World*, look at internal party organization and the effect of repression on the normalization process of Islamic parties.[127] One insight is that the more participatory the parties become, the less they use religious themes. However, competition with other religious parties tends to increase religious themes. Also highlighted is the specific dilemma of Islamic parties, which more than others are characterized by dual constituencies: religiously motivated voters and voters motivated by socioeconomic grievances. Repression by the state expands constituency beyond religious themes and facilitates coalition building.

As noted by scholars working outside Muslim countries, this kind of research does not allow for outliers, where inclusion into the system has not led to ideological moderation and can even prevent further democratization.[128] One reason for this limitation of the inclusion-moderation paradigm is that it focuses on strategies of political actors without taking into account the political culture in which they evolve. Thus moderation is not simply the outcome of the interactions of parties and state systems but is also shaped by the specificities of the state-society-religion dynamics. In this respect, the religious aspects of the national political culture are key to explaining the different trajectories of religious parties. When the party themes and motifs align with the national culture, there is less chance that it will ideologically and politically moderate; it can even reverse the democratization process. The evolution of the Justice and Development Party in Turkey in the last decade is a case in point.

Between 2008 and 2010, the democratic challenges of Turkey were curbing the military influence on the political system, resolving the Kurdish conflict, and overcoming religious-secular polarization. The AKP benefited from this context by forging alliances with historically marginalized forces in Turkey (including devout Muslims, liberals, and socialists). These alliances changed the balance of power at the expense of the Turkish bureaucracy and military. Structural reforms related to the prospect of joining the European Union (EU) intensified the political marginalization of the latter. The changes also enjoyed the strong support of the population, to the extent that "virtually all of the actors in Turkish politics [approved] of the reconfiguration of domestic power away from the bureaucracy."[129]

In these circumstances, the political marginalization of the military happened without violence. The military's suspicions of AKP rule, however, rooted in the ingrained Kemalist distrust of Islamic forces, came to a head in 2007 after Prime Minister Recep Tayyip Erdoğan nominated Abdullah Gül for the presidency. Concern over growing Islamization led the military to declare, "If necessary, the Turkish Armed Forces will not hesitate to make their position and stance abundantly clear as the absolute defenders of secularism."[130] In other words, it seemed that the military was poised to remove the country's rulers, as it had several times in the past.

However, no coup materialized—demonstrating the diminishing power of the military—and the government built on this inaction by prosecuting top military officials in the Ergenekon cases, bringing military spending under the aegis of the High Council of Auditors, and centralizing military control under the Ministry of Defense. The result was the rapid decline of the military's political influence. As Necati Polat notes, "For all practical purposes, the army seems to have been forced out of the equation in Turkish politics."[131] Thus, the rise of the AKP combined with the prospect of entering the EU and a coalition supporting reform—including liberals, intellectuals, and the AKP's core demographic of devout Muslims—to create favorable conditions for democratization. As a result, the inclusion of the AKP in the political system seemed to validate the inclusion-moderation approach.

Fast-forward a few years, and the conditions are different. Several successful elections later, the AKP is the dominant political force, with strong popular support. After his parliamentary victory in 2011, Erdoğan declared that his upcoming term would demonstrate the AKP's "mastership," which has translated into a return to authoritarianism. The AKP has forced its control on the media, muzzled freedom of expression, and become heavily intolerant of the opposition. Murat Somer notes that the party itself has become "less and less pluralistic and more and more dominated by charismatic leader Erdogan."[132]

Erdoğan's psychology and religious conservatism alone cannot explain the return to authoritarianism. It is also partially due to the fact that the ideology of the AKP is in line with the national political culture. In other words, the alignment of the ideology of the party with the national political culture limits, or in this case reverses, the political moderation previously gained with acceptance into the system. The Islamic dimension of the national identity has been strongly asserted under Erdoğan without undermining the secular political system initially built on a strong Turkification of Islam. Within this premise, Erdoğan's politics have appeared very much in line with the expectations and values of the majority of the population, especially the Islamist urban middle classes, or Anatolian tigers, who contributed to the economic growth of the country in the 1980s and 1990s. Does this mean that the convergence of AKP policies with the national political culture will ensure indefinite power for Erdoğan? Probably not, since other parameters will come into play to shape future political victories, mostly the economic prosperity and regional political stability strongly compromised with the rise of the caliphate on Turkey's border.

Conclusion

Islam's hegemonic nature entails more than its importance to the national identity. After all, this religious dimension of national identity also appears in multilinguistic and multicultural democracies such as the United Kingdom. The most distinctive feature is that state actions and laws regarding Islam reverberate throughout the national political culture. In other words, state law and national identity define Islam's political dimension.

Consequently, Islam is a defining feature of the state system and a parameter of the national identity, shared by all citizens, even if they are not Muslim. For example, during the discussion on the nature of the civil state after the 2013 military coup, an implicit agreement emerged in Egypt among all protagonists, from secularists to Salafis to religious minorities, about the inclusion or recognition of sharia in the civil state. Mohammed al-Salmawi, the deputy speaker of the 50 Council, claimed at the time that the higher constitutional court had the exclusive power to interpret sharia-related legislations, and no party should be based on religious motivations.[133] In the same vein, a group of professors at Cairo University proposed a new constitution for Egypt. Article I of the project stated that Egypt is a parliamentary, democratic republic that works to ensure the freedom, justice, and human dignity of its citizens, who are part of the Arab nation. The second article presented Islam as the state religion, Arabic as the official language, and the principles of Islamic sharia as the main source of legislation, with provisions applicable to non-Muslims based on the exercise of their religion and their personal rituals.[134]

Nader Marqas, a member of Saint Mark's Coptic Orthodox Cathedral, claimed that the new constitution should hold on to the concept of the civil state and the principles of the sharia. Joseph Malak, the cathedral's attorney, also supported Marqas's claims, stating that the concept of the civil state and the sharia are the base of the new constitution. He also added that a real civil state is based on the principle of equality and nondiscrimination among all segments of society, citing al-Azhar and the principles of Islamic sharia.[135]

As a result of the nationalization of religious institutions and personnel, this hegemonic form of political Islam is present across Muslim countries. A Moroccan state official declared in 2015 that the Moroccan constitution presents a clear image of what the Moroccan identity is, especially the sense of Islamic belonging. This declaration expressed his disapproval of a demand by the chair for human rights at the time to equalize inheritance between men and women. He added that Article 41 of the constitution clearly states, "The Supreme Scientific Council [as part of the government] is the only qualified body to issue fatwas, based on the principles and provisions of the sacred religion of Islam."[136]

According to my previous research, this hegemonic form of political Islam characterizes most of the fifty official Muslim countries. In a few cases, however, such as Indonesia and Senegal, Islam is a component of the national and social collectivity but is not absorbed into the state apparatus.

Notes

1. 'Ināyat, Ḥamīd. *Modern Islamic Political Thought*. Austin: University of Texas Press, 1982; Lapidus, Ira M. *A History of Islamic Societies*. Cambridge: Cambridge University Press, 1988.

2. Hourani, Albert Habib. *Arabic Thought in the Liberal Age: 1798–1939*. London: Oxford University Press, 1962, p. 212.

3. The concept of *syar* was developed in the early centuries of Islam by Muhammad al-Shaybani (748–805) and later codified by Muhammad b. Ahmad b. Abi Sahl Abu Bakr Al-Sarakhsī (d. 1101): "The *syar . . .* describes the conduct of the believers in their relations with the unbelievers of enemy territory as well as with the people with whom the believers had made treaties, who may have been temporarily (*musta'mins*) or permanently (*dhimmīs*) in Islamic lands; with apostates, who were the worst of the unbelievers . . . and with rebels." See Burgis, Michelle. "Faith in the State? Traditions of Territoriality, International Law and the Emergence of Modern Arab Statehood." *Journal of the History of International Law* 11, no. 1 (2009): 41–42.

4. Hassan, Riaz. *Faithlines: Muslim Conceptions of Islam and Society*. Karachi: Oxford University Press, 2002, p. 94.

5. "Al-Qaradawi's Statement on Shiites." Islamopedia Online. April 22, 2010. http://www.islamopediaonline.org/fatwa/al-qaradawis-statement-shiites.

6. This dominant political narrative does not necessarily reflect even the cultural and political evolution in the West. For example, in France, which is typically presented as the paradigm of political modernization associated with the disappearance of religion, the Jacobin phase of the French Revolution and its accompanying "Cult of Reason" went beyond the notion of "civil religion" as defined by Jean-Jacques Rousseau (see Chapter 4 in this book). As Mircea Eliade said, "The great majority of the irreligious are not liberated from religious behavior, from theologies and mythologies." See Eliade, Mircea. *Myths, Dreams, and Mysteries: The Encounter Between Contemporary Faiths and Archaic Realities*. New York: Harper, 1961.

7. The adjective "core" refers to an essentialized vision of culture and identity; most of the time, such essentializations drove political reforms. See Duara, Prasenjit. *Rescuing History from the Nation: Questioning Narratives of Modern China*. Chicago: University of Chicago Press, 1997.

8. Mufti, Malik. *Sovereign Creations: Pan-Arabism and Political Order in Syria and Iraq*. Ithaca, NY: Cornell University Press, 1996.

9. Cesari, Jocelyne. *The Awakening of Muslim Democracy: Religion, Modernity, and the State*. New York: Cambridge University Press, 2014.

10. Beaman, Lori G. "The Myth of Pluralism, Diversity, and Vigor: The Constitutional Privilege of Protestantism in the United States and Canada." *Journal for the Scientific Study of Religion* 42, no. 3 (2003): 311–325.

11. Grim, Brian J., and Roger Finke. *The Price of Freedom Denied: Religious Persecution and Conflict in the 21st Century*. New York: Cambridge University Press, 2011.

12. Grim and Finke, *The Price of Freedom Denied*, 208–209.

13. Tambiah, Stanley Jeyaraja. *Buddhism Betrayed? Religion, Politics, and Violence in Sri Lanka*. Chicago: University of Chicago Press, 1992.

14. Dessouki, Ali. "Official Islam and Political Legitimation in the Arab Countries." In *Islamic Impulse*, ed. Barbara Freyer Stowasser. London: Croom Helm, 1987, pp. 135–136.

15. Hallaq, Wael B. *An Introduction to Islamic Law*. New York: Cambridge University Press, 2009, p. 116.

16. Moustafa, Tamir. "The Islamist Trend in Egyptian Law." Simons Papers in Security and Development 2. School for International Studies, Simon Fraser University, Vancouver, May 2010.

17. This occurred also in Algeria in 1971, Libya in 1973, and the United Arab Emirates as late as 1980. See Saeed, Javaid. *Islam and Modernization: A Comparative Analysis of Pakistan, Egypt, and Turkey*. Westport, CT: Praeger Publishers, 1994, p. 120; see also Hallaq, *An Introduction to Islamic Law*, 138.

18. The mufti of the republic holds a symbolic role more than an active one. "The *mufti* is employed by the Ministry of Justice but is only vaguely related to the court system, primarily through the task of scrutinizing death sentences that have to be in conformity with the rules of *fiqh*. With the abolishment of the Shari'a courts in 1955, some minor tasks, previously the preserve of the chief qadi, were transferred to the State mufti, the most important of which today is the announcement of the beginning of the Islamic lunar months based on the observation of the new moon." See Skovgaard-Petersen, Jakob. *Defining Islam for the Egyptian State: Muftis and Fatwas of the Dār al-Iftā*. Leiden: Brill, 1997, p. 92.

19. The al-Azhar curriculum was also reformed with the addition of three new departments: medicine, agriculture, and commerce. It is important to note the lack of any disciplines in the social sciences. From Saeed, *Islam and Modernization*, 122.

20. Moustafa, Tamir. "Conflict and Cooperation Between the State and Religious Institutions in Contemporary Egypt." *International Journal of Middle East Studies* 32, no. 1 (2000): 3–22.

21. Saeed, *Islam and Modernization*, 134.

22. Walsh, Declan. "Egypt's President Turns to Religion to Bolster His Authority." *New York Times*. January 9, 2016. https://www.nytimes.com/2016/01/10/world/middleeast/egypt-abdel-fattah-el-sisi-islam.html.

23. Galal, Rami. "Sisi's Call for Religious Tolerance Divides Muslims." *Al-Monitor*. May 25, 2015. http://www.al-monitor.com/pulse/originals/2015/05/egypt-salafist-sufi-religion-extremism-azhar-quran-sheikh.html.

24. Hussein, Walaa. "Al-Azhar Rewrites Curricula." *Al-Monitor*. June 29, 2015. http://www.al-monitor.com/pulse/originals/2015/06/egypt-azhar-curriculim-revise-religious-discourse-extremism.html.

25. Ibid.

26. "Sisi Calls for 'Religious Revolution' at Cairo's Islamic University." *Jerusalem Post*. May 31, 2015. http://www.jpost.com/Middle-East/Sisi-calls-for-religious-revolution-at-Cairos-Islamic-University-404583.

27. Saeed, *Islam and Modernization*, 160.

28. Earle, Edward Mead. "The New Constitution of Turkey." *Political Science Quarterly* 40, no. 1 (1925): 86.

29. Ibid., 244.

30. Finkel, Andrew. "What's 4+4+4?" *Latitude* (blog), *New York Times*. March 23, 2012. http://latitude.blogs.nytimes.com/2012/03/23/turkeys-education-reform-bill-is-about-playing-politics-with-pedagogy.

31. Findley, Carter V. *Turkey, Islam, Nationalism, and Modernity: A History, 1789–2007*. New Haven, CT: Yale University Press, 2010, p. 252.

32. The Diyanet, or Ministry of Religious Affairs, was founded on May 3, 1924, as part of the Turkish constitution. Its main objective is "to execute the works concerning the beliefs, worship, and ethics of Islam, enlighten the public

about their religion, and administer the sacred worshiping places." It is responsible for drafting sermons delivered in mosques both in Turkey and abroad. It trains imams and provides children with Quranic education. See the Diyanet website (http://www.diyanet.gov.tr/en), accessed January 4, 2017.

33. Tremblay, Pinar. "Turkish Alevis Refuse 'Sunnification." *Al-Monitor*. September 11, 2013. http://www.al-monitor.com/pulse/originals/2013/09/turkey -shiites-alevis-sunnification-gulen-mosque-cemevi.html.

34. Gözaydın, İştar. *Diyanet, Türkiye cumhuriyeti'nde dinin tanzimi*. Istanbul: Iletisim Yayinlari, 2009.

35. Korkut, Senol. "The Diyanet of Turkey and Its Activities in Eurasia After the Cold War." *Acta Slavica Iaponica* 28 (2010): 117–139.

36. Ibid.

37. Kutlu, Sönmez. "Avrasya coğrafyasında Kadim dini bilginin kaynakları ve yeniden üretilmesi sorunu." Paper presented at the Seventh European Innovation Council, Ankara, Turkey, 2008.

38. Korkut, "The Diyanet of Turkey."

39. Başkanlığı, Diyanet İşleri. *Kuruluşundan günümüze Diyanet işleri başkanlığı: Tarihçe-teşkilat-hizmet ve faaliyetler (1924–1997)*. Ankara: Türkiye Diyanet Vakfı, 1999, p. 791.

40. Korkut, "The Diyanet of Turkey."

41. *Yili idare faaliyet raporu*. Ankara: Başbakanlık Aile ve Sosyal Araştırmalar Genel Müdürlüğü, 2009, p. 64.

42. Tremblay, Pinar. "How Erdogan Used the Power of the Mosques Against Coup Attempt." *Al-Monitor*. July 25, 2016. http://www.al-monitor.com/pulse /originals/2016/07/turkey-coup-attempt-erdogan-mosques.html.

43. "Groups claiming independent authority to interpret Islamic scriptures and transmit Islamic culture undermine one of the basic foundations of the state's moral legitimacy: its protection of the Islamic heritage, including the responsibility to provide children and youths with trustworthy religious guidance. Islam, the official religion of the Egyptian state, is a matter of vital government interest." Starrett, Gregory. *Putting Islam to Work: Education, Politics, and Religious Transformation in Egypt*. Berkeley: University of California Press, 1998, p. 5.

44. Ibid., 10.

45. Cesari, *The Awakening of Muslim Democracy*.

46. Aldeeb, Sami. "Religious Teaching in Egypt and Switzerland." Text sent to the symposium organized by the Movement for Human Rights, Beirut, Lebanon, 2000.

47. Toronto, James A., and Muhammad S. Eissa. "Egypt: Promoting Tolerance, Defending Against Islamism." In *Teaching Islam: Textbooks and Religion in the Middle East*, ed. Eleanor Abdella Doumato and Gregory Starrett. London: Lynne Rienner Publishers, 2007, p. 44.

48. Ibid.

49. *Seventh Year, Second Semester Islamic Education Textbook*, 2002–2003 school year, 30.

50. Ozlem, Altan. "Turkey: Sanctifying a Secular State." In *Teaching Islam: Textbooks and Religion in the Middle East*, ed. Eleanor Abdella Doumato and Gregory Starret, 197–214. Boulder, CO: Lynne Rienner Publishers, 2007, p. 212.

51. Yavuz, M. Hakan. *Islamic Political Identity in Turkey*. Oxford: Oxford University Press, 2003, p. 5.

52. Ibid., 212.

53. "Compulsory Religious Education an Abuse of Human Rights, Says European Court." National Secular Society. October 12, 2007. www.secularism .org.uk/compulsoryreligiouseducationanab.html.

54. Cornell, Svante E. "The Islamization of Turkey: Erdoğan's Education Reforms." *Turkey Analyst.* September 2, 2015. http://www.turkeyanalyst.org /publications/turkey-analyst-articles/item/437-the-Islamization-of-turkey -erdoğan's-education-reforms.html.

55. Ibid.

56. Ibid.

57. Ibid.

58. Prior to 2012, these classes were managed jointly by the Diyanet and the Ministry of Education.

59. Kaymakcan, Recep, and Oddbjørn Leirvik. *Teaching for Tolerance in Muslim Majority Societies.* Istanbul: Centre for Values Education (DEM) Press, 2007, p. 126.

60. Pink, Johana. "Nationalism, Religion and the Muslim-Christian Relationship: Teaching Ethics and Values in Egyptian Schools." Center for Studies on New Religions. 2004. www.cesnur.org/2003/vil2003_pink.html.

61. Kaymakcan and Leirvik, *Teaching for Tolerance,* 135.

62. *Tenth Year, Second Semester Islamic Education Textbook,* 2002–2003 school year, 74–77.

63. Toronto and Eissa, "Egypt: Promoting Tolerance," 29.

64. Doumato, Eleanor Abdella, and Gregory Starrett, eds. *Teaching Islam: Textbooks and Religion in the Middle East.* Boulder, CO: Lynne Rienner Publishers, 2007, p. 38.

65. Carre, Olivier. "L'idéologie politico-religieuse nassérienne à la lumière des manuels scolaires." *Politique Étrangère* 37 (1972): 535–553, 536. See excerpts from al-Sibai, Mustafa. "Islamic Socialism." In *Arab Socialism,* ed. Sami A. Hanna and George H. Gardner, 66–79. Leiden: Brill, 1969. For the complete text, see *Middle East Journal* 26 (winter 1972): 55–68. See also O'Kane, Joseph P. "Islam in the New Egyptian Constitution: Some Discussions in *al-Ahram.*" *Middle East Journal* 26 (spring 1972): 137–148.

66. Carre, "L'idéologie politico-religieuse."

67. The People of the Elephant refers to a story narrated in Sura 105 in the Quran. In the Year of the Elephant, when the Prophet Muhammad was born, Mecca was attacked by 60,000 invaders accompanied by elephants. God saved the Meccans by sending birds that dropped stones on the People of the Elephant and destroyed them. The story is a reminder that Allah can save his house (*al-Ka'bah*) by using a flock of birds to destroy an army of 60,000 people with elephants. See Mir, Mustansir. "Elephants, Birds of Prey, and Heaps of Pebbles: Farāhī's Interpretation of Sūrat al-Fīl." *Journal of Qur'anic Studies* 7, no. 1 (2005): 33–47.

68. *Al-tarbiyah al-waṭanīyah: Miṣr wa-dawruhā al-ḥaḍārī lil-ṣaff al-awwal al-thānawī.* Cairo: Jumhūrīyat Miṣr al-'Arabīyah, Wizārat al-Tarbiyah wa-al-Ta'līm, Qiṭā' al-Kutub, 2002–2003.

69. Raghavan, Sudarsan. "In New Egyptian Textbooks, It's like the Revolution Didn't Happen." *Washington Post.* April 23, 2016. https://www.washingtonpost .com/world/middle_east/in-new-egyptian-textbooks-its-like-the-revolution-didnt -happen/2016/04/23/846ab2f0-f82e-11e5-958d-d038dac6e718_story.html.

70. Ibid.

71. Tharoor, Ishaan. "Why Turkey's President Wants to Revive the Language of the Ottoman Empire." *Washington Post.* December 12, 2014. https://www

.washingtonpost.com/news/worldviews/wp/2014/12/12/why-turkeys-president
-wants-to-revive-the-language-of-the-ottoman-empire.

72. The sultan Abdulhamid II ruled the Ottoman Empire between 1876 and 1909. He adopted pan-Islamism to counter Western interference in the empire. To do so, he promulgated the first Ottoman constitution in 1876 and established eighteen professional schools as well as the University of Istanbul, known as Dar al Funun. See "Abdulhamid II." *Encyclopaedia Britannica.* April 4, 2011. https://www.britannica.com/biography/Abdulhamid-II.

73. Akyol, Mustafa. "Why Is Turkey Reviving an Ottoman Sultan?" *Al-Monitor.* September 29, 2016. http://www.al-monitor.com/pulse/originals/2016/09/turkey-reviving-sultan-abdulhamid-ii.html.

74. Ibid.

75. Ibid.

76. Doumato and Starrett, *Teaching Islam,* 5.

77. Ibid.

78. Kaymakcan and Leirvik, *Teaching for Tolerance,* 227.

79. Ibid., 123.

80. Ibid., 37.

81. The Ottoman constitution of 1876 was the model for constitutional development for the new Middle Eastern and North African states.

82. Brown, Nathan J., and Adel Omar Sherif. "Inscribing the Islamic Shari'a in Arab Constitutional Law." In *Islamic Law and the Challenges of Modernity,* ed. Yvonne Yazbeck Haddad and Barbara Freyer Stowasser. Walnut Creek, CA: Altamira, 2004.

83. "Personal Status Laws in Egypt: FAQ." Promotion of Women's Rights Project. Accessed January 3, 2017. http://www2.gtz.de/dokumente/bib-2010/gtz2010-0139en-faq-personal-status-law-egypt.pdf.

84. Sfeir, George N. "The Abolition of Confessional Jurisdiction in Egypt: The Non-Muslim Courts." *Middle East Journal* 10, no. 3 (1956): 248–256.

85. Ibid.

86. As much as the *Khul'* law has been praised as innovative, it is worth pointing out that classical Islamic jurisprudence already granted the rights offered to women in the new law. See Mashhour, Amira. "Islamic Law and Gender Equality: Could There Be a Common Ground? A Study of Divorce and Polygamy in Sharia Law and Contemporary Legislation in Tunisia and Egypt." *Human Rights Quarterly* 27, no. 2 (2005): 584, 595.

87. This allowed an individual to go outside his own personal school of law and select a resolution to his specific issue from the other three schools of law.

88. Johansen, Baber. "Apostasy as Objective and Depersonalized Fact: Two Recent Egyptian Court Judgments." *Social Research* 70, no. 3 (2003): 687–710.

89. Ibid., 687–710.

90. Ibid., 32.

91. With the short-lived 2012 constitution, for the first time in Egyptian history insulting the prophets became an unconstitutional act. This legal status was revoked by the 2013 constitution, returning to the situation before the January 2011 revolution.

92. Eltahawy, Mona. "Egypt's War on Atheism." *New York Times.* January 27, 2015. http://www.nytimes.com/2015/01/28/opinion/mona-eltahawy-egypts-war-on-atheism.html.

93. Ibid.

94. Greenslade, Roy. "Egyptian Student Jailed for Proclaiming That He Is an Atheist." *Guardian.* January 13, 2015. https://www.theguardian.com/media/green/slade/2015/jan/13/egyptian-student-jailed-for-proclaiming-that-he-is-an-atheist.

95. Laccino, Ludovica. "Egypt Writer Karam Saber Sentenced to Five Years in Jail for Atheist Book." *International Business Times.* June 5, 2014. http://www.ibtimes.co.uk/egypt-writer-karam-saber-sentenced-five-years-jail-atheist-book-1451453.

96. Mourad, Mahmoud. "Egyptian Poet Goes on Trial Accused of Contempt of Islam." Reuters. January 28, 2015. http://www.reuters.com/article/us-egypt-courts-poet-idUSKBN0L121M20150128.

97. Ibid.

98. Bryson, Jennifer S. "Egyptian Parliament Attempts to Repeal Blasphemy Law." *Arc of the Universe.* May 12, 2016. http://arcoftheuniverse.info/egyptian-parliament-attempts-to-repeal-blasphemy-law.

99. Hashemi, Kamran. *Religious Legal Traditions, International Human Rights Law and Muslim States.* Boston: Martinus Nijhoff Publishers, 2008, p. 23.

100. Berger, Maurits. "Apostasy and Public Policy in Contemporary Egypt: An Evaluation of Recent Cases from Egypt's Highest Courts." *Human Rights Quarterly* 25, no. 3 (2003): 720–740.

101. Hashemi, *Religious Legal Traditions*, 60.

102. Ibid., 83. *Tafriq* is a form of Islamic divorce different from *talaq. Talaq* is the unilateral divorce procedure initiated by the husband, while *tafriq* relies on the court to pronounce the divorce in the case of the husband's absence or if he refuses to consider his wife's petition for divorce.

103. American Center for Law and Justice. "Religious Freedom and Persecution in Egypt." 2009. http://media.aclj.org/pdf/egypt_memo.pdf.

104. "Religious Freedom and Apostasy." Islamopedia Online. Accessed August 10, 2016. http://www.Islamopediaonline.org/country-profile/egypt/religious-minorities-and-freedom-religion/religious-freedom-and-apostasy?page=253.

105. Abdelmassih, Mary. "Coptic Christian Woman Unwittingly Becomes Focal Point of Islamic Clash with Christianity." Assyrian International News Agency. November 12, 2010. http://www.aina.org/news/20101111233506.htm.

106. The 1926 Turkish civil code led to unity of the court system, replacing Mecelle, which was a code that employed sharia but was modeled after the 1912 Swiss civil code. The new law banned polygamy and gave women and men equal rights to divorce. The current Turkish civil code, reformed in 2001, is an updated version of the 1926 civil code, with an addition stating that family forms the basis of society and operates on equality between the spouses.

107. "Any person who openly disrespects the religious belief of a group is punished with imprisonment from six months to one year if such act causes potential risk for public peace." See "Turkey." End Blasphemy Laws. Accessed January 3, 2017. http://end-blasphemy-laws.org/countries/europe/turkey.

108. Fulton, Lauren. "A Muted Controversy: Freedom of Speech in Turkey." *Harvard International Review* 30 (2008): 26–29.

109. Harrod, Andrew. "Turkey PM Pushes International Blasphemy Laws." *Frontpage Mag.* September 18, 2012. http://www.frontpagemag.com/fpm/144562/turkey-pm-pushes-international-blasphemy-laws-andrew-harrod.

110. Ibid.

111. "Turkish-Armenian Scribe Sentenced to Thirteen Months for Blasphemy in Blog Post." *Hurriyet News Daily.* May 22, 2013. http://www.hurriyetdailynews

.com/turkish-armenian-scribe-sentenced-to-13-months-for-blasphemy-in-blog-post-.aspx?pageID=238&nID=47371&NewsCatID=341.

112. This section excerpts Cesari, Jocelyne, and Jonathan Fox. "Institutional Relations Rather Than Clash of Civilizations? How and When Religion Is Compatible with Democracy." *International Political Sociology* 10, no. 3 (2016).

113. For a more detailed discussion of the sources for the data, data-collection methodology, and data reliability, see Fox, Jonathan. *Political Secularism, Religion, and the State: A Time Series Analysis of Worldwide Data*. Cambridge: Cambridge University Press, 2015.

114. This based on a more detailed variable included in RAS2, which is coded as follows:

- There is no religious education in the public schools.
- Religious education is available in all religions for which there is a significant number of students (in cases where population is homogeneous, code this category).
- Religious education is available in some religions for which there is a significant number of students.
- Religious education is available for only one religion even though there are a significant number of students belonging to other religions.

Countries are deemed to have hegemonic religious education policies if the variable is coded as 3 or if the country is religiously homogeneous and coded as 1. The resulting variable is coded as 1 if the religious education policy is hegemonic and as 0 otherwise.

115. While a variable that accounts for the actual amount of funding for each religion would have been useful, this information is not available in a large number of states. This limits our measurement to this binary variable.

116. While in theory blasphemy laws are also part of the concept of hegemonic religion, we did not include this concept in our "hegemonic laws" variable. This is because the concept of democracy includes freedom of speech, which blasphemy laws limit. In fact the variables we use in this study include freedom of speech as one of their components. Thus, including blasphemy laws in the "hegemonic laws" variable would cause an issue of multicollinearity, which is methodologically unacceptable in this type of study.

117. We weight each of these types of laws equally because previous studies demonstrate that (1) there is no agreement among scholars as to how these laws should be weighted, and (2) weighting these items based on both scholarly opinion and factor analysis does not result in any substantial difference in the composite variable. See Fox, *Political Secularism*.

118. For more on the polity measure, see Jaggers, Keith, and Ted Robert Gurr. "Tracking Democracy's Third Wave with the Polity III Data." *Journal of Peace Research* 32, no. 4 (1995): 469–482; also see the polity website at http://www .systemicpeace.org/polity/polity4.htm.

119. The CIRI data provide yearly variables on human rights based on multiple sources, including US State Department reports and reports from human rights organizations such as Amnesty International. For more on the CIRI data set, see Abouharb, M. Rodwan., and David L. Cingranelli. *Human Rights and Structural Adjustment*. Cambridge: Cambridge University Press, 2007, and the CIRI homepage (http://www.humanrightsdata.com).

120. Fox and Sandler, *Bringing Religion into International Relations*.

121. This variable is taken from Barro, Robert J., and Rachel M. McCleary. *International Determinants of Religiosity.* Cambridge, MA: National Bureau of Economic Research, 2003.

122. The population variable was downloaded from the World Bank on April 23, 2010.

123. Isaac, Jeffrey C. "Analyzing Democracy." *Perspectives on Politics* 9, no. 2 (2011): 241–245.

124. Stepan, Alfred C., Juan J. Linz, and Yogendra Yadav. *Crafting State-Nations: India and Other Multinational Democracies.* Baltimore: Johns Hopkins University Press, 2011.

125. Schwedler, Jillian. *Faith in Moderation: Islamist Parties in Jordan and Yemen.* Cambridge: Cambridge University Press, 2007.

126. Wickham, Carrie Rosefsky. *The Muslim Brotherhood: Evolution of an Islamist Movement.* Princeton, NJ: Princeton University Press, 2015.

127. See Mecham, Quinn, and Julie Chernov-Hwang. *Islamist Parties and Political Normalization in the Muslim World.* Philadelphia: University of Pennsylvania Press, 2014; Cesari, *The Awakening of Muslim Democracy.*

128. Jaffrelot, Christophe. "Refining the Moderation Thesis: Two Religious Parties and Indian Democracy: The Jana Sangh and the BJP Between Hindutva Radicalism and Coalition Politics." *Democratization* 20, no. 5 (2013): 876–894.

129. Polat, Necati. "Regime Change in Turkey." *International Politics* 50, no. 3 (2013): 435–454.

130. Quoted in Cesari, *The Awakening of Muslim Democracy.*

131. Polat, "Regime Change in Turkey," 440.

132. Somer, Murat. "Conquering Versus Democratizing the State: Political Islamists and Fourth Wave Democratization in Turkey and Tunisia." *Democratization* 24, no. 6 (2016): 1–19.

133. Sadaqah, Hussam, Muhammed Ghareeb, and Mahmoud Ramzi. "Egypt Is a Civil Country and the Higher Constitutional Court Interprets the Shar'ia." *Al-Masry al-Youm.* November 21, 2013. http://www.almasryalyoum.com/news/details/344590.

134. Muhammed, Abu al-Saud, and Muhammed Kamel. "Parliamentarian Country and Shar'ia Is the Base of Legislation." *Al-Masry al-Youm.* December 3, 2012. http://www.almasryalyoum.com/news/details/166153.

135. Ramadan, Rajab. "Saint Mark's Coptic Orthodox Cathedral Supports the Civil State and the Islamic Shar'ia." *Al-Masry al-Youm.* July 4, 2012. http://www.almasryalyoum.com/news/details/193451.

136. "The Chair for Human Rights' Suggestion Does Not Correspond to the Moroccan Identity." *Jadid Presse.* November 1, 2015. http://www.jadidpresse.com/الوطني-المجلس-أطروحة-زعزاع-عبد-المالك.

4

Civil Islam

Robert N. Bellah's 1967 article "Civil Religion in America," in which he defines *civil religion* as a set of religious beliefs, symbols, and rituals shared by all citizens of a nation (religious or not), has dominated the contemporary debate on civil religion,[1] a debate also heavily shaped by American public culture's emphasis on citizens' actions and beliefs. As noted by Marcela Cristi, the dual meaning of civil religion has not been fully discussed.[2] Jean-Jacques Rousseau was the first scholar to introduce the concept, which he defined as a belief system designed and controlled by the state to authoritatively and sometimes coercively build a new citizenry. Although Rousseau coined the term *civil religion*, his state-centered definition did not really influence the American debate, which has instead prioritized Émile Durkheim's emphasis on the shared beliefs of citizens as the glue that holds the political society together. In other words, due to the specifities of the American context, contemporary scholarship on civil religion has understood it first and foremost as a shared set of beliefs at the societal level.

In the case of Muslim countries, however, Rousseau's analysis is much more relevant. As discussed in previous chapters, political Islam refers to political cultures shaped by nation-state building. I call the most common expression of this political culture "hegemonic Islam," defined as a state-centered Islam aimed at building a modern citizenry and national identity. Are there other forms of political Islam?

It is worth noting that Muslim countries without hegemonic Islam are strikingly few: Senegal, Indonesia, and Lebanon. Since the defining feature of Lebanon is sectarianism rather than civil religion, this chapter focuses primarily on Indonesia and Senegal, where the state has not absorbed Islamic institutions. For Indonesia, the term *civil Islam*, coined by Robert Hefner, describes the social dimension of political Islam.[3] I use it in a different way to refer specifically to Islam as the common reference for the public expression of all citizens under the same political rule.

There was no foundational fusion among state, Islam, and nation in either Senegal or Indonesia. Instead, a civil version of Muslim nationalism emerged, which acknowledged religious diversity and Islam's social rather than state-centered political influence. The civil version of Muslim nationalism has two main features:

1. The distinction between the state system and the religious establishment, although equidistance is an ideal more than a day-to-day reality
2. The acknowledgment of diversity at the foundation of the national identity

The Distinction Between State and Islam

The Pancasila Agreement and Recognition of All Religions

The foundation of Indonesian national identity is known as Pancasila, which literally means "five principles." The first principle, belief in God, is reflected in the country's constitution, which states, "The State shall be based upon the belief in the One and Only God."[4]

Pancasila was established at the time of Indonesian independence from the Netherlands in 1945. Sukarno (1901–1970), the first president of the independent state, was the original proponent of the five principles. Pancasila was further maintained by his successor, Suharto (1921–2008), who replaced him in 1967 and launched the political phase known as the New Order.[5] Despite the official adoption of Pancasila at the time of independence, debates on the status of Islam vis-à-vis the state and the nation have divided Muslim intellectuals and political leaders from the colonial era onward. Luthfi Assyaukanie identified three main polity models that have influenced state-Islam relations since independence:

1. The Islamic democratic state (IDS), in which Islam is a main feature of the state and the nation
2. The religious democratic state (RDS), which acknowledges the significance of all religions and establishes the state as the guardian of all faiths
3. The liberal democratic state (LDS), which emphasizes separation between state and religion[6]

Mohammad Natsir (1908–1993) coined the term *Islamic democratic state*: "The state based on Islam is not a theocracy. It is a democratic state. Neither is it a secular state. It is an Islamic Democratic State."[7] The IDS was therefore an attempt to adopt modern political values without ignoring Islamic doctrines in a way very similar to the modernist movement described in Chapter 1. In March 1945, the Investigating Committee for Preparatory Work for Indonesian Independence was formed. Although divided between Islamic and secular nationalists, the committee eventually agreed to adopt Islamic references for the new nation and state, then three months later was overruled by another committee, the Preparatory Committee for Indonesian Independence.

IDS advocates created the postindependence Masyumi party.[8] In their view, democracy and the Islamic state were synonymous; thus speaking of Islam and democracy was redundant.[9] They called for the unification of religion and state but rejected the notion of theocracy. Assyaukanie argues, "Seen from the viewpoint of classical Islamic political thought, Natsir's conception of the state is very progressive, because first, he saw the state as something to be attained through rational means. . . . [R]eligion is not the guarantee of the state; instead the state is the guarantee of religion."[10]

IDS advocates also opposed secularism, which they associated with the Western separation of religion and state. Their positions influenced the creation of the Ministry of Religious Affairs in 1946, which inserted religion into the state apparatus while confining it to one place.[11] The IDS partisans sought to win the 1955 elections to promote their cause but failed. None of the Islamic parties—such as the Islamic Tharikah Unity Party, the Islamic Victory Force, and the Islamic Association Party of Indonesia—managed to secure a majority of votes. The IDS model began to decline following the disbanding of Masyumi in the 1960s, not only because of the Suharto regime's repressive policy but also because citizens were slowly turning away from the idea of an IDS.

The religious democratic state model, which emphasized the need to uphold religious values rather than Islam specifically, was presented as a more reasonable alternative to the IDS. In this sense, the RDS was an attempt to take into account the religious diversity of Indonesia by emphasizing the crucial role of the state in protecting people's religious life.[12] The RDS is associated with Suharto and the New Order, as many partisans of this model backed Suharto. Nonetheless, the Suharto regime deliberately emphasized Pancasila as an independent ideology rather than an outcome of RDS input.[13] Suharto promoted the pluralistic principle of Pancasila as the only ideological basis. His argument won against the advocates of Islamic political ideologies because he convinced Muslim citizens that Islam orders its followers not to establish a certain type of political power, such as an Islamic state, but rather to found a society committed to basic religious principles of justice, equality, and freedom—principles that Pancasila did in fact foster.[14] As such, Pancasila was not presented as Islamic.

Nonetheless, RDS followers, often Muslim groups, did not view Pancasila as secular. Abdurrahman Wahid and Ahhmad Siddiq, members of the Nahdlatul Ulama (NU), argued in favor of the compatibility of Islam with Pancasila as follows:

1. Islam teaches *tawassut* (middle way) (Assyaukanie calls it "moderation").
2. The Quranic instruction to uphold the "equitable proposition" for pluralist Indonesia is best found in Pancasila.
3. Muslims can have both Islam and Pancasila: "Islam is a revealed religion while Pancasila is the result of human thinking."[15]

The Muhammadiyah was among the most reluctant Muslim movements to accept Pancasila.[16] An agreement was only made in

1985, after several rounds of negotiations. The leader of Muhammadiyah at the time praised the unifying power of Pancasila and encouraged people to see it as a philosophy disconnected from Suharto. Another prominent member of the movement, the writer Kuntowijoyo, explained that Pancasila is the result of looking at Islam and other religions objectively. He also emphasized that Pancasila would not replace religion because it was just an ideology. As Assyaukanie explains, "The exponents of RDS are fully aware that democracy cannot be built on Islamic ideology, since it will automatically exclude the participation of other religious communities."[17]

Interestingly, all RDS exponents reject the secularism that they associate with Western separation of religion and state by stating that Islam does not recognize a division between the religion and worldly domains. Dawam Rahardjo, an Indonesian academic, sees secularism as a violation of the democratic values and basic rights of religious people. He refers to the headscarf ban in France in these terms: "How could you claim democracy, while prohibiting people from what they wear?"[18] In other words, Indonesian intellectuals and politicians see Western secularism as an ideology hostile to religion and thus deliberately avoid using the term *secularism* to define their specific mode of state-religion interactions. This is a common attitude among Muslims across different countries, who see secularism as the Western imperialist project's ideological enterprise to eliminate religion.

RDS promoters endorse state establishment of religion but reject the concept of an Islamic state. Former member of the government Muhammad Syafaat Mintaredja was an early critic of the Islamic state model in the 1970s. He called it ill fitting within a religiously diverse country and theologically untenable. In the 1980s, the open critique of the Islamic state became systematic. Muhammad Amien Rais argued that an Islamic state is impossible because Islam doesn't specifically dictate everything about welfare and life.[19]

Additionally, the RDS holds that a political society must be religious and that religion is a significant element of communal life. As stated by Assyaukanie, in their view, "without religion, a state will be destroyed in anger by God."[20] RDS advocates envision an active role for the state in fostering religious education and religion in social life. They believe that religious education is essential to the morality of future generations and see it as a symbol of resistance against Western secular states.[21]

Although the majority of Indonesians agree about the importance of religion in education, the topic remains controversial because there is no consensus on the modalities of teaching it (content of the curriculum, religious identity of the teacher, religious diversity of the students), as evidenced by the National Education Bill about religion in public schools, which was submitted to Parliament three times before being adopted in 2003. One of the most disputed articles, Article 13(1), requires schools with ten or more students of any particular faith to employ religious education teachers of those faiths, so that students in all schools (state and private) could receive religious education in their own faith from a teacher of that faith. While Christians do not generally send their children to Islamic schools (hence Islamic schools are unlikely to be affected), many Muslims choose to send their children to Christian schools due to their superior educational standards. Secular nationalists as well as religious minorities have viewed this article as a violation of state neutrality in favor of Islam. Perhaps unsurprisingly, RDS partisans supported it.[22]

As a matter of fact, the state protection of religions as stated by the Pancasila agreement and endorsed by RDS partisans has translated into several bills that favor Islam. One example is the Marriage Law of 1974, perhaps the most controversial bill in Indonesian legislative history. Prior to 1974, there were marriage laws for different categories of citizens (i.e., citizens of European or Chinese origin, Indonesian Christians, and Muslims). Subject to customary Islamic family law, Muslims strongly criticized a primary version of the bill in 1973 for its restrictions on polygamy and its acceptance of interreligious marriages.[23] They protested that the bill would replace religious marriage with a secular institution. Due to the social unrest created by the law, an amended statute, enacted on January 2, 1974, permitted polygamous marriage and took out the provision that allowed interreligious marriages. Minorities and secular groups therefore came to see the Marriage Law of 1974 as "a law against the Christian community," with revised content modified to accommodate Muslims.[24]

Additionally, religious judicature's involvement with family law has consistently been a sensitive issue at the political-constitutional level. The Religious Judicature Bill adopted in 1989 reorganized the sharia court system and clarified its domains of intervention vis-à-vis the 1974 Marriage Law. The bill clearly asserted the power of sharia courts in all civil matters between Muslims (marriage, divorce, inheritance, and custody of children).[25] As such, Christian and secular groups saw it as state favoritism of Islam. The bill also enhanced the legal and institutional standing of Islamic courts by eliminating the 1931 rule that a civil court had to ratify their decisions.[26] Exponents of RDS downplayed the critiques of the bill and argued that all communities could have their own similar religious judicatures, if desired.[27]

Assyaukanie notes that while proponents of the RDS model are willing to work hand in hand with other religious communities to build a religious democratic state, "the adoption of certain religious values by the state" does not necessarily require the consensus of other religious communities.[28] In this respect, Muslims see unification between the state and Islam as a basis for pluralism, whereas Christians and other religious communities believe in a separation of religion and state.

Finally, the advocates of the third model, the liberal democratic state, believe that religion and state should be separated. Nurcholish Madjid (1939–2005) and former president of the country Abdurrahman Wahid (1940–2009) were known for their strong commitment to both religion and democracy.[29] In their view, recognition of diversity is conditioned by separation of religion from state. LDS advocates have gained popularity since the 1990s, mostly among younger Muslims critical of Suharto who are worried by the rise of Islamic groups attempting to bring Islam into the state system.

Madjid differentiates between the closed worldview of secularism operating like a counterreligion and the authentically emancipatory power of secularization. He goes on to argue that secularization permits Muslims to distinguish tradition from the transcendent and objects to Islamic political parties with the slogan "Islam, Yes. Islamic Party, No." LDS proponents believe that the many Muslims who do not agree with this slogan have misperceived it. Agiel Siradj, a board chairman of the Nahdlatul Ulama movement, refers to the Constitution of Medina under the Prophet Muhammad as secular and argues, "Islam was not designed to become a state institution."[30]

LDS partisans also criticize the Suharto model for lacking in neutrality and, more specifically, object to the following:

1. The creation of the Department of Religion, which they see as having made many concessions to Muslims to the detriment of non-Muslims.
2. The officialization of religion by which the government recognizes certain religions, which, in their view, discriminates against minority religions and minorities within religions.
3. Sharia, as part of state law, which once enforced by the state, loses meaning and provokes jealousy among those to which it does not apply.[31]
4. Religious freedom and pluralism. Wahid equates pluralism with liberalism.[32] Madjid argues that the state should not belong to certain people, citing the Constitution of Medina. Another proponent of this trend, Djohan Effendi, justifies the right to choose any religion, even excluded ones and atheism.[33] Madjid also defends the positive influence of atheism on religious reform.

Some beliefs of these contrasting views of state-religion interactions overlap, primarily with regard to the social importance of religion and religiously inspired public morality. The partisans of each model disagree on how to implement these ideas and how plural such a society should be. Jeremy Menchik describes this political culture as "godly nationalism."[34] In some ways endorsing the arguments of the LDS model, Menchik argues that godly nationalism does not preclude intolerance: although the constitution does have a provision for religious freedom, it only actually applies to religions formally recognized by the state.[35] Islam, Catholicism, and Protestantism received this recognition in 1951, and Hinduism and Buddhism were included in 1959 and 1966, respectively.

However, Ahmadiyyahs and other minority religions in Indonesia have yet to gain recognition.[36] As a result, these groups are very vulnerable to intolerance and social hostility and do not benefit from state protection or social support. In fact, surveys show that the majority of Indonesian Muslim leaders believe Ahmadiyyahs should be banned from public leadership positions and prohibited from building places of worship and teaching Islamic studies.

These same politicians, however, believe in giving Christians and Hindus greater political and religious freedom.

According to Menchik, "Indonesia contains a form of nationalism that is neither Islamic nor secular, but rather exclusively and assertively religious."[37] I, instead, prefer to apply the term *civil Islam* to this assertion of the importance of religion in society, and to a certain extent in politics, as a specific form of religious nationalism.

Indonesia's National Narrative of Civil Islam

The Indonesian education system is dual. Secular schools are under the purview of the Ministry of National Education, while religious schools are managed by the Ministry of Religious Affairs.[38] Students in both systems have the right to request religious instruction in any one of the six official religions as part of their education.[39]

A review of the national history textbooks currently used in both systems highlights the main features of Indonesian religious nationalism. Islam is described as the major religious player in Indonesian history and regarded as the best religion. However, the Indonesian nation is presented as diverse and inclusive, and all religions must be treated equally. These principles are disseminated in the following ways.

Islam as the best religion. The textbooks state that the Torah was for Jews and the Bible was for Christians, but the Quran is for everyone. It also declares that the Bible is corrupt.[40]

Equal treatment for other religions (Judaism, Christianity, etc.). The Constitution of Medina is presented as an example of how Jews and Muslims should interact with one another, cooperate in fighting, and help each other against their enemies. Furthermore, Jews should maintain their religion.[41] Medina is presented as a place of religious tolerance, where Muslims, Christians, and Jews were given freedom and guaranteed the right to worship.[42] It is asserted that Islam teaches tolerance for the believers of other religions. In Islam, there is no doctrine of hate or hostility to people of other faiths. Islam teaches Muslims to coexist in an atmosphere of peace, harmony, and mutuality.

Dawah (proselytization) must be undertaken peacefully, for "there is no compulsion in Islam."[43] A story is told about a Christian who became a Muslim after realizing how tolerant his Muslim neighbor was.[44] In one story, the Prophet Muhammad is mistreated by a group of Jews and yet shows them tolerance. As a result, the Jews became Muslims.[45] Another story presents a Muslim shopkeeper being extremely good to a Jewish shopper, even though the shopper once swindled him.

National identity and Islam. The Indonesian peninsula is presented as a diverse place, with explicit mention of the six officially recognized religions (Islam, Christianity, Catholicism, Hinduism, Buddhism, and Confucianism). One textbook emphasizes that this diversity is from Allah and that cooperation is a powerful force.[46] A diagram shows how Islamic values in the Indonesian cultural context should produce religious tolerance, preservation of Islam, and a proud nation.[47]

The challenge of unity in Indonesia is also discussed. The textbooks address attaining religious harmony, both between and within different religions. Educated people should participate actively in pursuing this harmony.[48]

A tenth-grade history textbook extensively describes the spread of Islam in the Indonesian peninsula but gives the other religions almost no mention.[49] The existence of Islam in Indonesia is inseparable from the country's history.[50] A twelfth-grade textbook on Islam argues at great length that Islam arrived in Indonesia very early on (in the seventh century AD rather than the thirteenth, as is sometimes taught) and came directly from Arab countries.[51]

One textbook discusses the current state of Islam in the world, giving different demographics for different places, and makes a point of mentioning that Indonesia has more Muslims than any other country.[52] A chapter on the universality of Islam lists dozens of different countries and how Islam entered them. Additionally, those who spread Islam in Indonesia preached with passion and sincerity and were well received. Muslims should therefore follow their example.

Any obstacle can be overcome through faith, intelligence, knowledge, and noble character. Islam is a rational religion in which the truth is manifested. It teaches peace and equality. The student of

Islam in Indonesia should therefore study diligently and show that the youth of Islam are tough, smart, and of good character.[53]

A state official in 1945 is quoted as calling for an Indonesia that is for all: not Christians for Indonesia, not Muslims for Indonesia, and so forth, but Indonesia for Indonesia.[54]

In an activity, students are asked to express how they feel about the following sentences using two thumbs up, one thumb up, or one thumb down:

1. Following regulations at a mosque
2. Preaching for the sake of Islam and not for any material or personal interest
3. Proselytizing in a peaceful (noncoercive, nonviolent) way, just as earlier preachers in Indonesia did
4. Using social media to preach
5. Being a proud citizen of the resource-rich, friendly Indonesia in which the majority of people are Muslims[55]

Islam and citizenship. For an assignment described in one textbook, a student who shows the following will get the highest mark:

1. That democratic values are in line with Islamic values
2. That Islamic values do not come only from Muslims
3. That Islam does not recognize the East/West divide and accommodates new ideas[56]

The same textbook mentions that this curriculum aims to help students become democratic and responsible citizens, to encourage them to engage in both religious and social rituals, and to promote competency to solve social problems.[57] Students receive extra points for acknowledging the social implications of their faith in both private worship (i.e., prayer) and public worship (i.e., social activities, or *aktifitas social*).[58]

The West, Europe, and the United States. One textbook presents Cordoba under Muslim rule as the cultural and civilizational achievement that inspired the scholars and scientists of Western nations.[59] Europe and the West were built not on their own but with the support of Islam. The textbook provides quotes from Barack

Obama and Montgomery Watt that emphasize Islam's contribution to the world. A textbook for eleventh-grade students predicts that Islam will one day predominate in the Western world.[60]

A grade-twelve textbook discusses the challenges faced by Islam in Europe and deems them more serious than those in Asia and Africa. It presents interfaith dialogue and the determination of preachers as tools to disseminate tolerance and recognition.[61] The European Union should be praised for handling diversity.[62]

Monolithic Islam. Across textbooks, there is no mention of Shias or Sunnis or Sufis or Ahmadiyyahs. Sufism is credited in one place as a factor that brought Islam to Indonesia.[63] There is no mention of minority religions that are not officially recognized by the state, such as Kebatinan, Kejawen, and Subud. There is one mention of atheism in the context of gratitude to the Prophet, whose message keeps us from it.[64]

Nation versus *ummah*. There are surprisingly few mentions of *ummah*. One chapter on pilgrimage mentions how pilgrimage creates a sense of unity among Muslims worldwide.[65] In one story, a father returning from pilgrimage performs prostration. When his son asks why he does so, he answers that he is showing gratitude to God for giving him strength to perform the pilgrimage and return to his "beloved" (*tercinta*) homeland.[66]

Diversity is seen as a gift from God and exemplified by Quranic quotations. One text points out how diverse Indonesia is and how grateful Indonesians must be to God for that. They should express their gratitude through mutual respect and peaceful relationships.[67]

The same text discusses Hilal bi Hilal, an Indonesian Islamic festival for building harmonious relationships. It states that although the name derives from Arabic, Arabs do not know what it means since Hilal bi Hilal arises out of Indonesian history.[68]

Senegalese Laïcité and Neutrality

Senegalese political culture constitutes another version of religious nationalism. Unlike in Indonesia, the separation between state and religion does not involve active intervention of the former to regulate or promote religious activities. Additionally, interactions between state and religion do not raise the same level of dispute as in Indonesia. The postindependence constitution (1959) reflects secular principles inherited from the French colonial era. According to its preamble, the nation is "secular, democratic, and social and Article 4 outlaws religious parties."[69] One of the first acts of national rulers was to abolish sharia courts and regional parties, giving the postcolonial state more control over society than the colonial power had. Nonetheless, Senegalese secularism differs from French secularism (*laïcité*). First, Senegalese secularism does not limit the public expression of religion.[70] Article 24 recognizes the right of religious communities to provide education, autonomously and without constraint, so long as they maintain law and order. Second, while French *laïcité* rests on the strict separation of state and religion, Senegalese *laïcité* allows for governmental involvement in religion as long as it does not privilege one religion over others.[71] Thus, from the presidency of Léopold Sédar Senghor (1906–2001) to the present, Senegalese political elites have agreed that "the state must support religions and brotherhoods in order to help Senegalese to better live their faith."[72] State support for pilgrimages for all religions, going back to colonial times in the case of the Hajj, illustrates this equal treatment perfectly. In this respect, the Senegalese government engages with religious communities in both official and unofficial ways. Political leaders have paid visits to and consulted religious leaders, as well as sought endorsements from them. Meanwhile, religious events, such as the Murids' Magal Touba, a major annual pilgrimage to the city of Touba, have included official government delegations.[73] President Abdoulaye Wade, once elected in 2000, pledged government support to finance projects in Touba and included prominent Murids in his politics.

Under these circumstances, Sufi orders have consistently been major political players and arbitrators between segments of society and the state. A few families with historical ties to the political elites dominate these orders. It is estimated that 92 percent of the population belongs to one of the four principal orders, or *confréries*—the Qadiriyya, Tijaniyya, Muridiyya, and Layene—making Senegal the Muslim country with the highest percentage of Sufis. Members of a Sufi order, or *tariqa*, follow the specific teachings of its founders, although it is not uncommon for followers of one order to attend the mosque of another.[74] Each order revolves around a shaikh, or marabout.[75]

The maraboutic model is characterized by its omnipresence in public life, from businesses to government offices and schools.[76] The *khalife* general, or the shaikh of *confrérie*, appoints the imams of *confrérie*-specific mosques, where they lead daily and weekly prayers and offer spiritual guidance to their followers. The founding families of each order also take on a significant role in contemporary Senegalese politics, as their endorsements can mobilize followers to vote for specific candidates. In the past, some faith leaders have given specific vote instructions (*ndigels*) to their disciples.

It is possible to identify a specific domain of social and political influence for each Sufi order. The Qadiriyya's main traditional activities are agriculture and commerce.[77] In 1989, disagreements over grazing rights at the Senegal-Mauritania border caused tens of thousands of Mauritanians in Senegal to repatriate.[78] The political strains led to closure of the border between the two countries.[79] The conflict left lasting animosity between Mauritanians and Senegalese. Today, however, the Qadiriyya emphasizes religious education as well as job training to prevent unemployment—particularly for youths and women. The Qadiriyya *confrérie* also provides health care to the less fortunate.[80]

The Niassène family, part of the Tijaniyya order, maintains a strong hierarchy very similar to the structure of a state. All members are dedicated to working for the *khalife*. As the *khalife* cannot be "everywhere at once," he has ambassadors and ministers to "assure directions are followed and objectives are achieved."[81] The Niassène family is also known as a provider of high-quality education, particularly for women.[82] In fact, parents from other countries as far away as Nigeria send their children to study with the family. As such, the Niassènes have followers in several countries.

The Omarien community is one of the oldest branches of Senegal's Tijaniyya. Focused primarily on religious education, it has developed Quranic schools as well as mixed institutions that combine Islamic education with science. The Omarien provide free health screenings for the needy and regularly mobilize their members in social campaigns, such as reducing poverty. The community's influence extends beyond Senegal to Mali, Mauritania, Niger, and Nigeria.[83]

The Sy family forms another branch of the Senegalese Tijaniyya. In the past, it has maintained both civil and collaborative interactions with French colonial authorities.[84] The family founder opened his own Islamic center in Tivaouane, which is credited with spreading Tijaniyya within present-day Senegal.[85] The family has also actively promoted Christian-Muslim dialogue as well as peace between the *confréries*.[86]

While not the largest order in Senegal, the Murids have significantly influenced Senegal's social, economic, and political development—particularly in the domain of agriculture, a mainstay of the national economy. In the past, Murid leaders held large areas of land, which their *talibes* (students or followers) cultivated for the population in exchange for spiritual guidance. By the end of the 1970s, the Murids dominated peanut production.[87] Even as recently as 2002, the Murid *khalife* was still Senegal's number one producer of peanuts.[88]

The Murid hierarchy is similar to that of the Niassène family. Commissions with various administrative responsibilities are assigned by the *khalife* to each branch of the twelve main families. Each branch is responsible for a different domain, such as education or health. A grandson of the *khalife* travels within the Senegalese diaspora as a so-called minister of foreign affairs.[89] Touba, the holy city for Murids, two hundred kilometers from Dakar, holds special administrative and political status. As an autonomous rural community, the city manages most of its own affairs, with the Murid marabouts having de facto legal power. The city population swells to several million during the annual Murid pilgrimage, or Magal Touba. Notwithstanding, Touba's status has been nothing short of controversial. In 2014, the city did not comply with Senegal's gender-parity law, as its political candidates were all men, causing outrage across the nation.[90] The government, however, took no action.

The Layene *confrérie* represents only 5 to 10 percent of Senegal's Muslim population. Its creed differs from orthodox Sunni Islam. Layenes believe that the Mahdi revealed himself as Seydina Limamou Laye on the Cape Verde peninsula of Senegal in 1883.[91] After Laye's death in 1909, his son, Issa, became leader of the Layenes, who see him as the second coming of Jesus.[92] Layenes are socially conservative, abstaining from dancing and other forms of entertainment.[93] Like the other orders, they are very engaged in community service, especially education, building Islamic schools and libraries.[94] They are also involved in media programs on television and radio.[95]

Generally speaking, Senegal's Sufi elites have evolved over time in their support for democratic institutions. From the 1960s to 1980s, they endorsed the single-party authoritarian system. In the 1990s and 2000s, they began creating spaces for serious political contestation and presidential turnovers. Since then, marabouts have consistently used their religious and popular legitimacy to facilitate peaceful conduct of elections. For example, Murid and Tijaniyya leaders helped ensure smooth transitions when Macky Sall replaced Abdoulaye Wade as president in 2012. The increasing role of Sufi elites in upholding democracy can be explained by social changes, such as deterioration of living conditions and urban riots associated with the economic crisis of the late 1980s. During these challenging times, it was in the interest of Sufi leaders to ensure good relationships with any political leader who could provide resources to their communities. On the downside, this new situation drew marabouts into electoral politics.[96] Consequently, corruption and clientelism have weakened the Senegalese social contract.

Nonetheless, it would be misleading to conclude that religious groups are the only movers and shakers in Senegalese politics. In fact, their religious influence coexists along with strong local identification and kinship. As noted by Etienne Smith, "Kinship is still the major conceptual framework irrigating Senegalese political culture that cuts across cleavages based on religion, language, or ethnicity. It remains a powerful ideological tool in triggering or silencing conflicts."[97] Based on his 2006 anthropological survey in Casamance, Smith notes that being part of the same ethnic group diffuses possible religious divisiveness. Circles of sociability are based on kinship, which allows for religious diversity within locally bound ethnic groups. Many families in Casamance have Catholic and Muslim members, which precludes the amalgamation of religious, local, and ethnic membership. Therefore, when asked about what makes good relations between citizens in Senegal, respondents unsurprisingly referred first to cultural values and practices such as *teranga* (hospitality) and *kalante* (kinship joke).[98] These practices express a sociability ethos that cuts across linguistic and religious divides.

The state also acknowledges this cultural diversity. In 1978, the constitution gave six languages the status of national languages (*langues nationales*). The 2001 constitution acknowledges cultural and linguistic diversity and expands the number of *langues nationales*.

In sum, in Senegal and Indonesia civil Islam is based on inter- and intrareligious diversity, which sets it apart from hegemonic Islam. This recognition of diversity does not translate, however, into the same state-society-religion interactions, as highlighted by the less intrusive role of the Senegalese state in religious legitimacy. Nonetheless, Islamically based civil activities shape both societies.

The Social Dimension of Religion

Activities based on Islam are not specific to Senegal or Indonesia and are actually shared by all contemporary Muslim societies. The difference is that Islamically based social organizations in Senegal and Indonesia interact directly with state institutions without the mediation of political parties or political institutions.

As presented above, Senegalese civil Islam is dominated by Sufi orders, which operate as mediators between state institutions and citizens. They also shape the daily social lives of citizens beyond worship and religious guidance, to the point that the secular-versus-religious divide loses its relevance. *Dahiras* (community groups) are the cornerstone of this civil life. Their actions in connection with the Sufi orders create a web of organizations and activities that the state has to take into account for any policy to succeed. Such a form of civil society presents similarities with the corporatist or consociationalist mode of democracy.[99] Unlike consociationalism, however, there is no institutional recognition of the Sufi orders since the interactions remain informal. Civil Islam is also more fluid than the consociationalist model, as attested by the rise of free riders such as the peripheral shaikhs (described below).

In Indonesia, Islamic parties have not successfully mediated between the state and citizens, likely because Islamic movements or organizations actually act as a go-between and communicate directly with the state as well as with all political parties. In other words, civil Islam loses its relevance when it becomes partisan as the electoral game goes hand in hand with divisiveness. This is because Islam is seen first and foremost as a feature of the consensual political culture and not so much as an ideology.

Dahiras

Dahiras provide Senegalese Muslims with an outlet for religious activity outside Friday prayers.[100] These community groups promote solidarity and unity among members of the same *confrérie* in the same geographical location. For citizens moving from rural to urban areas, *dahiras* often offer newcomers a way to build networks and access economic opportunities. The Murids in particular are known for their assistance to new urban dwellers.[101]

While *dahiras* operate independently from the Sufi orders, marabouts can solicit them for their participation in religious events, such as collective marriage ceremonies and preparation for religious pilgrimages. They also perform all kinds of charitable activities, such as collecting donations for prisoners and providing free medical consultations.[102]

Dahiras are oftentimes segregated by gender, with some women's groups being branches of co-ed *dahiras* and others being independently organized. These women's groups provide social and material support for members during critical moments, such as when giving birth. Women in *dahiras* also provide logistical support by cooking for religious gatherings.[103] *Dahiras* also include youth-focused groups, which mobilize members to perform charity work and care about religious values.[104]

Thus, by uniting followers of particular marabouts in "well-organized cells," *dahiras* place Sufi orders at the center of structured and dynamic social networks.[105]

Religious Rituals

Religious rituals in Senegal serve as the "meeting place" between society and the state.[106] As observed by Leonardo A. Villalón, they "shape and reflect the relationships among marabouts, between marabouts and their followers, and between marabouts and the state."[107] The *dahiras* plan and guarantee attendance at the ritual events. This allows marabouts to recruit disciples, as well as to assert their influence in the lives of their followers.[108]

Tijaniyya ceremonies (*gammus*) are held many times throughout the year, the most important being the Mawlud, or the birthday of the Prophet Muhammad.[109] Murid celebrations (*maggals*) culminate in the annual celebration in Touba, the order's "holy city."[110] Other, less visible celebrations, such as communal visits by disciples to their marabouts (*siyaare*),[111] are instrumental in fostering religious-based social networks, along with "communicating the strength of these networks to the state."[112]

Peripheral Shaikhs

Peripheral shaikhs are Sufi leaders who build clientelist relationships with secular politicians.[113] As a consequence, they "stifle" the traditional role of the *khalife* general as a transethnic religious mediator. Their actions fuel what Richard Joseph terms *prebendalism*, or "the use by elected officials of public resources in order to advance the interests of their ethnic or religious group."[114]

Electoral *ndigels*, traditionally religious voting commands issued by Sufi guides, are an example of such practices. Peripheral shaikhs, however, tend to issue them in support of a political party in exchange for rewards, which ensures their religious authority as well as their financial survival. These electoral *ndigels* can be explicit, for example, when shaikhs openly incite their followers to vote for a particular candidate, or implicit, such as when shaikhs provide "implied messages of support" for a particular politician during public addresses. For example, Bethio Thioune, a Murid shaikh, openly supported former president Wade in 2012.[115] Scholars tend to interpret electoral *ndigels* as limiting Senegalese democracy, because they normalize prebendalism and corruption.[116] They therefore undermine the corporatist mode of communication between the state and religious structures.

Islamic Parties and Civil Society

The oldest Islamic party in Indonesia, the United Development Party (PPP), was founded in 1973 under the Suharto regime. Most recently, in October 2015, the Indonesian music celebrity Rhoma Irama set up the Party of Peaceful and Safe Islam to show that Islam is a religion of peace.[117] In the 2014 election, four Islamic parties ran—the National Awakening Party (PKB), the National Mandate Party (PAN), the Prosperous Justice Party (PKS), and the United Development Party. (See the appendixes to this chapter for party descriptions and electoral data.)[118]

Yet the electoral influence of Islamic parties has never been significant. Despite Indonesia's 90 percent Muslim population, Islamic political parties have received less than 44 percent of the votes in the last four democratic elections. As recently as 2009, Islamic parties garnered only 29 percent of votes. This is the worst Islamic parties have done since Indonesian independence.[119]

Nonetheless, the minority status of Islamic political parties does not translate into the political decline of Islam. In fact, many laws promoting Islamic agendas have passed at both the national and local levels of government. These include a 2003 education bill and a 2008 antipornography bill, both of which had strong support across the political spectrum.[120] Additionally, on issues of religious violence against religious minorities such as the Ahmadiyya, there has been a lack of strong response from nationalist, secular, and Pancasila-based political parties. The Ahmadiyya religious practices are persistently threatened to the point that, to alleviate tensions, the central state put the blame on the victims and considered issuing a decree to prevent the group's followers from practicing their religious beliefs publicly![121]

In sum, Islamic agendas pervade the legal and political sphere despite a lack of Islamic political representation. Sunny Tanuwidjaja explains this paradox in two ways. First, the absence of explicit religious influence on voters is due to the lack of religious differentiation among political candidates.[122] Second, while electoral support for Islamic political parties is weak, nationalist and secular parties such as the Golkar and Demokrat parties have shifted their positions in recent years to be more accommodating of religious agendas.[123] In fact, many provinces considered "power bases" for Golkar contain districts that have passed sharia bylaws.[124]

Additionally, some Islamic parties have often been involved in high-profile corruption cases and scandals, which has tarnished their image as "religious" parties. Citizens instead turn to Islamic organizations, which adopt a soft approach by disseminating their ideas through social engagement.[125] Many religious elites, in fact, prefer to engage with Islamic movements rather than to participate in electoral politics. For example, Indonesia's Ulema Council (Majelis Ulama Indonesia, or MUI) is the top Muslim clerical group, comprising ulemas from all of Indonesian Muslim groups, including Nahdlatul Ulama as well as Muhammadiyah.[126]

The MUI was established by the New Order regime in 1975 to open a channel of communication between Muslims and the government. The council is government funded but acts independently. Nonetheless, the government often solicits MUI legitimization of its policies, which sometimes creates friction and tensions. For example, in the 1970s, the government asked the MUI to support its birth-control program criticized by many religious groups.[127] As noted by Martin Van Bruinessen, "The council [was] officially supposed to advise the government on matters of religious concern to the Ummah, but in practice most communication [went] in the other direction."[128]

The council also became increasingly conservative following the end of the New Order regime and issued fatwas that had particularly negative impacts on minority communities. Hefner notes that this increased conservatism was an attempt to establish further independence from the government.[129] This fundamentalist turn also reflected recruitment into the organization of members of Islamist groups to counter the influence of liberal Muslim groups. For instance, between 2005 and 2010, Muhammad Ismail Yusanto, national spokesperson for Hizb Tahrir Indonesia (HTI), held the position of vice chairman of the Commission of Research, which provides research-based suggestions for the issuing of fatwas. Meanwhile, Muhammad al-Khaththath, the first *mu'tamad*—the one that proclaimed the official position of HTI—was appointed to the *dawah* (preaching) commission.[130] During the tenure of these two HTI figures, MUI issued a fatwa condemning Ahmadiyyah as non-Muslim.[131]

To further its independence after the end of the Suharto regime, in most regions the MUI declared that it would go from being a "servant of the government" to being a "servant of the people." However, this was not the case in Aceh, where the MUI became a fully governmental organization and renamed itself as the Consultative Assembly of Ulema (Majelis Permusyawaratan Ulama, or MPU). Its main function is to guide and examine Aceh government's policies and regulations.[132] Nonetheless, Moch Nur Ichwan notes, "Some informal meetings have happened at the national level, but usually for the government's agenda (security concerns and disseminating government policies), and none at a provincial level."[133] Ichwan further adds that the MPU has not been given authority to interfere with the sharia courts, sharia police, policy development offices, or the Islamic treasury.

Other Islamic organizations—such as Komite Penerapan Syariat Islam and Gerakan Muslim Minangkabau—are considered key local players in West Sumatra. Hizbut Tahrir Indonesia, Majelis Mujahidin Indonesia, and the Islamic Defenders Front are active in the formalization of sharia laws in Java as well as West Sumatra.[134]

Under these circumstances, the influence of and support for political Islam should not be synonymous with the performance of Islamic parties. Political Islam has a strong hold at the local and national levels of Indonesian politics because of the influence of religion on social life.[135] Significant social groups and movements converge and sometimes work with Islamic parties to promote the political influence of Islam. For example, in 1948, Commander Kartosuwiryo formed Darul Islam in West Java to fight Dutch colonial forces. Darul Islam was also an attempt to establish an Islamic state in Indonesia. The leaders began to implement their own interpretation of sharia, which included amputations for thieves and executions for those it deemed apostates. Kartosuwiryo was captured and executed in 1962, and by 1965 Darul Islam had been terminated.[136]

Nevertheless, a splinter group of Darul Islam, called Jemaah Islamiyah, established an underground military wing in the early 1990s. Militants associated with the group went on to carry out a number of attacks on high-profile Western targets, including bombings at a beachfront pub in Bali in October 2002, the Marriott Hotel in Jakarta in August 2003, the Australian embassy in September 2004, and a tourist restaurant in Bali in October 2005.[137] In 2009, after arresting hundreds of other members, police cornered and killed the group's strategist.[138]

Expanding the Influence of Sharia

Despite proclaimed state neutrality or equidistance, Islamic prescriptions influence social and political life, especially in Indonesia, where criminalization of blasphemy has led to increasing hostility against Ahmadiyyahs. The other challenge to state neutrality is the hegemonic "temptation" of some Indonesian provinces dominated by Muslim populations.

Moralization of Public Life: Interreligious Marriages, Blasphemy, and Homosexuality

Indonesian sharia courts were reorganized in 1882 under Dutch courts. As a result, their role was significantly reduced to adjudicating matrimonial and inheritance disputes and only with permission from the civil courts.[139] In the 1930s, sharia courts were permitted on South Kalimanton, although jurisdiction over inheritance was transferred to the civil courts. In 1957, they were permitted anywhere there was a civil court.[140] As discussed previously, the Marriage Act of 1974 reduced the independence of the sharia courts vis-à-vis the civil courts, while the 1989 Judicature Bill granted them power over marriage, divorce, and custody of children.[141] At the same time, judges continued to produce judgments in the traditional way, by referring to classical *fiqh* (Islamic jurisprudence) and the methodology of the *shafi'i* school (dominant in the country).

Due to the extraordinary number of cases (several hundred thousand annually), it became difficult to recruit an adequate number of judges who had the juridical and linguistic skills to work with the traditional sources. The response to this challenge was the Presidential Decree of 1991 to codify Islamic law, known as Kompilasi Hukum Islam (Compilation of Islamic Law). As in most Muslim countries, the compilation unified family law and nationalized it further with the use of Indonesian instead of Arabic in the court systems. It also established the state administration as the sole authority to change the family code. These changes led to heated debates about polygamy, divorce, and inheritance.

The new law aimed to make polygamy more difficult by obliging a husband to seek permission from the court for each new marriage and giving the judge the authority to determine the legitimacy of requests—particularly with regard to fairness to all wives. The compilation also acknowledges the national Marriage Act of 1974, along with the condition that the wife must give her husband permission to marry another woman. Nonetheless, apparently practitioners of polygamy do not always comply with these limitations, since men can still contract religious marriages without the validation of state-appointed officials.

The 1974 Marriage Act obliges a husband to file for divorce in the religious court, taking away his unilateral and arbitrary ability to divorce his wife (*talaq*). Wives may now also file for divorce. The court has to hear both parts before finalizing the divorce.

The Compilation of Islamic Law introduced another provision unknown in traditional jurisprudence. Only a registered marriage is legal, which means that a couple wed religiously but without registration cannot claim legal benefits for this marriage. This has consequences for matters of inheritance. The Islamic tradition, in contrast, requires witnesses, rather than certification, for a marriage to be legal.[142]

Other changes brought by the compilation concern children's right to inherit. In classical Islamic law, an adopted child cannot claim his or her parent's inheritance, since filiation has not been established. Because adoption is very common in Indonesia, the compilation allows the adopted child to receive a portion of the inheritance through an obligatory bequest (*wasiat wajibah*).

Under the 1974 Marriage Act, the status of interreligious marriage has also raised heated discussions about the influence of sharia on social and political life. The law does not explicitly authorize intermarriages, but nor does it prohibit them. One interreligious marriage, which involved a Muslim woman and a Protestant man, particularly stirred a lot of debate. The Office of Religious Affairs would not formalize the wedding because the groom was not Muslim. The Civil Registry would not do so either because the bride was a Muslim. The result was a dead end caused by the Marriage Act clauses stating that non-Muslim marriages must be registered with the Civil Registry Office following the religious ceremony, while Muslim marriages must be registered with the local Office of Religious Affairs.[143] In the end, the Supreme Court ruled in 1989 that the union should be considered a non-Muslim marriage.[144] Currently, although not explicitly forbidden, interfaith weddings must adhere to the ritual of one of the religions shared by the bride or groom.[145]

The status of sharia in Senegal has similarities with that in Indonesia, in the sense that the state has taken away the independence of the sharia courts. The civil law is secular, and religious marriages are valid only after being registered first by a state official. However, each religious group has the right to perform marriages according to its own customs. As in Indonesia, the codification of Islamic family law in 1972 introduced provisions departing from tradition. For example, unilateral divorce is not recognized in the state law. Polygamy is permitted but conditioned by preregistration by the husband with a secular court.[146]

Another disputed law in Indonesia concerns freedom of speech and blasphemy. Both the 1965 law and the criminal code prohibit blasphemy.[147] As noted by a US Department of State Report on Religious Freedom in Indonesia,

> The law prohibits deliberate public statements or activities that express enmity with, abuse, or stain a religion adhered to in Indonesia, or have the intent of preventing an individual from adhering to a recognized religion. The law also forbids the dissemination of information designed to spread hatred or dissension among individuals and/or certain community groups on the basis of ethnicity, religion, or race. Individuals can be prosecuted for blasphemous, atheistic, or heretical statements under either of these provisions or under the laws against defamation, and can face a maximum jail sentence of five years.[148]

This law is particularly detrimental to Ahmadiyyahs, who are considered blasphemous and are not one of the recognized religions.[149] National law allows them to practice their religion within their community, but in some regions the local bylaws are more prohibitive. These include requirements to sign a form renouncing their faith "in order to get married or go on the pilgrimage to Mecca." The MUI issued a fatwa against the Ahmadiyyah community in 1980 (*Ahmadiyya Qadiyan*) requesting that the government review the legal status of Ahmadiyyahs in Indonesia and halt their spread.[150] This fatwa was reiterated in 2005 (*Aliran Ahmadiyyah*).

Ahmadiyyahs also fell victim to rising vigilantism at the end of Suharto's authoritarian regime. Hefner notes:

> The largest and most aggressive militias boasted of their Islamic credentials and had a far broader agenda than just combating crime. Citing the Islamic ethical principle to command right and forbid wrong, militants in groups like the Islamic Defenders Front (Front Pembela Islam) took advantage of the post-Soeharto vacuum of power to ransack nightclubs, bars, and other alleged centers of vice. The militants have attacked not only Ahmadiyyahs but also attacked liberal Muslims, Christians, and pro-democracy activists.[151]

Unlike Indonesia, Senegal has no law against blasphemy. However, homosexuality is a crime. Article 319, paragraph 3 of the penal code stipulates a prison sentence of one to five years, along with a fine of US$200 to US$3,000, for people convicted of homosexual acts.[152] In this respect, homosexual men are subject to violence and rejection. In a study of 250 homosexual Senegalese men, 43 percent of respondents had been raped at least once, with 13 percent reporting being raped by policemen. Almost half of them had experienced verbal abuse in the form of threats and insults, along with physical abuse in the form of stone throwing from family and police.[153] Furthermore, in two separate incidents in 2008, villagers desecrated the tombs of notable gay men because they "did not want them buried in their area."[154] As Islam bans homosexuality, religion is frequently used to justify this stigmatizing of and violence toward male homosexuals. A Muslim cleric explains, "When a Muslim shakes hands with a homosexual, a certain number of prayers are required for his purification."[155]

While there is no national prohibition against homosexuality in Indonesia, many local ordinances criminalize it, including the city of Palembang in South Sumatra and the city of Tasikmalaya in West Java.[156] Furthermore, homosexual couples are not allowed to adopt, according to government regulation No. 54/2007.[157] On March 4, 2015, the MUI issued a fatwa advocating caning and even the death penalty to punish homosexuals.[158] The head of the *fatwa* commission, Hasanuddin A. F., stated, "It doesn't matter that they love each other. The law still prohibits it. In Islamic law, it's a sexual act that must be heavily punished. It would be bad if the government allows same-sex marriage."[159]

The critique and discrimination of sexual minorities have been on the rise. In 2016 Muhammad Nasir (technology, research, and higher education minister), along with Anies Baswedan (culture and elementary and secondary education minister) and Ridwan Kamil (mayor of Bandung), argued for barring LGBTQ students from university campuses due to their moral corruptness.[160] In the same vein, in April 2017, a homosexual couple in Aceh was reported to the sharia police for illicit sexual acts; if charged they will face public flogging.[161]

Rampant Sharia

Although calls for nationally state-enforced sharia have proved unsuccessful with Indonesian voters, the influence of Islamic prescriptions on legislation and political debate remains strong and echoes similar debates we have described in the case of hegemonic Islam.

Laws 22/1999 and 25/1999 give greater power to local governments, creating opportunities for "sharia informed bylaws."[162] These laws were reinforced by Law 32/2004, which permits regional governments to pass their own legislation, called *peraturan daerah* (regional regulation), or *perda*. This law has allowed regional governments to pass Islamically based regulations (*perda syariah*) by referring to an article in the 2004 law authorizing regional and cultural habits.[163] Thus, local rulers present Islamic values as part of the local culture, thereby bypassing the national prohibition against laws based on the Quran or the Islamic tradition.

In short, regional regulations with strong Islamic influence became possible in a nation based on secular ideology (Pancasila), because religion was presented as the defining culture of the region.[164] Most of these bylaws concern the use of alcohol, gambling, and the mobility of women. They enforce Islamic devotional duties: in South Sulawesi, restaurants must close during Ramadan, and hotels must refuse rooms to unmarried couples.

Furthermore, in Padang Muslim villages, fornication and alcohol consumption are punished with lashes. Other regulations concern prostitution, Quranic education, and almsgiving.

Interestingly, Christian regions have also made use of Law 32/2004 to demand regulations inspired by religious values. In predominantly Christian Manokwari in West Papua, the government has proposed *perda injil*, or regional regulation inspired by biblical values. One of the most controversial aspects of this proposed *perda* is the banning of the hijab for public school students and civil servants.

Rampant sharia is also present in the Aceh region. Its status as a special province, granted in 1999, has facilitated the growth of its own legal system influenced by sharia.[165] Today, Aceh stands out in Indonesia as the only province that officially enforces sharia, including *hudud* penalties.[166]

In 2000, Law 5/2000, later clarified by 11/2002, introduced the Wilayatul Hisbah, a sharia police force. Officers have the power to "reprimand" and "advise" but not to formally charge, which remains the responsibility of the civil police and the prosecutor's office.[167] A Human Rights Watch report in 2010 notes that bylaw 11/2002 "contains a number of Shari'a obligations, requiring Muslims to refrain from disseminating deviant teachings, to attend Friday prayers, to observe the fast during Ramadan, to refrain from providing Muslims with an opportunity to break the fast during Ramadan, and to wear Islamic clothing."[168]

Moch Nur Ichwan argues that shariatization in Aceh was a "top-down political-elite-driven movement" initiated by the central government in order to dissuade independence movements and win over Muslims.[169] This took the form of a 2001 law, which gave more autonomy to Aceh, and a presidential decree (11/2003), which allowed for local interpretation of sharia law.[170] Subsequent Aceh bylaws include 12/2003, which prohibits the sale and consumption of alcohol; 13/2003, which bans gambling; and 14/2003 against "seclusion." These bylaws were implemented in June 2005.

In 2009, the Aceh parliament expanded the criminal code to allow for Islamic criminal punishment. Approved by the national house of representatives in 2014, this expansion was officially enforced starting in 2015.[171] The new laws allow the following punishments: for adultery, caning (100 lashes), a fine to be paid in gold, or imprisonment; for homosexuality, 100 lashes and a maximum fine of 1,000 grams of pure gold, or imprisonment of up to 100 months; for pedophilia, 200 lashes or a fine of up to 2,000 grams of fine gold, or maximum imprisonment of 200 months; for rape, at least 100 lashes up to a maximum of 200 lashes, or imprisonment of at least 100 months up to 200 months.[172] The penalties originally included stoning, although after widespread controversy, this punishment was later revoked.[173]

Conclusion

Senegalese civil Islam comes closest to the cohesive and unifying set of beliefs shared by all citizens emphasized by most definitions of civil religion. As discussed above, Sufi orders play a major role in interactions between citizens and contribute to the positive role attributed to religion in Senegalese society. But they do not exclusively shape the civil religion. The communities of believers are in fact embedded within kinship and local groups. As a result, religious leadership is ethnically diverse, leading to extended families encompassing Christians and Muslims. Etienne Smith notes that Cardinal Hyacinthe Thiandoum came from a Muslim family—it is even said that his uncle was an imam and that the muezzin of the mosque in the famous Catholic pilgrimage village of Popenguine is one of his nephews.[174] Therefore kinship relations and good neighboring influence interreligious communication. In this respect, the proportionate equidistance of the state from all groups and the acknowledgment of cultural and linguistic pluralism are as important as acknowledgment of religious diversity. As stated by Smith, "Senegal's imagined nation, or imagination, is a combination of a still omnipresent secular modern state, a lively religious society, as well as resilient cultural patrias and values."[175]

The deep impact of Léopold Sédar Senghor, the first president of Senegal, on Senegalese institutions partially explains this political culture. His double-minority background as a Catholic and Serer is significant for a country dominated by Muslims and Wolofs.[176] Senghor's origins certainly inspired his vision for the

Senegalese state. On one hand, he promoted the secular principle defined as equidistance vis-à-vis all religions. On the other hand, he recognized cultural and regional diversity.

Senegal's political elite has always reflected this religious and ethnic diversity. President Senghor had Muslim sisters. President Abdou Diouf, a Muslim, married a Catholic, and their children prolonged this familial ecumenism. President Abdoulaye Wade, a Muslim, married a Catholic. As for ethnicity, all the presidents have emphasized their local and kinship affiliations: Senghor traced his lineage back to the Mandinka nobility, Diouf presented himself as a Wolof with a Serer name, and the Wolof Wade often mentioned that his mother was of Mandinka origin from Casamance. Recognition of ethnic and regional diversity is not simply an elite strategy. It is also inscribed in the law with the recognition of national languages.

Political elites since Senghor have avoided the capture of state institutions by one religion or ethnicity at all costs. This has translated into a politics of equal respect, meaning that any recognition in favor of the majority groups (Muslims and/or Wolof) is associated with an equivalent acknowledgment of minorities. At the same time, the state proportions its policies according to the numeric importance of the groups. Thus state elite relations with major Sufi groups and Wolofs are more frequent than with Catholic or minor ethnic groups. Such a proportionate equidistance is not easy to maintain. The blatant Murid affiliation of President Wade (2000–2007) became a controversial topic not because it violated *laïcité* as such but because it did not conform to the proportionate equidistance.

In sum, Senegalese civil religion is shaped not simply by Islam or religion but also by ethnicity and secular principles and relies on tolerance among groups in society. This tolerance is explained by the fact that identities and religious affiliation do not line up, which allows for greater civility among citizens from different religious backgrounds (as long as they are acknowledged as members of families or kinship groups who share the same village or region). Through equal respect and proportionate equidistance, Senegalese political culture is a unique combination of local civility and civic secular principles protected by state institutions.

When we turn to Indonesia, civil Islam approximates the Rousseauian approach (meaning it operates first as a state-centered project). The cornerstone of Indonesia's civil Islam, the Pancasila agreement, defines the role of the state vis-à-vis religions and society and inscribes the recognition of religious diversity in the law. However, this official acknowledgment of toleration does not automatically translate into peaceful relations between religious groups. In fact, toleration and tolerance do not line up. The former refers to the legal protection of diversity, while the latter concerns individual and group relations. This distinction may seem artificial since law and behaviors mutually influence each other. But in the countries I have referred to as state-nations, the difference has relevance, because the law as an authoritative state-elite-driven initiative does not systematically match the identities or aspirations of the population.

In Indonesia, toleration is grounded in Islamic values and principles that allow for the recognition of other religions. In this respect, the Constitution of Medina as initiated by the Prophet Muhammad is presented in the national imagination as the best way to achieve tolerance. In other words, the ideal Indonesian civil Islam appears to be a multireligious Islamic state that upholds fundamental Islamic principles about family, gender relations, and freedom of speech, while protecting and recognizing some religions in line with these values and principles (Jews and Christians) and ostracizing others that contradict or violate them (Ahmadiyyahs, freethinkers, sexual minorities). Political elites widely share this political culture, as attested by the incapacity of liberal democratic state partisans to shift the state's biased treatment of religions toward greater neutrality. This is also why Islamic parties do not win elections. In fact, the political strength of Islam resides in its social mobilization through organizations and associations that interact with all political parties and do not channel their claims through Islamic parties.

The Senegalese and Indonesian examples shed light on the potential for civil religion to promote societal integration, in which religion is not subsumed into a secular civic creed but actually serves at the basis for this social integration. As Bellah once noted, Islam is in theory a civil religion and has functioned that way during several of its historical manifestations.[177] Such a civil religion, however, does not leave room for individual rights that challenge these religious principles.

In sum, the Senegalese and Indonesian cases illustrate that toleration and tolerance are not synonymous. Bellah's definition emphasizes the latter, but both dimensions are key in delineating the specific civil religion of any country. Senegalese civil Islam can be defined as the proportionate equidistance of the state (toleration) associated with intra- and interreligious pluralism (tolerance). Indonesian civil Islam, on the other hand, combines institutional recognition of religious diversity (toleration) with interreligious pluralism and intrareligious monism (or intolerance). In both cases, civil Islam is a hybrid between Rousseau's state-centered religion and Durkheim's shared-beliefs systems.

Appendix 4.1: Islamic Parties in Indonesia

PAN

Former Muhammadiyah chairman Amien Rais established the National Mandate Party (PAN) in 1998. PAN describes itself as open, pluralistic, and pro-democracy and encourages representation of diverse people (including those of different religions).[178] After its founding in 1998 it initially caused controversy through "intolerant and even radical statements." This led many moderate Muslims and Christians to leave the party.

PKB

The National Awakening Party (PKB) was founded in July 1998 by former Nahdlatul Ulama (NU) chairman and president of Indonesia Abdurrahman Wahid. NU leaders saw the resignation of Suharto as an opportunity for their organization to establish its own political party. On June 3, 1998, the NU executive board appointed a group of five members, known as "Team Five," to work on the creation of a new party. On July 23, 1998, the PKB was officially announced.

According to its *mabda' siyasi* (the foundational basis of the party), the PKB strives to safeguard the five *maqasid as-syariyyah* (foundational goals of Islamic law), namely, the body (*hifdz al-nafs*), the religion (*hifdz al-din*), the intellect (*hifdz al-'aql*), the lineage (*hifdz al-nasl*), and the property (*hifdz al-mal*). In interpreting these foundational goals, the PKB used the words *warga negara* (citizen) instead of "Muslim," signaling its wider interpretation of the principles to include all citizens of Indonesia regardless of their faith. The PKB specifically mentions that the party's distinct characteristic is its fostering of religious humanistic values under the banner of nationalism. Overall the PKB's goals, visions, and missions combine nationalistic values such as adherence to the constitution and the extension of Islamic humanism to non-Muslim citizens.[179] In August 2002, the party voted against including a constitutional provision for Islamic law, evidence that while religious, adherents are also secular nationalists.[180]

PPP

Founded in 1973 as an alliance among smaller Islamic parties, the United Development Party (PPP) professes to uphold human dignity and social justice, based on Islamic values.[181] In 1999 introduction of sharia law became one of its objectives.[182] The PPP proclaimed itself as the big house of the Indonesian *ummah*. It intends to become the place where all Muslims will return to fulfill their religious aspirations.

PKS

Established on July 20, 1998, the Prosperous Justice Party (PKS) was initially called the Partai Keadilan (Justice Party). It won 1.36 percent of the vote during the 1999 legislative election, which was below the 2 percent electoral threshold required for the party to participate in the next election in 2004. The party then reconstituted itself as the Partai Keadilan Sejahtera. It originally sought, through democracy, to establish an Islamic society based on sharia, but since 2004 it has turned away from the project of establishing an Islamic state.[183] The PKS was beset with sexual and corruption scandals in 2013.[184] Despite predicted losses for Islamic parties in 2014,[185] it actually made a slight comeback.[186] Expected to be hit much worse, it actually only fell by 1 percent.

Appendix 4.2: Indonesian Election Data

Table A.1 Election Data for PAN, PKB, PPP, PKS, and Remaining
Non-Islamist Parties (1999–2014)

Year	Party	Parliamentary Seats
1999	PAN	34
1999	PKB	51
1999	PPP	58
1999	PKS	7
1999	Remaining non-Islamist parties	350
2004	PAN	53
2004	PKB	52
2004	PPP	58
2004	PKS	45
2004	Remaining non-Islamist parties	292
2009	PAN	46
2009	PKB	28
2009	PPP	38
2009	PKS	57
2009	Remaining non-Islamist parties	331
2014	PAN	49
2014	PKB	47
2014	PPP	39
2014	PKS	40
2014	Remaining non-Islamist parties	325

Table A.2 Results of the 1999 Legislative Election
(24 Political Parties Participated)

Rank	Party	Parliamentary Seats (462 in Total)
1	PDIP (Partai Demokrasi Indonesia Perjuangan), Indonesian Democratic Party of Struggle	154
2	Golkar	120
3	PPP	59
4	PKB	51
5	PAN	35
6	PBB (Partai Bulan Bintang), Crescent Star Party	13
7	Partai Keadilan (Justice Party)	6
8	PKPI (Partai Keadilan dan Persatuan Indonesia), Indonesian Justice and Unity Party	6
9	PNU (Partai Nahdlatul Ummah), Nahdlatul Community Party	3
10	PDKB (Partai Demokrasi Kasih Bangsa), Love the Nation Democratic Party	3
11	PBI (Partai Buruh Indonesia), Labour Party of Indonesia	3
12	PDI (Indonesian Democratic Party)	2
13	Seven seats were distributed equally among seven different parties, with each receiving one seat.	7

Table A.3 Results of the 2004 Legislative Election
(24 Political Parties Participated)

Rank	Party	Parliamentary Seats (550 in Total)
1	Golkar	128
2	PDIP	109
3	PPP	58
4	Demokrat	55
5	PAN	53
6	PKB	52
7	PKS (Prosperous Justice Party)	45
8	Bintang Reformasi Party	14
9	Damai Sejahtera Party	13
10	Bulan Bintang Party	11
11	Persatuan Demokrasi Bangsa Party	4
12	Pelopor Party	3
13	Karya Pedula Bangsa Party	2
14	Indonesia Marhaenisme National Party	1
15	PKPI	1
16	Penegak Demokrasi Bangsa Party	1

Table A.4 Results of the 2009 Legislative Election (38 Political Parties Participated with 6 Local Parties of Aceh)

Rank	Party	Parliamentary Seats (560 in Total)
1	Demokrat	148
2	Golkar	106
3	PDIP	94
4	PKS	57
5	PAN	46
6	PPP	38
7	PKB	28
8	Gerindra	26
9	Hanura	17

Six other parties did not win any seats.

Table A.5 Results of the 2014 Legislative Election
(12 Political Parties Participated)

Rank	Party	Parliamentary Seats (560 in Total)
1	PDIP	109
2	Golkar	91
3	Gerindra	73
4	Demokrat	61
5	PAN	49
6	PKB	47
7	PKS	40
8	PPP	39
9	Nasdem	35
10	Hanura	16
11	PBB and PKPI	0

Table A.6 List of *Perda Syariah* in Indonesia

No.	Province	District	*Perda* Title	Description
2001				
1	West Sumatra	—	Peraturan Daerah Propinsi Sumatra Barat Nomor 11 Tahun 2001[187]	Prevention and eradication of immoral acts (e.g., adultery, gambling, consumption of alcohol and drugs)
2	West Sumatra	Solok	Perda Solok number 10/2001[188]	Obligatory Quran education for elementary school students up to high school students
3	West Sumatra	Tanah Datar	Surat Himbauan Bupati Tanah Datar number 451.4/556/Kesra-2001[189]	Obligation for female employees of the Education and Labor Department to dress according to Islamic values
2002				
1	East Nusa Tenggara	Dompu	Perda Dompu number 1/2002[190]	Obligation for women to wear the hijab and the requirement for civil servants and students to be able to read the Quran
2003				
1	West Sumatra	Padang	Perda Kota Padang number 6/2003[191]	Obligatory Quran education for elementary school students
2	West Sumatra	Solok	Perda Solok number 13/2003[192]	Regulation and guidelines on almsgiving (*zakat*)
3	West Sumatra	Sawahlunto	Perda Sawahlunto number 1/2003[193]	Requirement for students to be able to read the Quran to graduate from elementary, middle, and high school
4	West Sumatra	Sawahlunto	Perda Sawahlunto number 2/2003[194]	Obligation to dress according to Islamic values
5	West Sumatra	Pasaman	Perda Pasaman number 21/2003[195]	Requirement for students to be able to read the Quran to graduate from elementary, middle, high school, and university
6	West Sumatra	Pasaman	Perda Pasaman number 22/2003[196]	Obligation to dress according to Islamic values
7	West Sumatra	Limapuluh Kota	Perda Limapuluh Kota 6/2003[197]	Requirement for students to be able to read the Quran to graduate from elementary, middle, and high school
2004				
1	West Sumatra	Padang Pariaman	Perda Padang Pariaman number 2/2004[198]	Prevention and eradication of immoral acts (e.g., adultery, consumption of alcohol, gambling)
2	West Sumatra	Bukit Tinggi	Perda Bukit Tinggi number 29/2004[199]	Regulation and guidelines on almsgiving

continues

No.	Province	District	*Perda* Title	Description
2004				
3	West Sumatra	Pesisir Selatan	Perda Pesisir Selatan number 8/2004[200]	Mandatory Quran education and Quran literacy requirement for marriages
4	Bengkulu	Bengkulu	Instruction from the Mayor of Bengkulu number 3/2004[201]	Faith-building program for school children
5	Lampung	Lampung Selatan	Perda Lampung Selatan number 4/2004[202]	Prohibition of prostitution and gambling
6	Banten	Banten	Perda Banten number 4/2004[203]	Regulation and guidelines on almsgiving
7	East Java	Cirebon	Perda Cirebon number 77/2004[204]	Mandatory after-school Islamic-education class
8	South Borneo	Banjar	Perda Banjar number 4/2004[205]	Requirement for students to finish reading the whole Quran to graduate from elementary school
9	South Borneo	Banjar	Perda Banjar number 5/2004[206]	Prohibition for restaurants and shops to sell food and drink during Ramadan
10	East Nusa Tenggara	Dompu	Perda Dompu number 11/2004[207]	Requirement for candidates for village head to be able to read the Quran
2005				
1	West Sumatra	Pesisir Selatan	Perda Pesisir Selatan number Selatan 4/2005[208]	Obligation to dress according to Islamic values
2	West Sumatra	Agam	Perda Agam number 5/2005[209]	Requirement for students to be able to read the Quran to graduate from elementary, middle, and high school
3	West Sumatra	Agam	Perda Agam number 6/2005[210]	Obligation to dress according to Islamic values
4	West Java	Tangerang	Perda Tangerang number 7/2005[211]	Prohibition on selling and consuming alcohol
5	West Java	Tangerang	Perda Tangerang number 8/2005[212]	Prohibition of prostitution
6	West Java	Bandung	Perda Bandung number 9/2005[213]	Guidelines for almsgiving
7	East Java	Probolinggo	Perda Probolinggo number 5/2005[214]	Eradication of prostitution
8	East Java	Malang	Perda Malang number 8/2005[215]	Eradication of prostitution
9	East Java	Sidoarjo	Perda Sidoarjo number 4/2005	Guidelines and regulations on almsgiving
10	South Borneo	Banjar	Perda Banjar number 8/2005	Order to stop all activities during Friday prayer
11	South Borneo	Hulu Sungai Utara	Perda Hulu Sungai Utara number 19/2005[216]	Guidelines on almsgiving
12	South Borneo	Banjarmasin	Perda Banjarmasin number 4/2005[217]	Prohibition on open restaurants during Ramadan
13	South Sulawesi	Maros	Perda Maros number 15/2005[218]	Obligatory Quran education
14	South Sulawesi	Maros	Perda Maros number 16/2005[219]	Mandatory hijab for Muslim women
15	South Sulawesi	Maros	Perda Maros number 17/2005[220]	Guidelines on almsgiving

continues

Table A.6 continued

No.	Province	District	*Perda* Title	Description
2006				
1	West Sumatra	Sawahlunto	Perda Sawahlunto number 19/2006[221]	Prevention and eradication of immoral acts
2	West Sumatra	—	Perda Provinsi Sumatra Barat number 3/2007[222]	Mandatory Quran education
3	Riau	Kampar	Perda Kampar number 2/2006[223]	Regulation on almsgiving
4	Bangka Belitung	Bangka	Perda Bangka number 4/2006[224]	Regulation on almsgiving
5	Banten	Serang	Perda Serang number 1/2006[225]	Mandatory after-school religious education (*madrasah diniyah*)
6	East Java	Cianjur	Perda Cianjur number 3/2006[226]	Good moral-community movement (*akhlaqul karimah*)
7	South Kalimantan	Banjarbaru	Perda Banjarbaru number 5/2006[227]	Prohibition of the consumption of alcohol
8	South Sulawesi	Makassar	Perda Makassar number 5/2006[228]	Regulation on almsgiving
9	South Sulawesi	Pangkejene dan kepulauan	Perda Pangkejene dan Kepulauan number 11/2006[229]	Prohibition of the consumption of alcohol
10	South Sulawesi	Polewali Mandar	Perda Polewali Manda number 13/2006[230]	Supervision and control of the consumption of alcohol
11	South Sulawesi	Polewali Mandar	Perda Polewali Manda number 14/2006[231]	Quran teaching movement
12	South Sulawesi	—	Perda Provinsi Sulawesi Selatan number 4/2006[232]	Mandatory Quran education
13	South Sulawesi	Padang Muslim Village	Peraturan Desa Muslim Padang number 5/2006[233]	Punishment in the form of lashes for adulterers and alcohol drinkers
2007				
1	Yogyakarta	Bantul	Perda Bantul number 5/2007[234]	Prohibition of prostitution
2	East Java	Lamongan	Perda Lamongan number 5/2007[235]	Eradication of prostitution
3	South Borneo	Bankar	Perda Bankar number 10/2007[236]	Prohibition of prostitution and gambling
2008				
1	West Sumatra	Padang Panjang	Perda Padang Panjang number 7/2008[237]	Regulation and guidelines on almsgiving
2	Riau	Riau	Governor's Decree number 003.1/UM/08[238]	The use of Arabic letters for the naming of building
3	Central Java	Semarang	Mayor's Decree number 435/4687	Regulations for the open hours of nightclubs and bars
4	South Sulawesi	Bone	Circulated Letter Issued by the Division of Community Relations of Bone number 44/1857/VIII	The closure of restaurants and nightclubs during Ramadan and exhortation for hotels to refuse use of their facilities to unmarried couples
5	Banten	Tangerang	Mayor's Decree in August 2008	The closure of nightclubs during Ramadan
2012				
1	Gorontalo	Gorontalo	Perda Gorontalo number 6/2012[239]	Mandatory Quran education
2014				
1	South Borneo	Banjarmasin City	Perda Kota Banjarmasin number 1/2014[240]	Regulation and guidelines on almsgiving

Notes

1. Bellah, Robert N. "Civil Religion in America." *Daedalus* 134, no. 4 (2005): 40–55.
2. Cristi, Marcela. *From Civil to Political Religion: The Intersection of Culture, Religion and Politics.* Waterloo, ON: Wilfrid Laurier University Press, 2001.
3. Hefner, Robert W. *Civil Islam: Muslims and Democratization in Indonesia.* Princeton, NJ: Princeton University Press, 2000.
4. "The 1945 Constitution of the Republic of Indonesia." World Intellectual Property Organization (WIPO). Accessed December 23, 2016. http://www.wipo .int/edocs/lexdocs/laws/en/id/id048en.pdf.
5. Smith, Roger M., and Clark D. Neher. *Southeast Asia: Documents of Political Development and Change.* Ithaca, NY: Cornell University Press, 1974.
6. Assyaukanie, Luthfi. *Islam and the Secular State in Indonesia.* Singapore: Institute of Southeast Asian Studies, 2009.
7. Natsir was an Islamic scholar and Indonesia's fifth prime minister. See Assyaukanie, *Islam and the Secular State*, 60.
8. The advocates were Mohammad Natsir (1908–1993), Zainal Abidin Ahmad (1911–1983), and Sjafruddin Prawiranegara (1911–1989). See Assyaukanie, *Islam and the Secular State*, 60.
9. Ibid., 69.
10. Ibid., 59.
11. Ibid., 14.
12. Ibid., 97.
13. Muhammad Syafaat Mintaredja (b. 1921) and Abdul Mukti Ali (1923–2004) were allies of Suharto in his cabinet and RDS partisans. Further advocates for RDS include Muhammadiyah leaders Muhammad Amien Rais (b. 1944), Ahmad Syafii Maarif (b. 1935), Kuntowijoyo (1943–2005), and Muhammad Dawam Rahardjo (b. 1942) and Nahdlatul Ulama leaders Achmad Siddiq (1926–1991), Sahal Mahfud (b. 1937), and Ali Yafie (b. 1928).
14. Assyaukanie, *Islam and the Secular State*, 16.
15. Nahdlatul Ulama is an Islamic organization established in 1926 to counter the reformist modernist approach of Muhammadiyah. It upholds the schools of jurisprudence as well as local customs. It is the largest Muslim organization in the world, with more than 40 million members in 2003. See Ghosh, Ranjan. *Making Sense of the Secular: Critical Perspectives from Europe to Asia.* New York: Routledge, 2013, p. 202. See also Assyaukanie, *Islam and the Secular State*, 106.
16. Pancasila is a major Islamic nongovernmental organization established in 1912, with the goal of reforming Islamic practices and thinking along the lines of the modernist Salafiyya of Afghani and Abduh.
17. Assyaukanie, *Islam and the Secular State*, 108.
18. Ibid., 110.
19. Muhammad Amien Rais was a prominent Indonesian politician who led the reform movement that forced President Suharto to resign in 1998. He was also leader of Muhammadiyah from 1995 to 2000.
20. Assyaukanie, *Islam and the Secular State*, 17.
21. Ibid., 119.
22. Indonesia has two educational systems, one regulated by the Ministry of Education and one by the Ministry of Religious Affairs. The ongoing issue of teaching religion has to do with the former system, not the latter.
23. Butt, Simon. "Polygamy and Mixed Marriage in Indonesia: Islam and the Marriage Law in the Courts." In *Indonesia: Law and Society*, ed. Tim Lindsey. Sydney: Federation Press, 1999.

24. Assyaukanie, *Islam and the Secular State*, 116.

25. The 1974 Marriage Act gave the general courts power to dissolve a marriage. However, if the marriage concerned two Muslims, the sharia court had to validate the divorce.

26. Cammack, Mark. "Indonesia's 1989 Religious Judicature Act: Islamization of Indonesia or Indonesianization of Islam?" *Indonesia* 63 (1997): 143–168; Assyaukanie, *Islam and the Secular State*, 116.

27. Assyaukanie, *Islam and the Secular State*, 116.

28. Ibid.

29. Nurcholish Madjid was a prominent Muslim intellectual known for his support for modernization within Islam. Upon completion of his PhD in the United States under the guidance of Fazlur Rahman, he returned to Indonesia in 1984 and created Paramedina, an organization devoted to a pluralistic approach to the Islamic tradition.

30. The Constitution of Medina refers to the document drafted by the Prophet Muhammad when he ruled over the Medina population from AD 622 to 632. This document acknowledged not only Muslims but also Christian and Jewish tribes and regulated their coexistence. It is often considered as the reference for the existence of a multireligious Islamic state. See conclusion of this chapter as well as Assyaukanie, *Islam and the Secular State*, 149.

31. This is according to Masdr Masudi, a santri intellectual, who had an orthodox religious upbringing.

32. Abdurrahman Wahid was an Indonesian Muslim religious and political leader and the president of Indonesia from 1999 to 2001.

33. Djohan Effendi (b. 1939) served as state secretary during Wahid's presidency, between 2000 and 2001. In 2001 he founded the Indonesian Circle for Pluralism and Peace.

34. Menchik, Jeremy. *Islam and Democracy in Indonesia: Tolerance Without Liberalism*. New York: Cambridge University Press, 2016.

35. "The State guarantees all persons the freedom of worship, each according to his/her own religion or belief" ("The 1945 Constitution of the Republic of Indonesia").

36. An Islamic religious movement, founded in Punjab in 1889 by Mirza Gulam Ahmad (1835–1908), that emphasizes the need to restore Islam to its true and original form. Ahmad claimed to be a *mujaddid* (renewer) and the Mahdi. For this reason, the movement is not acknowledged in mainstream Islam because the Mahdi will come only at the end of time, and there can be no prophet after Prophet Muhammad. At the death of Ahmad, a minority of followers broke away and founded the Lahore Ahmadiyyah movement because they did not acknowledge Ahmad as a prophet and Mahdi.

37. Menchik, *Islam and Democracy in Indonesia*, 559.

38. "School's In." *Economist*. December 13, 2014. http://www.economist .com/news/asia/21636098-indonesias-schools-are-lousy-new-administration -wants-fix-them-schools.

39. "Indonesia 2014 International Religious Freedom Report." United States Department of State. Accessed December 22, 2016. http://www.state.gov /documents/organization/238510.pdf.

40. *Buku guru: SMP/KTs kelas 08 pendidikan agama Islam dan budi pekerti*. Jakarta: Kementerian Pendidikan dan Kebudayaan, 2013, p. 19.

41. *SMP/KTs kelas 07 pendidikan agama Islam dan budi pekerti*. Jakarta: Kementerian Pendidikan dan Kebudayaan, 2014, p. 163.

42. *SMP/KTs kelas 09 pendidikan agama Islam dan budi pekerti*. Jakarta: Kementerian Pendidikan dan Kebudayaan, 2015, p. 182.

43. Ibid.

44. Ibid., 187.

45. *SMP/MTs kelas 07*, 187.

46. *SMP/KTs kelas 09*, 176.

47. Ibid., 238.

48. *SMA/MA/SMK/MAKs kelas 11 pendidikan agama Islam dan budi pekerti.* Jakarta: Kementerian Pendidikan dan Kebudayaan, 2013, p. 186.

49. *SMA/MA/SMK/MAKs kelas 10 semester 2 sejarah Indonesia.* Jakarta: Kementerian Pendidikan dan Kebudayaan, 2014, pp. 20–105.

50. *Kelas 12 buku siswa pendidikan agama Islam dan budi pekerti.* Jakarta: Kementerian Pendidikan dan Kebudayaan, 2015, p. 166.

51. Ibid., 190.

52. *SMP/KTs kelas 09*, 166.

53. Ibid., 93–94.

54. *SMP/KTs kelas 07*, 36.

55. *Buku guru: SMP/MTs kelas 09 pendidikan agama Islam dan budi pekerti.* Jakarta: Kementerian Pendidikan dan Kebudayaan, 2015.

56. *Buku guru: SMP/MTs kelas 09*, 103.

57. *Buku guru kementerian kelas 11–12 pendidikan agama Islam dan budi pekerti.* Jakarta: Kementerian Pendidikan dan Kebudayaan, 2015.

58. Ibid., 156.

59. *SMP/KTs kelas 08 pendidikan agama Islam dan budi pekerti.* Jakarta: Kementerian Pendidikan dan Kebudayaan, 2013, p. 87.

60. *SMA/MA/SMK/MAKs kelas 11*, 70.

61. *SMA/MA/SMK/MAKs kelas 12 pendidikan agama Islam dan budi pekerti.* Jakarta: Kementerian Pendidikan dan Kebudayaan, 2014, p. 212.

62. *Kelas 10 bahasa Indonesia wahana pengetahuan.* Jakarta: Kementerian Pendidikan dan Kebudayaan, 2013, p. 82.

63. *Kelas 12 buku siswa pendidikan*, 173.

64. *Kelas 10 pendidikan agama Islam dan budi pekerti.* Jakarta: Kementerian Pendidikan dan Kebudayaan, 2014, p. 45.

65. *SMP/KTs kelas 09*, 177.

66. *SMP/KTs kelas 08*, 54.

67. *SMP/KTs kelas 09*, 167.

68. Ibid., 242.

69. "Constitution de la République du Senegal." Government of Senegal. 2001. http://www.wipo.int/edocs/lexdocs/laws/fr/sn/sn013fr.pdf. Translation by author.

70. Ibid.

71. Stepan, Alfred. "Stateness, Democracy, and Respect: Senegal in Comparative Perspective." In *Tolerance, Democracy, and Sufis in Senegal*, ed. Mamadou Diouf. New York: Columbia University Press, 2013, p. 216.

72. Smith, Etienne. "Religious and Cultural Pluralism in Senegal: Accommodation Through 'Proportional Equidistance'?" In *Tolerance, Democracy, and Sufis in Senegal*, ed. Diouf Mamadou, 147–179. New York: Columbia University Press, 2013, p. 161.

73. Ibid.

74. "World Faiths Development Dialogue." *Faith and Development in Focus: Senegal.* Berkley Center for Religion, Peace, and World Affairs, Georgetown University, May 2016.

75. Qadiriyaa was founded by Abdul-Qadir Gilani in 1119. The order advocates adherence to Islamic fundamentals and is widespread in the Arab-speaking world. The Tijaniyya was founded by Ahmad al-Tijani in the 1780s. The order emphasizes the personal commitment of the believer, along with culture and

education. The Muridiyya was founded by Amadou Bamba in 1883. The order believes that Bamba was a *mujaddid*, a renewer of Islam sent by God every hundred years. The Layene was founded by Seydina Limamou Laye in 1884. This order believes that its leader is the reincarnation of Muhammad (Mahdi). Most of its members are Lebous living in fishing communities in Cape Verde peninsula, Senegal. See Villalón, Leonardo A. "Generational Changes, Political Stagnation, and the Evolving Dynamics of Religion and Politics in Senegal." *Africa Today* 46, no. 3/4 (1999), 133.

76. Ibid., 134.

77. Leichtman, Mara A. "Revolution, Modernity and (Trans)National Shi'i Islam: Rethinking Religious Conversion in Senegal." *Journal of Religion in Africa* 39, no. 3 (2009): 319–351.

78. Parker, Ron. "The Senegal-Mauritania Conflict of 1989: A Fragile Equilibrium." *Journal of Modern African Studies* 21 (1991): 155–171.

79. Ibid.

80. "Diversity and Tolerance in the Islam of West Africa." Africa Online Digital Library. Accessed December 23, 2016. http://aodl.org/islamictolerance.

81. "A Conversation with El Hadji Baye Lamine Niass, Niassene Family of the Tijaniyya Confrérie in Senegal." Berkley Center for Religion, Peace, and World Affairs. November 17, 2014. https://berkleycenter.georgetown.edu/interviews /a-conversation-with-el-hadji-baye-lamine-niass-niassene-family-of-the-tijaniyya -confrérie-in-senegal.

82. Lliteras, Susana Molins. "A Path to Integration: Senegalese Tijanis in Cape Town." *African Studies* 68, no. 2 (2009): 215–233.

83. Ibid.

84. Glover, John. *Sufism and Jihad in Modern Senegal: The Murid Order*. Rochester, NY: University of Rochester Press, 2007.

85. Wright, Zakariya. "Al-Hajj Malik Sy." Tariqa Tijaniyya. 2016. http:// www.tijani.org/al-hajj-malik-sy.

86. Mané, Mamadou. "Les valeurs culturelles des Confréries musulmanes au Senegal." UNESCO. 2012. http://www.unesco.org/new/fileadmin/multimedia /field/Dakar/pdf/EtudeconfréríesSenegal4Dec2012.pdf.

87. Diouf, Mamadou. "The Senegalese Murid Trade Diaspora and the Making of a Vernacular Cosmopolitanism." Translated by Steven Rendall. *Public Culture* 12 (2000): 679–702.

88. Guèye, Cheikh. *Touba: La capitale des mourides*. Paris: Karthala Editions, 2002.

89. "A Discussion with Sheikh Saliou Mbacke, Continental Coordinator of IFAPA." Berkley Center for Religion, Peace, and World Affairs. July 3, 2014. https://berkleycenter.georgetown.edu/interviews/a-discussion-with-sheikh -saliou-mbacke-continental-coordinator-of-ifapa.

90. Senegal's law on gender parity requires half of the candidates on party lists to be women.

91. In the Islamic eschatology, the Mahdi is the redeemer who will come before the end of time to return Muslims to the path of righteousness. This prophesied redeemer arrived in the form of a fisherman named Limamou Thiaw, who became Limamou Laye. Following the revelation he received, Limamou Thiaw's family, friends, and community ostracized him before many of them came to accept his teachings.

92. "Issa Rohou LAHI fils de l'imam de tous les imams, imam des deux lieux saints." Layene. Accessed January 5, 2017. http://www.layene.sn/new/l _francais/rohoulaye.php.

93. "They marry young to protect their children from perdition, and children begin Muslim rites such as fasting as early as age five. Layene education focusses on purity, sincerity, non-violence, and non-discrimination. Last names are not used—rather everyone is called 'Laye'—as a way to place all members on an equal level" ("A Discussion with Cheikh Djibril Diop Laye, Imam and Member of the Layene Order of Senegal." Berkley Center for Religion, Peace, and World Affairs. November 17, 2014. https://berkleycenter.georgetown.edu/interviews /a-discussion-with-cheikh-djibril-diop-laye-imam-and-member-of-the-layene -order-of-senegal). See also Glover, John. "The Prophet Muhammad Reincarnated and His Son, Jesus: Re-centering Islam Among the Layene of Senegal." *Journal of Historical Geography* 42 (2013): 24–35; Laborde, Cécile. *La Confrérie layenne et les Lébou du Sénégal.* Bordeaux: Centre d'Étude d'Afrique Noire, Institut d'Études Politiques de Bordeaux, Université Montesquieu-Bordeaux IV, 1995.

94. "Presentation de l'Association Nurul Mahdi." Layene. Accessed January 5, 2017. http://www.layene.sn/new/nurul_mahdi.php.

95. Ibid.

96. Diallo, El Hadji Samba, and Catherine Lena Kelly. "Sufi Turuq and the Politics of Democratization in Senegal." *Journal of Religious and Political Practice* 2, no. 2 (2016): 9.

97. Smith, "Religious and Cultural Pluralism," 15.

98. This anthropological term refers to the practice between two persons or groups of exchanging jokes or partaking in a form of banter that follows a specific cultural code.

99. *Consociationalism* refers to power sharing in which different social, ethnic, or religious groups build their specific modes of influencing decisionmaking at the institutional level. See Lijphart, Arend. "Constitutional Design for Divided Societies." *Journal of Democracy* 15, no. 2 (2004): 96–109.

100. Babou, Cheikh Anta. "Brotherhood Solidarity, Education, and Migration: The Role of the *Dahiras* Among the Murid Muslim Community of New York." *African Affairs* 101, no. 403 (2002): 151–170; Villalón, Leonardo A. *Islamic Society and State Power in Senegal: Disciples and Citizens in Fatick.* Cambridge: Cambridge University Press, 2006.

101. Babou, "Brotherhood Solidarity, Education, and Migration."

102. Fondation Sonatel, http://www.sonatel.com/prise-en-charge-gratuite-des -personnes-agees. Accessed September 5, 2017.

103. Thiam, Rokhaya. "Étude sur les associations et réseaux de femmes religieuses au Sénégal." Internal Report, *World Faiths Development Dialogue.* 2014.

104. Gueye, Mame Safiétou Djamil. "Genre et gouvernance urbaine au Sénégal: La participation des femmes à la gestion urbaine." *Thèse de la Faculté des sciences économiques, sociales, politiques et de communication.* Louvain-la-Neuve, Belgium: Presses Universitaires de Louvain, 2009.

105. Villalón, "Generational Changes," 134.

106. Villalón, Leonardo A. "Sufi Rituals as Rallies: Religious Ceremonies in the Politics of Senegalese State-Society Relations." *Comparative Politics* 26, no. 4 (1994): 416.

107. Ibid., 416.

108. Ibid., 434.

109. Ibid., 418.

110. Ibid., 418.

111. Ibid., 419.

112. Ibid., 434.

113. Camara, Samba. "Political Islam and the Negotiation of Political Roles Among Peripheral Sufi Leaders in Senegal." *International Journal of Political Science and Development* 2, no. 6 (2014): 105.

114. Joseph, Richard. "Prebendalism and Dysfunctionality in Nigeria." Brookings Institution. July 26, 2013. https://www.brookings.edu/opinions/prebendalism -and-dysfunctionality-in-nigeria.

115. Camara, "Political Islam," 106.

116. Ibid., 114.

117. Daslani, Pitan. "Commentary: Rhoma's Idaman Party Promotes Islam as Religion of Peace." *Jakarta Globe.* December 2, 2016. http://jakartaglobe.id /opinion/commentary-rhomas-idaman-party-promotes-islam-religion-peace.

118. Otto, Ben, and Sara Schonhardt. "Islamic Political Parties Make a Comeback in Indonesian Election." *Wall Street Journal.* April 10, 2014. http://www .wsj.com/articles/SB10001424052702303873604579493311138076926.

119. Tanuwidjaja, Sunny. "Political Islam and Islamic Parties in Indonesia: Critically Assessing the Evidence of Islam's Political Decline." *Contemporary Southeast Asia* 32, no. 1 (2010): 29–49.

120. "Indonesia: Controversial Education Bill Is Passed." EA Foundation. June 2003. http://www.ea.org.au/ea-family/Religious-Liberty/Indonesia--Controversial -education-bill-is-passed-1.

121. Ibid., 41.

122. Ibid., 31.

123. Ibid., 44.

124. Ibid., 41.

125. Wanto, Adri. "The Paradox Between Political Islam and Islamic Political Parties." *Al-Jamiah* 50, no. 2 (2012): 330–368.

126. Croft-Cusworth, Catriona. "Why Islamic Parties Don't Win Indonesian Elections." Lowy Institute. March 31, 2014. https://www.lowyinstitute.org/the -interpreter/why-islamic-parties-dont-win-indonesian-elections.

127. Bruinessen, Martin Van. "Islamic State or State Islam? Fifty Years of State-Islam Relations in Indonesia." In *Indonesien am Ende des 20*, ed. Ingrid Jahrhunderts, 19–34. Hamburg: Abera-Verlag, 1996.

128. Ibid.

129. Hefner, Robert W. *Shari'a Politics: Islamic Law and Society in the Modern World.* Bloomington: Indiana University Press, 2011, p. 282.

130. This is a surprising turn of events, since HTI has been known to promote the abolition of Indonesia as a nation-state and the return to the caliphate. By contrast, MUI is known for advocating the implementation of sharia law without undermining the state.

131. Fahlesa Munarabi, "Islamic Activism: The Socio-political Dynamics of the Indonesian Forum of Islamic Society (FUI)." PhD diss., University of New South Wales, 2016, p. 102.

132. The MPU has legally been given a privileged part in the process of forming legislation to introduce sharia in Aceh. Officially it stands in equal partnership with the government of Aceh and can issue edicts on the government's activities. Qunun no. 9/2003 even implies the MPU is in fact superior to other state institutions. "To date, however," as pointed out by Cammack and Feener, "the MPU has been unable to exercise all of these powers" and in fact has faced some considerable obstacles in terms of internal fractiousness, competition for influencing policy, and resources and facilities." See Cammack, Mark, and Michael Feener. "The Islamic Legal System in Indonesia." *Pacific Rim Law & Policy Journal* 21, no. 1 (2012); Ichwan, M. N. "Official Ulema and the Politics of Re-Islamization: The

Majelis Permusyawaratan Ulama, Sharilhringatization and Contested Authority in Post–New Order Aceh." *Journal of Islamic Studies* 22, no. 2 (2011): 183–214.
133. Ibid.
134. Komite Persiapan Penegakan Syariat Islam (KPPSI), or the Islamic Shari'a Implementation Preparation Committee, was founded in October 2000 during the South Sulawesi Muslim Congress. Its first leader was Azis Kahar Muzakkar, the son of Kahar Muzakkar, a prominent figure of Darul Islam, an organization that, in the 1950s, aimed at building an Islamic state in South Sulawesi. KPPSI aims at implementing Shari'a law by demanding a special autonomy of South Sulawesi province from the central government. KPPSI received support from numerous Muslim public figures, such as Jusuf Kalla, who would later become the vice president of Indonesia. See Amal, T. A. *Politik syariat Islam: Dari Indonesia hingga Nigeria*. Ciputat, Jakarta: Pustaka Alvabet, 2004, p. 82.

Gerakan Muslim Minangkabau, or Minangkabau Muslim Movement, was established on August 17, 1999, by four West Sumatran ulema: Abusamah Siregar, H. Nurman Agus, H. Rusman Nipon RS, and H. Muhammad Ma'ad Makkah bin Achin RB. It aims to develop missionary activities in West Sumatra in order, through religious, social, and education programs, to prevent Muslim conversion to Christianity.

Hizbut Tahrir Indonesia (HTI) is the official branch of Hizbut Tahrir, an international pan-Islamic political organization aiming to reestablish the caliphate. It was first established in Palestine in 1958 and reached Indonesia in the early 1980s. In Indonesia, HTI refuses to be called a social organization and claims to be a political party based on Islam, although it has not registered as such yet. The group was disbanded by the Indonesian Government on July 18, 2017. See http://www.aljazeera.com/news/2017/07/indonesia-hizbut-tahrir-group -banned-protect-unity-170719050345186.html. Accessed September 5, 2017.

Majelis Mujahidin Indonesia (https://majelismujahidin.wordpress.com, accessed January 6, 2017) is the umbrella organization of Indonesian Islamist groups, founded by the former leader of Jemaah Islamiyah, Abu Bakar Bashir, in 2000. It declared the implementation of sharia as its ultimate goal.

Front Pembela Islam, or the Islamic Defenders Front, is a radical organization created in 1999 and known for its violence. Its most notorious actions include the raiding of nightclubs and prostitution areas and forced closings of restaurants during Ramadhan. It has also accused the Christian Chinese mayor of Jakarta of blasphemy. See also Wanto, "The Paradox Between Political Islam and Islamic Political Parties," 333.
135. Tanuwidjaja, "Political Islam," 44.
136. Hefner, Robert W. "Indonesia: Shari'a Politics and Democratic Transition." In *Shari'a Politics: Islamic Law and Society in the Modern World*, 280–318. Bloomington: Indiana University Press, 2011; Formichi, Chiara. "Preface." In *Islam and the Making of the Nation: Kartosuwiryo and Political Islam in Twentieth-Century Indonesia*. Leiden: KITLV, 2012.
137. Hefner, "Indonesia: Shari'a Politics and Democratic Transition," 290–292.
138. Ibid.
139. Cammack and Feener, "The Islamic Legal System in Indonesia."
140. Hefner, "Indonesia: Shari'a Politics and Democratic Transition."
141. A Muslim man is still legally allowed up to four wives. However, he must be able to support each equally and obtain the permission of his first wife, a condition not easy to meet in practice.
142. This issue was intensely debated in 2012 when famous singer Aisyah Mochtar claimed marriage to Moerdiyono, a public figure and former minister. The marriage was conducted according to Islam with the presence of witnesses

and a *wali* but without the presence of a government-appointed official, because Moerdiyono was already married and did not want to comply with the polygamy regulations introduced by the 1991 compilation. The problem entailed Moerdiyono's refusal to provide financial support for Iqbal, the son born of his marriage with Mochtar, and her lack of legal recourse since their marriage was not registered. It got worse when Moerdiyono died, leaving significant wealth that his first wife refused to share with Mochtar and her son. Mochtar filed a claim with the religious court that was unsuccessful since the marriage did not legally exist. Mochtar filed an appeal with the supreme court, claiming that Iqbal's rights as a child had been violated because of the absence of a document. The supreme court required Mochtar to prove her son's paternity by means of DNA testing. The test proved Mochtar's claim and Iqbal's biological relationship to Moerdiyono. Based on the test, the supreme court ruled in favor of Mochtar and ordered Moerdiyono's family to include Iqbal and Mochtar in the inheritance. Interestingly, the head justice of the supreme court mentioned at the time that DNA testing could be used to prove paternity for couples who are not legally married, which will influence the power of the religious court in the future. It is unclear how. See Butt, Simon. "Asia-Pacific: Illegitimate Children and Inheritance in Indonesia." *Alternative Law Journal* 37, no. 3 (2012): 196–198; "MK: Laki-Laki." Hukumonline.com. February 17, 2012. http://www.hukumonline.com/berita/baca/lt4f3e288a2589c/mk-lakilaki-buaya -darat-wajib-bertanggung-jawab.

143. "Indonesia: Inter-religious Marriage." Law Library of Congress. July 2015. https://www.loc.gov/law/help/inter-religious-marriage/indonesia-inter-religious -marriage.pdf.

144. Ibid.

145. The possibility of interreligious marriage, however, is very slim, especially since the administrative decisions of 1983 and 1984. The former is a presidential decision that instructed the Civil Registry to refuse to formalize marriages involving Muslims; the latter, from the Ministry of Religion, instructed marriage registry officials at the Office of Religious Affairs only to register marriages between Muslims. See "Indonesia 2014 International Religious Freedom Report."

146. Despite this regulation, Senegal has one of the highest rates of polygamy in Africa, which can be explained by specific social and cultural factors. In the Wolof-speaking parts of Senegal, because women play a large role in domestic work, reproduction, and food production, it has been argued that monogamous marriages would place an "unbearable burden" on single wives. Additionally, in some parts of Senegal, men consciously maintain competition among their spouses and use secrecy as well as the threat to take additional wives to assert dominance. Finally, in certain communities, men are likely to marry a cousin first to fulfill familial expectations and then to marry another woman afterward for love. See Kringelbach, H. N. "'Marrying Out' for Love: Women's Narratives of Polygyny and Alternative Marriage Choices in Contemporary Senegal." *African Studies Review* 59, no. 1 (2016): 155–174.

147. Parlina, Ina. "Constitutional Court Rejects Blasphemy Review Request." *Jakarta Post.* September 20, 2013. http://www.thejakartapost.com/news/2013 /09/20/constitutional-court-rejects-blasphemy-review-request.html.

148. "Indonesia 2014 International Religious Freedom Report," 3–4.

149. Gelling, Peter. "Indonesia Bans Sects It Deems Blasphemous." *New York Times.* November 16, 2007. http://www.nytimes.com/2007/11/16/world/asia /16indo.html.

150. *Aliran Ahmadiyyah* (2005)—"the fatwa placed the government in a hierarchically lower position than the MUI by insisting that it enforce the fatwa" and

halt the spread of the Ahmadiyyah movement. It "states that (1) although the MUI have issued a fatwa condemning the Ahmadiyyah in 1980 and that this movement has been forbidden, the Ahmadiyyah still exists and spreads its teachings in Indonesia; (2) the existence and the activities of the Ahmadiyyah have created unrest or disharmony in society; (3) some people in society have requested the MUI to reaffirm the previous fatwa on the status of the Ahmadiyyah because of the controversies and social actions related to this movement; (4) to answer the demand from society and to protect the purity of Islam, the MUI concludes that it is needed to reissue the previous fatwa." Sekretariat MUI 2010, p. 41

151. Hefner, *Shari'a Politics: Islamic Law*, 43.

152. M'Baye, Babacar. "The Origins of Senegalese Homophobia: Discourses on Homosexuals and Transgender People in Colonial and Postcolonial Senegal." *African Studies Review* 56, no. 2 (2013): 109–128.

153. Niang, Cheikh Ibrahima, et al. "'It's Raining Stones': Stigma, Violence and HIV Vulnerability Among Men Who Have Sex with Men in Dakar, Senegal." *Culture, Health & Sexuality* 5, no. 6 (2003): 499–512.

154. "Senegal: Growing Intolerance Towards Gay Men." *HIV AIDS Policy Law Review* 14, no. 1 (2009): 31.

155. Niang, "It's Raining Stones."

156. "Being LGBT in Indonesia: Country Report." UNDP in Asia and the Pacific. 2014. http://www.asia-pacific.undp.org/content/dam/rbap/docs/Research%20&%20Publications/hiv_aids/rbap-hhd-2014-blia-indonesia-country-report-english.pdf.

157. Ibid.

158. Laia, Kennial Caroline. "Rights Activists Lash Out at MUI's Anti-LGBT Fatwa." *Jakarta Globe*. March 15, 2015. http://jakartaglobe.beritasatu.com/news/rights-activists-lash-muis-anti-lgbt-fatwa.

159. Ibid.

160. The Support Group and Resource Center on Sexuality Studies at the University of Indonesia also offers counseling for LGBT students. See Yosephine, Liza. "Komnas HAM Slams Vilification of LGBT by Officials." *Jakarta Post*. February 5, 2016. http://www.thejakartapost.com/news/2016/02/05/komnas-ham-slams-vilification-lgbt-officials.html.

161. See "Indonesia: 2 Men in Aceh Face Caning for Homosexual Intercourse." Asian Correspondent. April 8, 2017. https://asiancorrespondent.com/2017/04/indonesia-men-aceh-caning-homosexual-intercourse/#ehCy87K5-72wTfv7y.99.

162. Hefner, "Shari'a Politics and Democratic Transition."

163. Law no. 32/2004, article 216.

164. *Perda syariah* passed since 2004:

Year	Number of *Perda Syariah*	Regions
2004	18	7 provinces
2005	25	10 provinces
2006	13	8 provinces
2007	3	3 provinces
2008	5	5 provinces
2009	1	1 province

165. Ichwan, "Official Ulema."

166. Hefner, "Shari'a Politics and Democratic Transition."

167. Cammack and Feener, "The Islamic Legal System in Indonesia."

168. Human Rights Watch. "Policing Morality: Abuses in the Application of Shari'a in Aceh, Indonesia." Human Rights Watch. 2010. https://www.hrw.org/sites/default/files/reports/indonesia1210WebVersionToPost.pdf, p. 21.

169. Ichwan, "Official Ulema."

170. United States Commission on International Religious Freedom (USCIRF). "USCIRF 2013 Annual Report: Indonesia." USCIRF. 2013. http://www.uscirf.gov/sites/default/files/resources/Indonesia%202013.pdf.

171. Simanjuntak, Hotli. "'Qanun Jinayat' Becomes Official for All People in Aceh." *Jakarta Post*. October 23, 2015. http://www.thejakartapost.com/news/2015/10/23/qanun-jinayat-becomes-official-all-people-aceh.html.

172. Ichwan, "Official Ulema."

173. Simanjuntak, "'Qanun Jinayat' Becomes Official for All People in Aceh."

174. Smith, "Religious and Cultural Pluralism," 154.

175. Ibid., 152.

176. Serer is the third-largest ethnic group in Senegal.

177. Bellah, Robert. "Islamic Tradition and the Problem of Modernization." *Beyond Belief: Essays on Religion in a Post-traditional World*, 146–167. New York: Harper & Row, 1991.

178. "Prinsip Dasar." Partai Amanat Nasional. Accessed December 23, 2016. http://www.pan.or.id/prinsip-dasar; "Tentang Pan." Partai Amanat Nasional. Accessed December 23, 2016. http://www.pan.or.id/tentang-pan.

179. "Partai Kebangkitan Bangsa (PKB)." Pemilu Indonesia. Accessed December 23, 2016. http://www.pemilu.com/pkb.

180. Woischnik, Jan, and Philipp Muller. "Islamic Parties and Democracy in Indonesia." Konrad Adenauer Stiftung. 2013. http://www.kas.de/wf/doc/kas_35685-544-2-30.pdf?131015120646, p. 64.

181. "Visi dan Misi PPP." Partai Persatuan Pembangunan. September 20, 2016. http://ppp.or.id/page/visi-dan-misi-ppp.html.

182. Woischnik and Muller, "Islamic Parties," 65.

183. Ibid., 63.

184. Cochrane, Joe. "'Beef-Gate' Transfixes Scandal-Prone Indonesia." *New York Times*. May 16, 2013. http://www.nytimes.com/2013/05/17/world/asia/beefgate-transfixes-scandal-prone-indonesia.html.

185. Woischnik and Muller, "Islamic Parties," 67.

186. Otto and Schonhardt, "Islamic Political Parties Make a Comeback in Indonesian Election."

187. "Peraturan Propinsi Sumatera barat nomor: 11 tahun 2001." Mahkamah Konstitusi RI. Accessed January 10, 2017. https://portal.mahkamahkonstitusi.go.id/eLaw/mg58ufsc89hrsg/128b5a9a195240689ef9fae8e17224006917a0087.pdf.

188. "Peraturan daerah kabupaten solok nomor 10 tahun 2001." Peraturan.go.id. Accessed January 10, 2017. http://peraturan.go.id/perda/kabupaten-solok-nomor-10-tahun-2001-11e452bd02244d10883d313634303436.html.

189. "Perda busana Muslim di 'Tanah Datar Sumbar' Juga Disikat Jokowi." Media Pribumi. June 16, 2016. http://www.mediapribumi.com/2016/06/perda-busana-muslim-di-tanah-datar.html.

190. "Perda syariat dicabut, MUI dompu: Itu kesalahan fatal!" Jurnalislam. June 18, 2016. https://jurnalislam.com/perda-syariat-dicabut-mui-dompu-kesalahan-fatal.

191. "Pemerintah kota Padang." Kota Padang. Accessed January 10, 2017. http://jdih.padang.go.id/po-content/uploads/23No%206%20Tahun%202003.pdf.

192. "Peraturan daerah kota Solok nomor: 13 tahun 2003 tentang pengelolaan zakat." Jaringan Dokumentasi dan Informasi Hukum Kota Solok. Accessed January 10, 2017. http://jdih.solokkota.go.id/perda/peraturan-daerah-kota-solok -nomor-13-tahun-2003-tentang-pengelolaan-zakat.

193. "Peraturan daerah kabupaten Sawahlunto/Sijunjung nomor: 1 Tahun 2003." Accessed January 10, 2017. http://ditjenpp.kemenkumham.go.id/files/ld /2003/sawahlunto2-2003.pdf.

194. "Peraturan daerah kabupaten Sawahlunto/Sijunjung nomor: 2 tahun 2003." Kementerian Hukum dan Hak Asasi Manusia Republik Indonesia. Accessed January 10, 2017. http://ditjenpp.kemenkumham.go.id/files/ld/2003 /sawahlunto2-2003.pdf.

195. "Lembaran daerah kabupaten Pasaman." Melborne Law School. 2003. http:/law.unimelb.edu.au/__data/assets/pdf_file/0008/1546379/LembaranDaer ahKabupatenPasamanNomor48Tahun2003SeriDLembaranDaerahKabupaten-Pasaman2.pdf.

196. Ibid.

197. "Peraturan daerah kabupaten Lima Puluh kota." Kementerian Hukum dan Hak Asasi Manusia Republik Indonesia. Accessed January 10, 2017. http://ditjenpp .kemenkumham.go.id/files/ld/2003/limapuluhkota6-2003.pdf.

198. "Peraturan daerah kabupaten padang pariaman nomor 2 tahun 2004." Peraturan.go.id. Accessed January 10, 2017. http://peraturan.go.id/perda/kabupaten-padang -pariaman-nomor-2-tahun-2004-11e452bd19f37540bc9b313634313236.html.

199. "Peraturan daerah kota Bukit Tinggi nomor 29 tahun 2004 tahun 2004." Peraturan.go.id. Accessed January 10, 2017. http://peraturan.go.id/perda/kota -bukit-tinggi-nomor-29-tahun-2004-tahun-2004.html.

200. "Peraturan daerah kabupaten Pesisir Selatan nomor 8 tahun 2004." Peraturan.go.id. Accessed January 10, 2017. http://peraturan.go.id/perda/kabupaten -pesisir-selatan-nomor-8-tahun-2004-11e452bd2205bba08081313634313430.html.

201. Nugraha, M. "Revitalisasi peran sekolah dalam penguatan pendidikan dan akhlak mulia bagi anak." Academia.edu. Accessed January 10, 2017. http:// www.academia.edu/19655885/Revitalisasi_Peran_Sekolah_dalam_Penguatan _Pendidikan_dan_Akhlak_Mulia_bagi_Anak.

202. "Peraturan daerah kabupaten Lampung Selatan nomor 4 tahun 2004." Peraturan.go.id. Accessed January 10, 2017. http://peraturan.go.id/perda/kabupaten -lampung-selatan-nomor-nomor-4-tahun-2004-tahun-2004.html.

203. "Peraturan daerah Provinsi Banten nomor 4 tahun 2004." Peraturan.go.id. Accessed January 10, 2017. http://peraturan.go.id/perda/provinsi-banten-nomor -4-tahun-2004-11e452bd1e6ea3d0a3ea313634313334.html.

204. "Peraturan daerah." Jdih.cirebonkab.go.id. Accessed January 10, 2017. http://jdih.cirebonkab.go.id/prodkum.php?cat_id=7&orderby=download_title &sort=DESC.

205. "Perda 2000–2004." Kabupaten Banjar. April 1, 2014. http://hukum .banjarkab.go.id/index.php/perda/perda-2000–2004.

206. Ibid.

207. "Perda syariat dicabut, MUI Dompu: Itu kesalahan fatal!"

208. "Peraturan daerah kabupaten Pesisir Selatan." Jdih.setjen.kemendagri .go.id. Accessed January 10, 2017. http://www.jdih.setjen.kemendagri.go.id/files /KAB_PESISIR%20SELATAN_4_2005.pdf.

209. "Direktori Download." Pemerintah Kabupaten Agam. Accessed January 10, 2017. http://agamkab.go.id/?agam=download&se=kategori&id=4&page=35.

210. Ibid.

211. "Perda kota Tangerang nomor 7 dan 8 tahun 2005." LANSKAP. Accessed January 10, 2017. http://lanskap-regulasi.blogspot.com/2008/02/perda-kota-tangerang-nomor-7-dan-8.html.

212. "Peraturan daerah kota Tangerang nomor 8 tahun 2005 tahun 2005." Peraturan.go.id. Accessed January 10, 2017. http://peraturan.go.id/perda/kota-tangerang-nomor-8-tahun-2005-tahun-2005.html.

213. "Peraturan daerah kabupaten Bandung nomor 9 tahun 2005." Peraturan.go.id. Accessed January 10, 2017. http://peraturan.go.id/perda/kabupaten-bandung-nomor-9-tahun-2005-11e452bd2febb16084c4313634323033.html.

214. "Peraturan daerah kabupaten Probolinggo." Mahkamah Konstitusi RI. Accessed January 10, 2017. https://portal.mahkamahkonstitusi.go.id/eLaw/mg58ufsc89hrsg/Perda_Probolinggo_5_Tahun_2005.pdf.

215. "Peraturan daerah kota Malang." JDIH. Accessed January 10, 2017. http://jdih.jatimprov.go.id/?wpfb_dl=13811.

216. "Peraturan daerah kabupaten Hulu Sungai Utara." Lembaran Daerah Kabupaten Hulu Sungai Utara Prov. Kalimantan Selatan. Accessed January 10, 2017. https://kumhsu.files.wordpress.com/2011/08/peraturan-daerah-thn-2005-no-19-ttg-pengelolaan-zis-doc1.pdf.

217. See http://www.jdih.setjen.kemendagri.go.id. Accessed January 10, 2017.

218. "Gerakan bebas buta aksara dan pandai baca alquran dalam wilayah kabupaten Maros." SIMPERDA. Accessed January 10, 2017. http://simperda.maroskab.go.id/web/detail/909023949.

219. See http://www.jdih.setjen.kemendagri.go.id. Accessed January 10, 2017.

220. Ibid.

221. "Peraturan daerah kabupaten Sawahlunto/Sijunjung." Sijunjung.go.id. http://sijunjung.go.id/Download/perda2006/19thn2006.pdf.

222. "Peraturan daerah propinsi Sumatera Barat." Badan Pembinaan Hukum Nasional. Accessed January 10, 2017. http://www.bphn.go.id/data/documents/perda_pempov_sumbar_no._3_tahun_2007.pdf.

223. "Pelaksanaan perda nomor 2 tahun 2006 tentang pengelolaan zakat, infak dan shadaqah di Bazda kabupaten Kampar (studi pasal 20)." UIN Suska Riau Repository. Accessed January 10, 2017. http://repository.uin-suska.ac.id/1885/1/2011_2011150.pdf.

224. "Salinan peraturan daerah kabupaten bangka." Mahkamah Konstitusi RI. Accessed January 10, 2017. https://portal.mahkamahkonstitusi.go.id/eLaw/mg58ufsc89hrsg/1441f9528bdff91980a5924bc9e71dd78f4a8da26.pdf.

225. "Peraturan daerah (PERDA)." JDIH Kabupaten Serang. Accessed January 10, 2017. http://jdih.serangkab.go.id/kategoridownload-1-0-peraturandaerah.html.

226. "Kab Cianjur 3 2006." Jdih.setjen.kemendagri.go.id. Accessed January 10, 2017. http://www.jdih.setjen.kemendagri.go.id/download.php?KPUU=13036.

227. "Kota Banjar Baru 5." Jdih.setjen.kemendagri.go.id. Accessed January 10, 2017. http://www.jdih.setjen.kemendagri.go.id/download.php?KPUU=14575.

228. "Kota Makassar 5 2006." Jdih.setjen.kemendagri.go.id. Accessed January 10, 2017. http://www.jdih.setjen.kemendagri.go.id/download.php?KPUU=4665.

229. "Peraturan daerah kabupaten Pangkajene dan kepulauan nomor 11 tahun 2006." Peraturan.go.id. Accessed January 10, 2017. http://peraturan.go.id/perda/kabupaten-pangkajene-dan-kepulauan-nomor-11-tahun-2006-11e452bd.a4a04.2092ab313634323230.html.

230. Basmal, Andi. "Fungsi pengawasan dewan perwakilan rakyat daerah terhadap pelaksanaan peraturan daerah di kabupaten Polewali Mandar." PhD diss., Universitas Hasanudin, 2011.

231. Ibid.

232. "Peraturan daerah Provinsi Sulawesi Selatan nomor 4 tahun 2006." Peraturan.go.id. Accessed January 10, 2017. http://peraturan.go.id/perda/provinsi-sulawesi -selatan-nomor-4-tahun-2006-11e452bd3671a1d09553313634323134.html.

233. Asmawaty, Andi Cipta, and Aflina Mustafaina. *Dekonstruksi agensi perempuan dalam konteks Muslim: Membuka topeng implementasi syariat Islam di level lokal.* Report, Solidaritas Perempuan, 12.

234. "Kab Bantul 5 2007." Jdih.setjen.kemendagri.go.id. Accessed January 10, 2017. http://www.jdih.setjen.kemendagri.go.id/download.php?KPUU=9593.

235. "Peraturan daerah." Accessed January 10, 2017. http://kablamongan.jdih .jatimprov.go.id/?page_id=929.

236. "Kab Banjar 10 2007." Jdih.setjen.kemendagri.go.id. Accessed January 10, 2017. http://www.jdih.setjen.kemendagri.go.id/download.php?KPUU=7612.

237. "Peraturan daerah kota Padang Panjang nomor 7 tahun 2008." Mahkamah Konstitusi RI. Accessed January 10, 2017. https://portal.mahkamah konstitusi.go.id/eLaw/mg58ufsc89hrsg/18a64b98a5cd062a03ee8b9fac2597ef5 e14fac2.pdf.

238. Candraningrum, Dwei. *The Challenge of Teaching English in Indonesian's Muhammadiyah Universities (1958–2005): Mainstreaming Gender Through Postcolonial Muslim Women Writers.* Berlin: Lit, 2008, p. 123.

239. "Peraturan daerah kota Gorontalo nomor 6 tahun 2012." JDIH Gorontal Province. Accessed January 10, 2017. http://jdih.gorontaloprov.go.id/peraturan /nomor%206%20tahun%202012.pdf.

240. "Peraturan daerah kota Banjarmasin." BPK RI. Accessed January 10, 2017. http://banjarmasin.bpk.go.id/wp-content/uploads/2014/10/Perda-1-2014.pdf.

5

The Globalization
of Political Islam

It may seem that the main argument of this book—that politicization and nationalization go hand in hand—is contradictory to the rise of al-Qaeda and the Islamic State (ISIS). After all, Abu Bakr al-Baghdadi's efforts to overcome the nation-state system and rebuild the caliphate can be seen as an attempt to return to the historical abode of Islam. Nonetheless, the global political projects of al-Qaeda and ISIS should be understood as a globalization of the national forms of Islam rather than a return to the premodern form of polity before nationalism. As argued in previous chapters, political Islam resulted from the globalization of nationalism and the adoption of the nation-state framework in Muslim territories. In these circumstances, global jihadism operates on the nationalized versions of sharia, jihad, and the *ummah*. In other words it is the most recent and radicalized version of political Islam.

Along with scholars such as Liah Greenfeld, I argue that political globalization is the dissemination of concepts, initially framed within nations but now spreading beyond national boundaries.[1] Even if opposed to nationalism, pan-Islamists were also influenced by it—especially after decolonization, when the nation became the "natural" political space instead of being perceived as "foreign" or Western. Thus, Islamist movements gradually used

Islam more as an alternative to the secular nationalism promoted by state elites and less as a way to promote return to the caliphate.

In this sense, Islamist movements have increasingly operated within the context of the newly defined national political community. When Muhammad Abduh's disciple, Hassan al-Banna (1906–1949), founded the Muslim Brotherhood in 1928, he did not oppose the ideas of nationalism and the nation-state. His political platform called for violent resistance against Western powers and the restoration of Muslim sovereignty, which did not necessarily clash with Egyptian nationalist goals. He declared that the Muslim Brotherhood would, first, free the "Islamic homeland" from foreign authority and, second, establish an Islamic state within the freed homeland, acting according to Islam's precepts, applying its social regulations, advocating its "sound principles," and broadcasting its mission to all mankind.[2] Egypt was the "logical and historically right place for Islam to base itself. . . . Egypt had a unique role to play in Islam's resurgence."[3] In al-Banna's own terms, "The Muslim Brothers, true to the faith, plead that the nation be restored to Islam. Egypt's role is unique, for just as Egyptian reform begins with Islam, so the regeneration of Islam must begin in Egypt, for the rebirth of 'international Islam,' in both its ideal and historical sense, requires first a strong 'Muslim State' [*dawla muslima*]."[4]

So, although al-Banna sought to build an Islamic political system, his vision was not entirely pan-Islamic. This may explain why the Muslim Brotherhood would operate more and more within the national Egyptian framework in the decades to come.

Acceptance of the nation framework, however, did not systematically translate into alliance and cooperation between nationalists and Islamists. After the death of al-Banna in 1949, then the Free Officers' coup to remove the monarchy from power in 1952, the relationship between the Muslim Brotherhood and the state changed from one of cooperation to mistrust. At first, the Brotherhood was allowed to continue as an organization under Gamal Abdel Nasser, despite the abolition of existing political parties in 1953. However, the Brotherhood's refusal to grant legitimacy to a regime that did not implement sharia soon led to organized demonstrations against it. In October 1954, a young member of the Muslim Brotherhood allegedly attempted to assassinate President Nasser. As a result, the Brotherhood was outlawed. Members were arrested and jailed; some even received death sentences.

Such political changes modified the Muslim Brotherhood's strategy to directly oppose the state but did not debase the group's initial national grounding. These changes also accounted for the divides in the movement regarding how to interact with the state. On one hand, the vast majority of the Ikhwan (Brothers, short for Muslim Brothers) decided to work within the state system, while a minority, such as Sayyid Qutb (1906–1966), chose to destroy it and eventually left the Brotherhood. Hassan al-Hudaybi (1891–1973), successor to al-Banna and emir of the Muslim Brotherhood until 1973, explicitly criticized Qutb's *takfiri* ideology in *Preachers, Not Judges* (*Du'a la quda*).[5] Al-Hudaybi questioned Qutb's idea of jihad and instead preached faith, patience, and perseverance. He argued that the duty of all Muslims is "to enact all of God's orders and statutes and to pave the way for the establishment of His religion."[6] More specifically, under Hudaybi, the Muslim Brothers began to discuss their (1) involvement in Egyptian political life, (2) compromise with the Egyptian state, and (3) acceptance of democratic rules, including for women and minorities.

On the other hand, Sayyid Qutb's redefinition of jihad as the fight against the unjust ruler was instrumental to the systematic use of violence for political purposes. It also gave jihad a national dimension that, from Hezbollah to Hamas, remains very relevant.

Global jihad—also known as Salafi jihadism—is a unique combination of the jihadi war of Qutb or Muhammad abd-al-Salam Faraj (1954–1982) and Saudi Wahhabi religious doctrine.[7] The national form of jihad defined in the Egyptian context became global notably with the internationalization of the Afghan jihad against the Soviet Union.[8] The fundamentalist, literalist, and exclusivist vision of the *ummah* comes from Wahhabism.[9] It is fundamentalist in that it reaches back to the fundamentals (Quran and Hadith), submitting them to a literal reading by which the believer strives to imitate the Prophet Muhammad at Medina. It is exclusivist in its condemnation of all other interpretations or doctrines and excommunication of Muslims who follow them. The combination of these three features set Wahhabism in stark contrast with most Sunni modes of interpretation that do not operate on a direct and decontextualized reading of the revealed sources. Rejection of other theological interpretations is also at odds with the built-in pluralism of the Islamic tradition (*ikhtilaf*).[10]

For example, expanded use of the term *kafir* (infidel, heretic) is also a defining feature of the Wahhabi doctrine. Nonetheless, in classical Islamic tradition, this term was used for polytheists and theoretically not for members of competing monotheistic faiths. In globalized fundamentalist groups the term has been extended to include Jews, Christians, and even nonpracticing Muslims.[11] Global jihad movements also separate the various aspects of life—family, work, leisure—and classify them according to the opposition between *haram* (forbidden) and *halal* (permitted). Everything that did not already exist or happen during the time of the Prophet is an innovation and thus *haram*. This is further contrasted with the traditional classification of religious acts, which consisted of several nuances between *haram* and *halal*.

In sum, with the rise of al-Qaeda, national jihad has become globalized and justified by a fundamentalist and exclusivist religious project. The semantic evolution of the terms *ummah* and *jihad* illustrates this dual transformation of religious nationalism.

The *Ummah* as a Global Imagined Community

Western observers generally regard the *ummah* as a religious community for Islam analogous to that of Jews, Christians, or Hindus. However, the definitions of *ummah* within the Islamic tradition are more complex and more historically fluid than the confessional diversity and steady depoliticization of faith observed in post-Westphalian Europe.[12] The Quran contains no definitive or unitary concept of the *ummah*. Frederick M. Denny highlights at least eight meanings or motifs used to describe community in the Quran. In the most prevalent definition, the *ummah* is a human collective that uniquely receives guidance from Allah in the form of revelations (*ummah wahida*), given even to Jews and Christians (Ahl al-Kitab).[13]

The Quran also mentions *ummah muslimah* (Muslim community) and *ummah wasat* (community of the middle path), both concepts that refer to the Muslim community built by the Prophet Muhammad at Medina. Initially the *ummah* was a type of political confederation, codified in the Constitution of Medina, that included Jews and Christians.[14] The concept of the *ummah* continued to develop through the time of the Prophet's surviving Companions, and especially in the three decades of the first four caliphates (AD 632–661). Numerous popular books and pamphlets of the first caliphs and the other Companions across Muslim cultures illustrate the paradigmatic quality of the Prophet Muhammad as the model human being for every generation of Muslims.

While the congruence of the political power and the *ummah* diminished after the death of the Prophet Muhammad, it nonetheless remains an ideal. An important part of being Muslim is a developed and powerful consciousness of the pristine community of Medina in the time of the Prophet Muhammad and his immediate successors as God's prototype for human society. The model *ummah* existed in the golden age of Muhammad and, for Sunnis, at least the Medinan caliphate after him.[15] The idealized early *ummah* was maintained as the political model and continued its "unchallenged role in later Muslim thinking about politics."[16]

The dissonance between political power and the *ummah* emerged when caliphal rule became associated with a leader's ability to maintain and extend the Prophet's message through conquest and empire.[17] The word *khalīfa*, or caliph, derives from the Arabic verb *khalafa* (to follow or succeed). Abu Bakr (AD 573–634), the first caliph, expressed the interrelationship between religion and politics, saying, "I am not a successor to God, I am a successor to God's Messenger." Although political disputes arose following the death of the Prophet, Muslims later sought to overcome these differences by depicting the period of the first four caliphs as one of consensus and compromise.[18]

In principle, the caliphate was the representative institution of the community of God. In reality, geography rendered it comparable to other secular dynasties ruling multiple ethnic and religious groups.[19] This tension, manifested in the geographic and institutional split in the system of governance, is apparent in the distinction between sharia and *syar*. Sharia refers to the laws that apply to Muslims; *syar* refers to the laws that apply to non-Muslims living under caliphate rule or to the relations between the caliphate and non-Muslims at the international level. The concept of *syar* was developed in the early centuries of Islam by Muhammad al-Shaybani[20] (AD 748–805) and later codified by Muhammad b. Ahmad b. Abi Sahl Abu Bakr al-Sarakhsī (d. 1101). According to Michelle Burgis, "The *syar* is the conduct of the believers in their relations with the unbelievers of enemy territory as well as with the people with whom the believers had made treaties, who may have been temporarily (*musta'mins*) or permanently (*dhimmīs*) in Islamic lands; with apostates, who were the worst of the unbelievers . . . and with rebels."[21]

The Ummah *as a Nation for Muslims*

The key turning point in the politicization of the term *ummah* came in the nineteenth century with the advent of reform movements against the backdrop of the rise of European imperial expansion and the decline of the Ottoman Empire. During this period, both activists and ideologues revisited the Islamic tradition as part of their efforts to confront the challenges of modernization spurred by Europe.

Antonio Gramsci's differentiation between organic ideology and willed ideology captures the distinction between activists and ideologues.[22] *Organic ideology* refers to mass expectations and imagination and best describes efforts to mobilize the *ummah* at the grassroots level. *Willed ideology* refers to the intellectual work and rhetoric conducted by elites through publications, newspapers, and diplomatic and intellectual exchanges.[23] The confluence of the organic and willed ideological forces in the nineteenth century resulted in a radical redefinition, and ultimately politicization, of terms that had hitherto the purview of religious authorities.

The revivalist movements that emerged in the nineteenth century in Asia and Africa attempted to regenerate the moral foundations of Muslim local communities by revisiting the Islamic tradition. They called for the adoption of a pristine faith and made periodic attempts to mobilize the masses to return to the "purity" of Islam, in ways comparable to past rebellions and protests to return the caliphate to its original message.[24] Members of these movements were neo-Sufis, egalitarian and mobilized at the grassroots level. For example, the Sokoto Caliphate led by Usman Dan Fodio (1754–1871) was an amalgam of local governments whose unity came not from their territorial contiguity but rather from their dedication to revive the *ummah* as a political community defined by the rule of Islam.[25]

Some of these revivalist movements served the pan-Islamist project of the Ottomans, who were struggling against western powers to maintain caliphal rule over multiple groups and territories. In the shadow of the French and British seizure of parts of the empire, the activism of these local groups transformed *nas* (people) and *ummah* (community) from perfunctory ideas into political entities. Their success with grassroots mobilization shifted the power of the regulatory institutions of the Muslim community from the ulemas to the community as a whole.

The intellectual work of nineteenth-century reformers who comprehended European modernization, nation-building, and secularization through the lens of Islamic terminology amplified the efforts of these movements. For example, Jamal al-Din al-Afghani (1838/39–1897) and Muhammad Abduh (1849–1905) referred to the *ummah* as a "modern nation."

Borrowing François Guizot's (1787–1874) conception of civilization as comprising intellectual and moral achievements that contribute to the unity and greatness of a people, Abduh viewed Islamic civilization, the foundation of pan-Islamism, as a common cultural stream that fed the national political aspirations of such distinct countries as India, Persia, and Egypt. Abduh saw Islam in civilizational rather than religious terms. He argued that ideals such as social egalitarianism, popular sovereignty, and the pursuit and preservation of knowledge had their origins not in Christian Europe but in the *ummah*. He held that the Prophet Muhammad's revolutionary community had introduced the concept of popular sanction over the ruling government, while dissolving all ethnic boundaries between individuals and giving women and children unprecedented rights and privileges. To achieve lasting social, political, and economic reform, the *ummah* had to internalize the enduring Muslim values that underlay the first Muslim community.[26]

Muhammad Abduh's most notable disciple, Mohammad Rashid Rida (1865–1935), advocated for the restoration of the caliphate and the reaffirmation of the unity of spiritual and temporal aspects of Islam against the Turkish- and Arabic-derived aspects of secularism. In his treatise on the caliphate, Rida lays down the specific conditions necessary for this revival of caliphal rule and examines the routes that do not involve a return to the Ottoman Empire.[27] His restoration would create an elected caliphate through the political mobilization of the *ummah* around a Muslim ruler chosen for his capacity to maintain and protect Islamic principles. Yet, paradoxically, Rida also praised Muslim territorial conquests, noting, "The greatest glory in the Muslim conquests goes to the Arabs, and that religion grew and became great through them; their foundation is the strongest, their light the brightest, and they are indeed the best umma brought forth to the world. . . . [A] little knowledge of past and present history shows that most of the countries where Islam was established were conquered by the Arabs."[28]

In sum, through the combined work of activists and ideologues, the *ummah* came to represent an ideal political community. The dominant scholarly literature often describes pan-Islamism, nationalism, and pan-Arabism as in competition throughout the nineteenth and twentieth centuries; interestingly, however, despite the differences in their political objectives, actors from each of these movements used the term *ummah* to describe their respective groups, instilling each definition with political motivation. When pan-Arabists such as the Ba'ath party leaders challenged pan-Islamists, they referred to the *ummah* as *ummah arabiya wahida maa risalit khalida* (one Arab nation with an eternal mission). Even with this more secular identification, a connection to Islam was maintained in the very use of the term, alongside terms with religious connotations, such as *risala* (message) and *mujahidin* (combatants).[29] Thus, the politicization of the *ummah* expanded beyond the community of Muslim believers and described a political community in which religious belief is subordinated to the political goals of independence, sovereignty, and civilizational influence.

Meanwhile, the meaning of a revelation-based community guided by the message of the Prophet Muhammad remained. This web of meanings gives the term *ummah* its equivocality: one can refer to the national community of Muslims as a whole, to Arabs, or solely to nationals such as Egyptians. The term can also refer to the return to caliphal rule or to a transnational community without a central Islamic state. The postcolonial states further instrumentalized the ambiguity of the Muslim or Arab *ummah* in their different attempts to unify across national boundaries, as exemplified by the short-lived fusions of Syria with Egypt (1958–1961) and Libya with Egypt (1972–1977). The *ummah* was presented as the ultimate goal of these unifications, reinforcing its meaning as a political entity.

Similarly, the "mythification" of intellectual figures such as Jamal al-Din al-Afghani in modern Egypt illustrates the shift in meaning of the *ummah* from revelation-based community to Muslim nation. Afghani favored the political framework of the Ottoman Empire and offered no direct praise for modern Egypt. Contemporary historians of Egypt, however, often present his project as a combination of Egypt, the Arab world, and all Muslims in one imagined community that traces Egypt's national identity to a nineteenth-century narrative of renewal and resistance. In this perspective, Afghani epitomizes the self-view of the nineteenth century Egyptian reform movement. He led the country to national emancipation while guiding the Arab world in its rise against the Ottoman Empire and its struggle against the West.

It therefore came as no surprise that Lewis Awad's 1975 studies on Afghani, depicting him as an outsider who failed to combine religious and political ideas, engendered deep controversy.[30] Awad argued that Afghani did not play a significant role in leading the Egyptians to revolt against the Ottoman suzerain. In his view, Afghani played an active role in resisting Western influence and, "faced with a dilemma between Ottoman despotism and Western colonialism," ultimately fought Western colonialism "within the framework of Ottoman unity."[31] With this deviant portrayal of Afghani, Awad intended to demonstrate the incompatibility between religion and politics.[32] Rudi Matthee interprets his revisionist conclusions as "an attempt to demythologize Afghani for the Egyptian home audience and thereby to counter newly politicized Islam's claim to legitimacy and appropriation of history."[33]

One of the most noted reactions to Awad's interpretation came from Muhammad Imara, whose defense of Afghani's goals and principles reflected a conception of Islam centered in Arab lands, with Cairo as its capital and no reference to non-Arab Muslims.[34] In contrast to Awad, Imara reaffirmed "Afghani's commitment to Egypt's liberation and his role in the reawakening of the Egyptian consciousness."[35] He argued that Afghani supported the Ottoman Empire, which was not the enemy, as it defended the *ummah* from the West and thus acted as a buffer against the real enemy, which was Western imperialism. Most importantly, Imara makes an ideological connection between Afghani and the concept of Arab preeminence in the *ummah* and further claims, "Afghani even emphasized the distinguished role of Egypt in the revival of Arab preeminence."[36]

In the same vein, the politicized concept of the *ummah* has pervaded contemporary political discourse in the most secular regimes. For example, in the case of Iraq, Adeed Dawisha argues that Saddam Hussein shifted the focus of Iraq's identity in three main phases to legitimize his regime: to the Arabist identity during the Iran-Iraq War, to the Islamist identity during the Gulf War, and to the tribalist identity after the Gulf War. However, even during the Arabist and tribalist identity phases, the influence of Islam remained in Hussein's political discourse, as seen in his reference to Islamic terms such as *ummah* and *jihad*. Interestingly, the first records of Hussein's use of these words date to the onset of the Iran-Iraq War. Despite his emphasis on the Arabist identity during this war, he "occasionally found it prudent to reiterate his own commitment, as well as Iraq's adherence, to Islam and its principles."[37] Three years into the conflict in 1983, he declared, "Many people welcomed the Iranian revolution at its inception. Many pinned hopes on it. Many expected good from it. Some people said that the revolution will be a support for the *ummah*, while others hoped that it would not be a burden on the *ummah*."[38]

In this quote, Hussein confirmed and upheld his own, as well as Iraq's, firm participation in the *ummah*, as he criticized Ayatollah Ruholla Khomeini's actions for disappointing all Muslims. Additionally, more than a year after the Gulf War, he invoked the *ummah* again in the following statement: "This rancor [of the West] seeks to destroy us and our achievements, as well as every genuine orientation and action based on active interaction with our nation's faithful, balanced heritage, about which God has said: Thus we have made of you an *ummah* justly balanced, that you might be witness over the nations, and the messenger a witness over you."[39]

After the US aerial bombardment on January 17, 1991, Hussein stated, "When the forces of infidelity attack the Iraqis, they [Iraqis] will fight as they wished them to fight and perhaps in a better way, and . . . their promise is of faith and jihad. . . . It remains for us to tell all Arabs, all the faithful strugglers, and all good supporters wherever they are: You have a duty to carry out *jihad* and struggle in order to target the assembly of evil, treason, and corruption everywhere."[40] In this statement, Hussein called on the faithful to engage in jihad in order to protect the *ummah* against the vices of the West. From this speech onward, he ended his discourses with "God is great, God is great, and accursed be the lowly." After the Allies' ground attack, he again invoked the importance of jihad: "They will realize after a while that God's unshakable desire will prevent them from inflicting evil on the people of faith and jihad. . . . As men collide with each other, the weapons of supremacy will disappear and the only thing that remains to decide the final result will be the faith of the faithful and the courage of those who adhere to their noble, nationalistic, and faithful stand of jihad."[41]

In every speech marking the anniversary of the Gulf War, Hussein extolled the merits of the faithful who carried out jihad. He even made symbolic references to God and jihad in speeches marking the July Ba'athist Revolution:

O great people; O sons of our glorious Arab nation: The Mother of Battles, the anniversary of the military aggression of which we are currently marking, is the jihad of faithful people to earn the pride of their people and their nation. It is the embodiment of their patience during jihad and the sufferings it entails to safeguard the faith.[42]

July, with the help of Almighty God and the Iraqi people's determination, has become a beacon for the nation and for the criteria of right and sacrifice in this age. It has also become a beacon for other peoples and nations and the criteria of their struggle and jihad.[43]

Iraqi political rhetoric offers a typical illustration of the instrumentalization of the *ummah* in contemporary political discourses. Three tropes emerge from Hussein's rhetoric that are recurrent across nationalist discourses and central to al-Qaeda's vision as well:

- The Arab or Muslim community is based on shared virtue.
- The duty of the Muslim is to defend the *ummah.*
- The concept of community embodied in the *ummah* is associated with a modern pan-Arab and/or pan-Islamic concept.[44]

These layered meanings of the *ummah* as a political project pervade even the spiritual dimensions of the Islamic discourse today. As early as 1881, the shaikh of al-Azhar, Husain al-Marsafi, in his *Risalat al-kalam al-thaman* (Tract on eight words) defined the *ummah* as a community united not only by faith but also by language and territory. Today, after several decades of socialization under the nation-states, self-identification as a believer often means that Muslims commit to the political project of the *ummah* as defined in the terms of national or transnational Islamic groups. The position of Yusuf al-Qaradawi illustrates how existing clerics use *ummah* to emphasize the unity of Muslims as a global nation that has to be protected from internal dissent and external political attacks. Similarly, Iraqi grand ayatollah al-Baghdadi discourages the participation of Muslims in international political organizations "since these organizations are established on principles that are incompatible with our religion and with Shari'a and since they aim at fragmenting the ummah."[45]

The Ummah *as the Combatant Community*

Under these circumstances, the politicization of the *ummah* was not initiated but radicalized in the writings of Islamist ideologues such as Sayyid Qutb (1906–1966) and Abul Ala Maududi (1903–1979). Their input provided crucial intellectual influences on the redefinition of the *ummah* not only as a political but also as an activist collectivity.

In *Milestones* (*Ma'alim fi al-Tariq*), Qutb divided social systems into two categories: the order of Islam and the decadent, ignorant order of *jahiliyyah*—which existed in Arabia before the Prophet Muhammad received the word of God—and has now returned with the rise of corrupted rulers who do not follow Islam. Qutb expressed this division as follows: "*Jahiliyyah* is now present not only in the capitalist West and the Communist East, it has also infected the world of Islam. All that is around us is *Jahiliyyah*. Peoples' imaginings, their beliefs, customs, and traditions, the sources of their culture, their art and literature, their laws and statutes, much even of what we take to be Islamic culture, Islamic authorities, Islamic philosophy, Islamic thought: all this too is of the making of this *Jahiliyyah*."[46] This presentation of *jahiliyyah* as a state of ignorance, barbarity, and idolatry pervading the Muslim world after the revelation of the Prophet Muhammad departs starkly from the classical religious view that the revelation sent to the Prophet Muhammad ended the state of *jahiliyyah*.

In Qutb's view, the "true Muslims," the *tali'ah* (vanguards), are and must remain set apart from the ambient infidel society as a sort of "countersociety." During the trial that culminated in his execution, Qutb declared, "We are the ummah of the believers, living within a jahili society. Nothing relates us to state or to society and we owe no allegiance to either. As a community of believers we should see ourselves in a state of war with the state and the society."[47]

Such a definition is at odds with the traditional concept in which *ummah* is a canopy for Muslims and non-Muslims under the rule of the caliphate as the protector of the abode of Islam (*dar al-Islam*). The quest for a virtuous order transformed the community of the faithful (the *ummah*) into what Mawlana Azad called the *hizbullah*, the party (or followers or partisans) of God, a term used by Maududi as well.[48] In other words, Islamist opponents of the 1960s have transferred the concept of political resistance that Muslim societies developed during the colonial period to contemporary national and domestic arenas. Through these efforts, the *ummah* becomes not simply the Muslims who embrace the Prophet Muhammad's message but also those who commit to combat the political and social decadence in Muslim societies. Thus, *ummah*, sharia, and jihad become associated with political resistance.

Global jihadi groups refer to the *ummah* in a way that relies on the term's political meaning, but with a radical bent. In other words, the *ummah*, as used by al-Qaeda, is an ultraradicalized version of the imagined community embedded in the social imaginary of contemporary Muslim societies. For al-Qaeda, the *ummah* is the collective of committed Muslims who fight to reinstate Islamic rules. In declaring jihad against the United States in 1996, Osama bin Laden instrumentalized the medieval figure of Ibn Taymiya (1263–1328) to "[arouse] the ummah of Islam against its enemies."[49] In his declaration of jihad, he stated, "It is essential to hit the main enemy [the Zionist-Crusader alliance] who divided the ummah into small and little countries and pushed it, for the last few decades, into a state of confusion."[50] In a later interview, he added, "The nation [*ummah*] is asked to unite itself under this Crusaders' campaign, the strongest, most powerful, and most ferocious [*ashad wa a`naf wa ashras*] Crusaders' campaign to fall on the Islamic nation [*ummah*] since the dawn of Islamic history."[51]

It is worth mentioning that al-Qaeda's radical *ummah* is only one definition among many in a repertoire that mixes social responsibility, activism, and resistance. As already mentioned, Qutb and Faraj understood the *ummah* as a combative community that stands in violent opposition to oppressive nation-states and rulers. Al-Qaeda, however, promotes the understanding that the *ummah* stands in opposition not only to unjust rulers but also to all Muslims who do not identify with the *ummah* as a combative community.

Such radicalization has been interpreted as a postmodern vision or an ultra-individualization of Islam. Devji Faisal notes that the logic of the extreme politicization of the *ummah* leads to a preeminence of individual choice.[52] The individual makes the decision to join the *ummah* as a combatant, and that personal decision to participate in the combatant group creates the community. This reverses the logic of the *ummah wahida*, in which Allah created the community to disseminate his message to all of humanity. The *ummah*, from this politicized perspective, is the community of Muslims who have chosen to fight to defend Islamic values, particularly against corruption by decadent Muslim rulers or by the West. It projects a pattern of purity and resistance opposed to the West and its allies, as well as to Muslims who do not make the choice to fight.

ISIS's political project is the most recent iteration of this militant *ummah*. It differs from al-Qaeda in that it aims to ground this pure and homogenous community of combatants in a territory. Here are some statements from ISIS's propaganda magazine, *Dabiq*, that express the grounding of the combatant *ummah* via the Islamic State:

> As the mujāhidīn of the Islamic State continue their march against the forces of kufr there is a new generation waiting in the wings, eagerly anticipating the day that it is called upon to take up the banner of īmān. These are the children of the Ummah of jihād, a generation raised in the lands of malāhim (fierce battles) and nurtured under the shade of Sharī'ah, just a stone's throw from the frontlines.[53]

> The Islamic State has taken it upon itself to fulfill the Ummah's duty towards this generation in preparing it to face the crusaders and their allies in defense of Islam and to raise high the word of Allah in every land. It has established institutes for these ashbāl (lion cubs) to train and hone their military skills, and to teach them the book of Allah and the Sunnah of His Messenger (sallallāhu 'alayhi wa sallam). It is these young lions to whom the Islamic State recently handed over two agents caught spying for Russian Intelligence and an agent caught spying for the Israeli Mossad, to be executed and displayed as an example to anyone else thinking of infiltrating the mujāhidīn.[54]

> This firāsah (perception/insight) and deep understanding of the dīn is as Abū 'Umar al-Baghdādī mentioned in his words, "O ummah of Islam, when we announced the Islamic State and said that it was a state of hijrah and jihād, we were not lying against Allah and thereafter against the people, nor were we talking about false dreams, rather, by the bounty of Allah ta'ālā, we are more capable of understanding Allah's sunnah in this jihād." This understanding is derived from the blood of the mujāhidīn amongst the muhājirīn and ansār, after we witnessed their character and methodology with our eyes [Hasād as-Sinīn]. His Messenger (sallallāhu 'alayhi wa sallam) said, "Indeed, Allah gathered the Earth for me, and thus I saw its eastern and western extents, and indeed the reign of my Ummah will reach what

was gathered for me from the Earth" [Sahīh Muslim on the authority of Thawbān].[55]

Furthermore, there is no doubt that ISIS has attempted to build state institutions, such as currency:

> In an effort to disentangle the Ummah from the corrupt, interest-based global financial system, the Islamic State recently announced the minting of new currency based on the intrinsic values of gold, silver, and copper. This initiative is a significant step towards shifting the Ummah away from the usage of currencies that are no longer backed by any precious metals, and whose values are constantly manipulated by the central banks of their respective nations.[56]

Other efforts have been reported in the domain of education and city administration. But overall, ISIS works to maintain the determination of its fighters and secure a steady flow of combatants. Internally, the search for purity has superceded the building of state institutions. This has resulted in the destruction of groups (non-Muslim and Muslim) who do not accept ISIS rule, along with religious and historical sites that are irrelevant to this homogenous community of combatant Muslims. This way of fighting derives from the national forms of jihad and al-Qaeda and the conception of a unified community of believers. The theological justification for this purification comes from the literalist and unhistorical readings of the Quran and the Hadith of the Wahhabi doctrine. The combination of jihad and Wahhabi interpretation of Islam leads to a politico-religious vision that resembles the communist and fascist totalitarian projects of the twentieth century.

Here is how Islamist strategist Abu Bakr Naji describes some Muslim groups working across sectarian lines in *The Management of Savagery*. "These groups are like the [Arab] Christians and the propagandists of nationalism among the secular, apostate parties; their like is legion. They even directed some people to hold meetings with the Arab Christians and the secular parties in order to find fault with the activities of the groups of jihad, which [they contend] will split apart the nation. God is sufficient for us; an excellent Guardian is He (cf. Qur'an 3:173)."[57] Similarly, issue 8 of *Dabiq* and *The Management of Savagery* describe two features of this community of combatants: jihad and *hijra* (migration).

> All this, after Allah had granted the imam of The Islamic State the blessing of performing hijrah and fighting jihad in His cause, on top of already having been characterized by his noble lineage, sound intellect, and a prestigious level of knowledge and religious practice. . . . The goal of establishing the Khilafah has always been one that occupied the hearts of the mujahidin since the revival of jihad this century. . . . The jama'ah would use the absent obligation of jihad as its fundamental means for change, implementing Allah's command, (And fight them until there is no fitnah and [until] the religion, all of it, is for Allah) [Al-Anfal: 39].[58]

> The Umma which faces hardships and struggles with difficulties and whose sons live in constant struggle and continuous jihad is the Umma which deserves life and for which permanence and triumph are ordained.[59]

This global community of fighters does not reflect most political uses of the *ummah*, which is still very much associated with a national fight. In fact, the latter clashes with the former. For example, Hamas and Hezbollah have condemned al-Qaeda's tactics.[60] Hamas has also attacked members of the al-Qaeda network.[61] Abu Muhammad al-Maqdisi, a Salafi theologian and mentor of Abu Musab al-Zarqawi, former leader of al-Qaeda in Iraq, stated that al-Qaeda and Hamas share "neither ideology nor doctrine."[62] Al-Zarqawi condemned Hezbollah as the "enemy of the Sunnis."[63] Finally, Hezbollah leader Hassan Nasrallah called al-Qaeda "the worst, the most dangerous thing that this Islamic revival has encountered."

Nevertheless, the common point between national and global jihad is the apprehension of *ummah* as a militant political community. Both are outcomes of the nationalization of Islam. The two differ in the boundaries of this political community and the modes of creating it.

The Western Echo:
The Ummah *Is a Political Threat*

Ironically, the dominant political narrative of the West now reinforces the perception of a unified politicized *ummah*. Unlike the terms *jihad* and *sharia*, the term *ummah* does not appear in Western political and media discourses. But the perception of an Islamic threat to Western civilization reinforces the significance of the *ummah* as a "deterritorialized community of Muslims," committed to a political project that is anathema to the democratic values of the West.

After the collapse of the Soviet Union, Islam emerged as the new political enemy of the West with two major features in political rhetoric. First, Islam is a unified, utopian ideology that offers a platform for critique of industrial and Western society. Second, Islamic ideology stands in opposition to Western ideology: it is despotic, militant, retrograde, and undemocratic. Together, these characteristics strip Islam of nuance and reinforce the politicized use of Islamic terminology.

The Western perception of a clash between Western civilization and the "Muslim world of the Greater Middle East," first advanced by Samuel P. Huntington in the early 1990s, has become the academic validation of this political perception. In *The Clash of Civilizations*, Huntington rejected Francis Fukuyama's claim that all the important ideological and military conflicts ended with the fall of the Soviet Union. He argued that conflict would continue in the post–Cold War world, ordered along civilizational rather than big-power lines. "The fault lines between civilizations," Huntington wrote, "will be the battle lines of the future."[64] In a troubling convergence with al-Qaeda's ideologues, Huntington saw Islam as a single civilization unified by a religious message in violent conflict with Christianity and therefore the West. As Huntington wrote of the West and Islamic civilizations, "Each has been the other's Other. . . . Across the centuries the fortunes of the two religions have risen and fallen in the sequence of momentous surges, pauses and counter surges."[65]

This vision of a unified political community lies at the core of the current securitization of policy toward Islam in Europe and in the United States. Since 9/11, and even more so with the rise of

ISIS, policies toward Muslim groups across Europe have sought the most efficient representatives of an *ummah*, seen implicitly as a political project and a threat to domestic political stability. Toby Archer argues that the perception of a radicalized *ummah*, and therefore, the search for religious representatives who could counter it, has shaped recent British policies toward Muslims. This perception, Archer discusses, is only recent; for several decades before 9/11, British Muslim-related policies prioritized localized and ethnically conscious versions of the Muslim community.[66]

The controversy over the construction of a mosque near the site of the 9/11 attacks in New York City in 2006 illustrates the same perception: the *ummah* is a direct threat to American interests and values. Valerie Dixon, blogging for the *Washington Post*, writes, "People who oppose this project see Islam as not only a religion, but as an ideology that fuels a determination to destroy the United States."[67] Furthermore, movements against a perceived Islamization of the United States have sprung up across the country, as documented by the partisan blog Real-Courage.org.[68] These movements oppose the construction of mosques, growth of Muslim communities in America, and neutral or favorable policies toward American Muslims. They understand the Muslim community as a combative *ummah* and fear its impact on American political and social interests. The rise of ISIS and increased attacks in Europe and the United States since 2014 have exacerbated this vision.

In light of the semantic evolution of the *ummah*, it would be erroneous to see the current extreme jihadi version as predominant over other religious and political meanings. In fact, all meanings from the revelation-based community to Muslim nations, and now communities of combatants, coexist side by side and can be activated for different causes and purposes in multiple contexts.

Jihad: From Theory of War to Personal and Global Resistance

The term *jihad* is even more multilayered than *ummah*. The root *jhd* means "to strive." As such, most theological meanings of *jihad* relate to the efforts of the believer to implement the revelation-based community defined by the message of Islam. In this sense, theologians usually qualify jihad by pacific means (heart, mouth, and pen) as greater jihad, in contrast with the lesser jihad of the sword.

Interestingly, in the ongoing objections by Muslim authorities to the jihad conducted by al-Qaeda or ISIS, there is very little allusion to the fact that in the Islamic tradition, jihad was a theory of war that shaped the international relations of the Muslim empires. Though there have been multiple interpretations, a *doxa* did in fact emerge in classical Islam on how to conduct war in the path of God, or jihad. It rested on the *summa* division between *dar al-Islam* (abode of Islam) and *dar al-harb* (abode of war) and was transmitted through numerous treatises, such as *The Law of Nations*, published by Muhammad al-Shaybani at the end of the eighth century. As noted by Haider Ala Hamoudi, "The ultimate aim of the House of Islam was to bring the entire world within the House of Islam. War, or the jihad, is no more and no less a means to this end in Shaybani's vision, one that is only taken when and where the enemy has refused to submit to Islam's call and it is military [*sic*] advantageous to launch an attack."[69]

In a way similar to the just-war tradition, al-Shaybani described the modes of initiating war (*jus ad bellum*) as well as conducting war (*jus in bello*). Later on, Ibn Rushd (1126–1198), or Averroes, synthesized the following rules of war as they applied in his time:[70]

1. Jihad, as war in the path of god, is validated by the body of ulema and then waged by the caliph.
2. Clerics have systematically disapproved of jihad by individuals. Scholars agree that jihad is a collective not a personal obligation. According to the majority of scholars, the compulsory nature of the jihad is found at Sura 2:216: "Prescribed for you is fighting, though it be hateful to you." That this obligation is a collective and not a personal one—that is, that the obligation, when it can be properly carried out by a limited number of individuals, is cancelled for the remaining Muslims—is found at Sura 9:122: "It is not for the believers to go forth totally"; at Sura 4:95: "Yet to each God has promised the reward

most fair"; and, lastly, on the fact that the Prophet never went to battle without leaving some people behind.[71]

3. Conduct in war follows rules and distinguishes between combatant and noncombatant, based on the Prophet's statements: "Do not slay the old and decrepit, children, or women. Do not purloin what belongs to the spoils. . . . Do not slay women, nor infants, nor those worn with age" [while the Prophet commanded] "slay the polytheists but spare their children."[72] Opinions vary as to the damage that may be inflicted on their property, such as buildings, cattle, and crops. For example, Imam Malik allowed the felling of trees, the picking of fruit, and the demolishing of buildings, but not the slaughter of the cattle and the burning of the date palms. Others disapproved of the felling of the fruit-trees and the demolishing of buildings, regardless of whether the buildings in question were churches or not. According to an authoritative tradition, the Prophet set fire to the palm trees of Banu Nadir. However, it has been related as an irrefutable fact that Abu Bakr said: "Do not fell trees and do not demolish buildings."[73]

4. The end of the war has to follow rules. Some consider truce to be permitted from the very outset and without an immediate occasion, provided that the imam deems it in the interest of the Muslims. Others maintain that it is only allowed when Muslims are pressed by sheer necessity, such as a civil war and the like. As a condition for truce, it may be stipulated that the enemy must pay a certain amount of money to the Muslims. This is not poll tax, because that would require that they come under Islamic rule. Such a stipulation, however, is not obligatory.[74]

In sum, jihad as war was a tool of the caliph to preserve or expand his international authority, among other objectives of good governance. It was a collective duty, following rules comparable to those of the tradition of just war. The last example of such traditional jihad was the one waged by the Ottoman sultan in 1915 before the collapse of the caliphate.[75]

Once the French and the British asserted their authority over most of the Muslim territories, jihad lost its relevance for international relations. Instead, it became a way for the Muslim elites to mobilize the masses and resist the colonial project in order to create new nations. For example, nationalist groups fighting against the French in Algeria called themselves *mudjahidin*, while the *mujahidat* were the female fighters (usually young women wearing "Western clothes").[76] In other words, jihad turned from a theory of war aimed at maintaining and expanding the caliphate into a form of resistance to the colonial power. Jihad became a term expressing the pursuit of what international law calls "the right of people to rule themselves."

In some cases, jihad came to define any kind of fight for the growth and development of the new nations. Take, for example, Habib Bourguiba, who in 1968 stated on television during the month of Ramadan, "A modern nation cannot afford to stop for a month every year," while drinking a glass of orange juice. He even asked the grand mufti of Tunisia to proclaim a fatwa delegitimizing fasting during Ramadan. The mufti refused and thus lost his position.

Jihad as a Personal Act of Piety

The decisive step toward a radicalization of jihad came from Qutb. Contradicting the classical interpretation, Qutb advocated for individual jihad.[77] In his view, human-based rulings and military powers are true obstacles to Islam. It is necessary to remove them by force to righteously and openly reach out to people's hearts and minds. In this respect, he saw personal jihad as an act of freedom:

> Since the objective of the message of Islam is a decisive declaration of man's freedom, not merely on the philosophical plane but also in the actual conditions of life, it must employ Jihad.
> . . . When Islam strives for peace its objective is not that superficial peace which requires that only that part of the earth where the followers of Islam are residing remain secure. The peace which Islam desires is that the religion (i.e., the Law of the society) be purified for God, that the obedience of all people be for God alone, and that some people should not be lords over

others. . . . [T]he eternal struggle for freedom of man will continue until the religion is purified for God.[78]

In contrast to al-Shaybani and Ibn Rushd,[79] he downplayed the warfare associated with jihad, to make it a personal spiritual act, and remarked, "It is a battle against himself, against Satan, against his own desires and ambitions . . . against every obstacle which comes into the way of worshipping God, and the implementation of the Divine authority on earth."[80]

Jihad thus becomes the obligation of the believer to fight against the immoral order of the unjust ruler. The boundaries established by the canonical definition disappear: jihad becomes an individual moral act perpetrated against the unjust ruler, who is not really a Muslim since he does not apply the laws of Islam. We see here the influence of modern revolutionary ideology on Qutb's approach, where the political fight is to take initiative to radically transform the political order. It is worth noting that Qutb read Maududi, who elaborated an activist vision of Islam and was very much influenced by communist ideology.

The creation of al-Qaeda illustrates another decisive reorientation: jihad as the use of indiscriminate violence against all enemies of Islam, Muslims and non-Muslims, politicians and civilians alike. For example, in the fatwa declaring jihad against the United States, bin Laden stated,

> The ruling to kill the Americans and their allies—civilians and military—is an individual duty for every Muslim who can do it in any country in which it is possible to do it, in order to liberate the al-Aqsa Mosque and the holy mosque from their grip, and in order for their armies to move out of all the lands of Islam, defeated and unable to threaten any Muslim. This is in accordance with the words of Almighty God: "and fight the pagans all together as they fight you all together," "and fight them until there is no more tumult or oppression, and there prevail justice and faith in God." This is in addition to the words of Almighty God: "And why should ye not fight in the cause of God and of those who, being weak, are ill-treated and oppressed—women and children, whose cry is 'Our Lord, rescue us from this town, whose people are oppressors; and raise for us from thee one who will help!'" We—with God's help—

call on every Muslim who believes in God and wishes to be
rewarded to comply with God's order to kill the Americans and
plunder their money wherever and whenever they find it.[81]

In another statement, Bin Laden asserted,

> This immense obligation [i.e., jihad] . . . has no place among the
> clerics today who do not speak of it. They all, except for those upon
> whom Allah has had mercy, are busy handing out praise and words
> of glory to the despotic imams [i.e., Arab rulers] who disbelieve
> Allah and His Prophet. They send telegrams praising those rulers
> who disbelieve Allah and His Prophet. Their newspapers and media
> spread heresy against Allah and His Prophet. Other telegrams are
> sent from the rulers to these clerics, praising them for deceiving the
> nation. The nation has never been as damaged by a catastrophe like
> the one that damages them today. In the past, there was imperfec-
> tion, but it was partial. Today, however, the imperfection touches
> the entire public because of the communications revolution and
> because the media enter every home. . . . Faithful clerics possess
> characteristics described in the book of Allah. . . . The most promi-
> nent characteristics are faith and jihad for the sake of Allah. . . .
> Those who do hijrah, and those who support Allah and His Prophet
> and wage jihad for the sake of Allah, are the faithful ones.[82]

The meanings of jihad in globalized radical Islam entail combat as a personal mode of salvation to defeat the forces of chaos
and confusion that pervade all Muslim countries, the West, and
elsewhere. All the parameters of the *jus ad bellum* and *jus in bello*
in the traditional theory of war dissolve to promote indiscrimina-
tory violence that does not distinguish between combatant and
noncombatant or Muslim and non-Muslim.

Although al-Qaeda condemned ISIS in 2014, the two organizations' differences in this respect are strategic rather than ideological.[83] A review of *The Management of Savagery* reveals the same
tropes, only more strongly asserted: jihad is not simply military and
territorial but also ontological, as a fight between good and evil.[84]
Furthermore, in *A Message to the Mujahidin and the Muslim
Ummah in the Month of Ramadan*, al-Baghdadi addresses the Muslim communities across the world as *mujahidin* in the Islamic
ummah. He states, "We congratulate the ummah (people) of Islam,

in the East and in the West, on the advent of the blessed month of Ramadan, and we praise Allah (the Exalted) for allowing us to reach this virtuous month."[85] He then emphasizes, "There is no deed . . . better than jihad in the path of Allah," and exhorts all Muslims, "Go forth, o mujahidin in the path of Allah."[86] Another statement by al-Baghdadi also illustrates the division of the world between good and evil: "O ummah of Islam, indeed the world today has been divided into two camps and two trenches, with no third camp present: The camp of Islam and faith, and the camp of kufr and hypocrisy—the camp of the Muslims and the mujahidin everywhere, and the camp of the Jews, the crusaders, their allies, and with them the rest of the nations and religions of kufr, all being led by America and Russia, and being mobilized by the Jews."[87]

Similarly, Naji sees the West no longer as a geographical location but as a situation of extreme abuse and malevolence. In *The Management of Savagery*, he calls for two different levels of strategy:

> a media strategy targeting and focusing on two classes. [The first] class is the masses, in order to push a large number of them to join the jihad, offer positive support, and adopt a negative attitude toward those who do not join the ranks. The second class is the troops of the enemy who have lower salaries, in order to push them to join the ranks of the mujahids or at least to flee from the service of the enemy. . . . Developing the media strategy such that it reaches and targets the heart of the middle leadership of the armies of apostasy in order to push them to join the jihad. This is no doubt necessary, but there should be more concentration on a presentation tailored to the mentality of the people and [which addresses] the ideas that prevent them from joining the ranks of the jihad, particularly [emphasizing] to them that they have a way of thinking and a sentiment that is different from the mentality of "the two ways"![88]

What all of these jihadi and Wahhabi movements have in common is the ideal of a homogenous global Muslim community. Thus the world is divided into Muslims and infidels, and the image of the West, automatically associated with moral depravity, is always a negative one. Everything that did not already exist or happen during the time of the Prophet is an innovation, thus *haram* (forbidden). All share the vision of the superiority of Islam as well as the resolve to make the *ummah* uniform.

Notes

1. Greenfeld, Liah, ed. *Globalization of Nationalism: The Motive-Force Behind Twenty-First Century Politics.* Colchester, UK: ECPR Press, 2016.

2. Al-Banna, Hassan. *Bayn al-ams wa'l-yawm* (Between yesterday and today). Beirut: Ar-Risalah, n.d., p. 250.

3. Mitchell, Richard P. *The Society of the Muslim Brothers.* New York: Oxford University Press, 1993, p. 217.

4. Ibid., 232.

5. A doctrine or ideology is *takfiri* when Muslims who do not comply with it are rejected as infidels. Al-Hudaybi was the second "general guide" for the Society of Muslim Brothers and is best known for *Preachers, Not Judges* (*Du'at la qudat*), which is a refutation of Sayyid Qutb's *Milestones*. He was trained as a lawyer and a judge and recognized for his careful scholarship. In 1965, he was imprisoned in a crackdown against the Brotherhood by Nasser, but he was released in 1971 by Nasser's successor, Anwar Sadat. See Zollner, Barbara H. E. *The Muslim Brotherhood: Hasan al-Hudaybi and Ideology.* London: Routledge, 2009, p. 63.

6. Johnston, David L. "Hassan al-Hudaybi and the Muslim Brotherhood: Can Islamic Fundamentalism Eschew the Islamic State?" *Comparative Islamic Studies* 3, no. 1 (2007): 43.

7. Sayyid Qutb was a writer and literary critic who, after sojourning in the United States as a student, became convinced that Western secularism and culture were corrupt and decided to join the Muslim Brotherhood upon his return to Egypt. He was imprisoned under Gamal Abdel Nasser's rule and tortured. During his time in prison, Qutb wrote several books, including *Signposts in the Road* (1964), which became a template for modern Sunni militancy. See "Sayyid Qutb." *Encyclopaedia Britannica.* April 2014. https://www.britannica.com/biography/Sayyid-Qutb. Muhammad abd-al-Salam Faraj (1954–1982) was head of the Islamist group al-Jihad (also Tanzim al-Jihad), known for its attacks on political personnel and civilians. In his pamphlet "The Neglected Obligation," he argued for jihad as the sixth pillar of Islam. He was executed in 1982 for his role in coordinating the assassination of President Anwar Sadat that year.

8. Gerges, Fawaz A. *Why Jihad Went Global.* Cambridge: Cambridge University Press, 2005.

9. These three qualifications are not synonymous. Some movements can go back to the fundamentals to create contextualized and modernist interpretations, like Abduh in the nineteenth century. Some movements can be both fundamentalist and literalist without excluding the believers who do not follow their interpretation. It happens that Wahhabism combines these three features.

10. *Ikhtilaf* refers to differences of opinion or disagreement in religious interpretations. Variety in opinions is permissible as long as they don't transgress the basic Islamic principles. "*Ikhtilāf* permits a Muslim to choose the interpretation of religious teachings that best suits his own circumstances and causes the least harm." See "Ikhtilaf." *Encyclopaedia Britannica.* July 20, 1998. https://www.britannica.com/topic/ikhtilaf.

11. Cesari, Jocelyne. *Why the West Fears Islam: An Exploration of Muslims in Liberal Democracies.* New York: Palgrave Macmillan, 2013.

12. Piscatori, James P. *Islam in a World of Nation-States.* Cambridge: Cambridge University Press, 1986.

13. Denny, Frederick Mathewson. *Islam and the Muslim Community.* San Francisco: Harper & Row, 1987, p. 48.

14. Indonesian writer Munawir Syadzali, in *Islam and the Governmental System: Teachings, History, and Reflections*. Jakarta: University of Indonesia Press, 1990, argues that since the Constitution of Medina did not mention Islam as the religion of the state, the Prophet did not actually call for the establishment of a theocracy.

15. Graham, William A. "Traditionalism in Islam: An Essay in Interpretation." *Journal of Interdisciplinary History* 23, no. 3 (1993): 495–522.

16. "Yet, if the Muslim umma was caught up in the cut and thrust of politics, Muslim political thought evolved in a way that safely shielded the Islamic religio-political idea from worldly compromise. The first step in this evolution had been taken with the denial of the right to fix orthodoxy to any individual or group (whether caliph or ulama)." See Brown, L. Carl. *Religion and State: The Muslim Approach to Politics*. New York: Columbia University Press, 52, 53.

17. Burgis, Michelle. "Faith in the State? Traditions of Territoriality, International Law and the Emergence of Modern Arab Statehood." *Journal of the History of International Law* 11, no. 1 (2009): 50.

18. Houtsma, M. T. *E.J. Brill's First Encyclopaedia of Islam, 1913–1936*. Leiden: E. J. Brill, 1987. The first four caliphs following the death of the Prophet Muhammad were: Abu Bakr (632–634), Umar (634–644), Othman (644–656), and Ali (655–661). They are known as the Rightly Guided Caliphs or *Rashidun*.

19. Hourani, Albert Habib. *Arabic Thought in the Liberal Age, 1798–1939*. London: Oxford University Press, 1983, p. 12.

20. Muhammad al-Shaybani (749–805) was an Islamic jurist of the Hanafi School. One of his notable works is "Introduction to the Islamic Law of the Nations," published at the end of the eighth century. See Chaumont, E. "Al-Shaybānī, Abū ʿAbd Allāh Muḥammad b. al-Ḥasan b. Farḳad." In *Encyclopaedia of Islam*, ed. P. Bearman et al. Brill Online. 2008.

21. Burgis, "Faith in the State," 52.

22. Karpat, Kemal H. *The Politicization of Islam: Reconstructing Identity, State, Faith, and Community in the Late Ottoman State*. New York: Oxford University Press, 2001.

23. Ibid.

24. Gramsci, Antonio, and David Forgacs. *The Gramsci Reader: Selected Writings, 1916–1935*. London: Lawrence and Wishart, 1999, pp. 189–222.

25. The Sokoto Caliphate (West Africa, 1804–1903) was established by Usman Dan Fodio, the leader of the Maliki school of thought and Qadiri branch of Sufism. He took on the quest to revive the role of Islam in West Africa and led an uprising to initiate reforms. He wrote more than one hundred books concerning religion, government, society, and culture.

26. al-Afghani, Jamal al-Din. "Wa-I'tasimu bi-habl Allah jami'an wala tafarraqu." *Al-Manar* 24 (1923): 28–32. This article originally appeared in *Al-'Urwa al-Wuthqa* 5 (1884). See Kudsi-Zadeh, Albert. "Jamal al-Din al-Afghani: A Select List of Articles." *Middle Eastern Studies* 2, no. 1 (October 1965): 66–72.

27. "Al-Khilafah au al-Imamah al-'Uzma" originally appeared in *Al-Manar*, the organ of the Salafi movement, between December 1922 and May 1923. French translation by H. Laoust (Beirut, 1938). See Fakhry, Majid. "The Theocratic Idea of the Islamic State in Recent Controversies." *International Affairs* (Royal Institute of International Affairs 1944–) 30, no. 4 (October 1954): 450–462.

28. Zoubeida, Sami. "Islam and Nationalism: Continuities and Contradictions." *Nations and Nationalism* 10, no. 4 (2004): 407–420. Quoted in Haim, Sylvia G. *Arab Nationalism: An Anthology*. Berkeley: University of California Press, 1962,

pp. 22–23. Islamists opposed nationalism under the postcolonial nation-state. While the Islamists of the early twentieth century shared with the nationalists the objective of ending colonial domination, the Islamists under Nasser were firmly repressed and persecuted by a nationalist regime after the British had been ejected. Qutb conceived of the Nasserist regime as a *jahiliyyah*, a term referring to an age of barbarism and ignorance to be confronted by true Muslims fortified by faith and following in the footsteps of the first Islamic vanguard of Muhammad and his followers. Faith here replaced nation as a basis of solidarity and struggle to establish the sovereignty of God against that of the nationalist tyrant.

29. Halliday, Fred. "The Politics of the Umma: States and Communities in Islamic Movements." *Mediterranean Politics* 7, no. 3 (autumn 2002): 20–41.

30. Awad, Lewis. "Bahth jari can Jamal al-Dyn al-Afghani; al-Irani al-ghamid ft Misr." *Al-Tadamon* (April 16–September 10, 1983): 1:1–1:22.

31. Matthee, Rudi. "Jamal al-Din al-Afghani and the Egyptian National Debate." *International Journal of Middle East Studies* 21, no. 2 (May 1989): 162.

32. Ibid., 161.

33. Ibid., 156.

34. Imara, Muhammad. *Jamal al-Din al-Afghani: Al-Amalal-kamila*. 2nd ed. 2 vols. Beirut: Dar Al Shuruq, 1979. For a detailed description of the different components of the Anwar/Imara controversy, see Matthee, "Jamal al-Din al-Afghani and the Egyptian."

35. Ibid., 162.

36. Ibid., 163.

37. Dawisha, Adeed. "'Identity' and Political Survival in Saddam's Iraq." *Middle East Journal* 53, no. 4 (1999): 553–567.

38. *Text of Saddam Husayn 27 Apr Al-Anba Interview*. Daily Report. Middle East & Africa, FBIS-MEA-83-085, May 2, 1983, E3.

39. *Saddam Address Ba'th Party Congress 5 October*. Daily Report. Near East & South Asia, FBIS-NES-92-195, October 7, 1992, p. 22.

40. *Saddam Speech 20 Jan (After Aerial Bombardment on 1991-01-17)*. Daily Report. Near East & South Asia, FBIS-NES-91-014, January 1–22, 1991, p. 36.

41. *Saddam Speaks on Allies' Ground Attack 24 Feb*. Daily Report. Near East & South Asia, FBIS-NES-91037, February 25, 1991, p. 33–34.

42. *Saddam Husayn Anniversary Speech*. Daily Report. Near East & South Asia, FBIS-NES-93-011, January 19, 1993, p. 39.

43. *Saddam 17 Jul Revolution Anniversary Speech*. Daily Report. Near East & South Asia, FBIS-NES-94-137, July 18, 1994, p. 36.

44. Halliday, "The Politics of the Umma."

45. On the weekly talk show "Life and Religion" broadcast by Doha Al Jazeera television, on October 5, 2008, shaikh Yousuf al-Qaradawi discussed the *ummah* as an "Islamic Nation." In his view, the Islamic nation is a reality and refers to one nation, one state, one caliphate. He acknowledged, however, that religious minorities are a part of this Islamic nation. "Egyptian Cleric al-Qaradawi discusses the concept of Islamic Nation." Al Jazeera, *BBC Monitoring the Middle East*, London, October 20, 2008. "Grand Ayatollah Al-Baghdadi of Iraq Discourages the Participation of Muslims in International Policy Organizations." Islamopedia Online. April 22, 2010. http://www.islamopediaonline.org/fatwa/grand-ayatollah-al-baghdadi-iraq-discourages-participation-muslims-international-policy-organi.

46. Qutb, *Milestones*.

47. Tamimi, Azzam S. "Democracy in Islamic Political Thought." Ireland Online. Accessed January 4, 2017. http://ireland.iol.ie/~afifi/Articles/democracy.htm.

48. Mohiuddin Ahmad (1888–1958), better known as Mawlana Abul Kalam Azad, scholar, writer, and statesman, played a leading role in the Indian struggle for independence and then later in the Indian government, remaining a symbol of Muslim coexistence in religiously diverse India. Among his many writings were his acclaimed Urdu translation and interpretation of the Quran.

49. "Declaration of Jihad Against Americans Occupying the Land of the Two Holy Mosques." CENGAGE. Accessed January 4, 2017. http://college.cengage.com/history/primary_sources/world/two_holy_mosques.htm.

50. Ibid.

51. "Document—the Unreleased Interview with Usamah bin Laden—21st October 2001." Terrorisme.net. August 19, 2016. http://www.terrorisme.net/2002/08/19/obl-interview.

52. Faisal, Devji. *Landscapes of Jihad: Militancy, Morality, Modernity.* Ithaca, NY: Cornell University Press, 2005.

53. Islamic State. *Shari'ah Alone Will Rule Africa. Dabiq* 8 (Jumada Al-Akhirah 1436): 20.

54. Ibid.

55. Islamic State. *Remaining and Expanding. Dabiq* 5 (Muharram 1436): 8.

56. Ibid.

57. Naji, Abu Bakr. *The Management of Savagery: The Most Critical Stage Through Which the Umma Will Pass.* Translated by William McCants. Cambridge, MA: John M. Olin Institute for Strategic Studies at Harvard University, 2006.

58. Islamic State. "The Islamic State Is a True Imamah." In *The Return of Khilafah. Dabiq* 1 (Ramadan 1435): 26.

59. See "Section Ten: Mastering Education Within the Movement Just as It Was in the First Age of Islam," in Naji, *The Management of Savagery.*

60. For examples, see Gardella, Rich. "Insurgent Groups Condemn al-Qaida Tactics." *NBC News.* October 16, 2007. http://www.msnbc.msn.com/id/21267335; Dakroub, Hussein. "Beheading Condemned by Hamas and Hizbollah." *Independent.* May 14, 2004. http://www.independent.co.uk/news/world/middle-east/beheading-condemned-by-hamas-and-hizbollah-563351.html.

61. Beaumont, Peter. "Hamas Destroys al-Qaida in Violent Gaza Battle." *Guardian.* August 16, 2009. http://www.guardian.co.uk/world/2009/aug/15/hamas-battle-gaza-islamists-al-qaida.

62. Altikriti, Anas. "Hamas Is Not al-Qaida." *Guardian.* September 21, 2009. http://www.guardian.co.uk/commentisfree/2009/sep/21/hamas-al-qaida.

63. Wright, Robin. "Inside the Mind of Hezbollah." *Washington Post.* July 16, 2006. http://www.washingtonpost.com/wp-dyn/content/article/2006/07/14/AR2006071401401.html.

64. Huntington, Samuel P. *The Clash of Civilizations and the Remaking of the World Order.* New York: Simon & Shuster, 1998, p. 209.

65. Ibid.

66. Archer, Toby. "Welcome to the Ummah: The British State and Its Muslim Citizens Since 9/11." *Cooperation and Conflict* 44, no. 3 (2009): 327–349.

67. Dixon, Valerie. "Land of the Free, Home of the Mosque near Ground Zero." *On Faith* (blog), *Washington Post.* July 21, 2010. http://newsweek.washingtonpost.com/onfaith/panelists/valerie_elverton_dixon/2010/07/the_mosque_a_fitting_response.html.

68. "Coast-to-Coast Anti-Islam Movement Results in Protests, Attacks Against Mosques." Real Courage. July 22, 2010. http://www.realcourage.org/2010/07/coast-to-coast.

69. Hamoudi, Haider Ala. "'Lone Wolf' Terrorism and the Classical Jihad: On the Contingencies of Violent Islamic Extremism." *Florida International University Law Review* 11, no. 1 (2015): 106.

70. Ibn Rushd, or Averroes (1126–1198), was a theologian and philosopher from the *maleki* school of jurisprudence, born in Spain (Cordoba).

71. Peters, Rudolph. *Jihad in Classical and Modern Islam: A Reader.* Princeton, NJ: Markus Wiener, 1996, p. 29.

72. Bostom, Andrew G. *The Legacy of Jihad: Islamic Holy War and the Fate of Non-Muslims.* Amherst, NY: Prometheus Books, 2005, pp. 151, 152.

73. Ibid., 153.

74. Peters, *Jihad in Classical and Modern Islam,* 38–39.

75. The sultan announced the call for jihad one month after Russia's declaration of war. His announcement was supported by a fatwa released by Shaikh al-Islam, the most prominent religious figure in the caliphate. The fatwa asked Muslim groups living in the colonies of France, Russia, and Britain to resist their oppressors. It also affirmed that fighting against the Ottoman Empire was considered a critical sin, for which its Muslim subjects would be severely punished in the hereafter. The fatwa, however, was not fully embraced by Muslim populations and was actually contested by religious figures in different provinces of the Ottoman Empire.

76. Vince, Natalya. "Colonial and Post-colonial Identities: Women Veterans of the 'Battle of Algiers.'" *French History and Civilization* 2 (2009): 153–168.

77. Qutb. *Milestones.*

78. Qutb, Sayyid. *Ma'alim fi al-Tariq.* Cairo: Kazi Publications, 1964.

79. Peters, *Jihad in Classical and Modern Islam,* 29.

80. Toth, James. *Sayyid Qutb: The Life and Legacy of a Radical Islamic Intellectual.* Oxford: Oxford University Press, 2013.

81. "World Islamic Front Statement Urging Jihad Against Jews and Crusaders." Federation of American Scientists. Accessed January 9, 2017. https://fas.org/irp/world/para/docs/980223-fatwa.htm.

82. "A New Bin Laden Speech." Middle East Media Research Institute. July 18, 2003. https://www.memri.org/reports/new-bin-laden-speech.

83. In 2014, al-Qaeda leader Ayman al-Zawahiri publicly condemned ISIS as "extremists" and insisted that the group "is not a branch of al-Qaeda." Al-Qaeda "has no connection with the group called the ISIS, as it was not informed or consulted about its establishment. It was not pleased with it and thus ordered its suspension. Therefore, it is not affiliated with al-Qaeda and has no organizational relationship with it." And "we distance ourselves from the sedition taking place among the *mujahidin* factions [in Syria] and the forbidden bloodshed." He warned that *mujahidin* must acknowledge the "enormity of the catastrophe" led by "this sedition." Back then, Abu Bakr al-Baghdadi attempted to merge his Iraq-based group with the al-Nusra Front, al-Qaeda's group in Syria. But his attempt failed after al-Zawahiri rejected the coalition.

84. Abu Bakr Naji, al-Qaeda's strategist in Iraq, published *The Management of Savagery* online in 2004. His manifesto became a reference for the military strategy of ISIS. See Naji, *The Management of Savagery.*

85. Al-Baghdadi, Abu Bakr. "A Message to the Mujahidin and the Muslim Ummah in the Month of Ramadan." Al-Hayat Media Center. 2014. https://www.gatestoneinstitute.org/documents/baghdadi-caliph.pdf.

86. Ibid.

87. Ibid.

88. "Mastery of the Art of Management," in Naji, *The Management of Savagery.*

6

The Riddle
of Political Islam

At least since the Islamic Revolution in Iran, there has been no shortage of predictions about the decline of political Islam. The military crush against the short-lived Muslim Brotherhood government in Egypt since 2013, the ruthless repression of the Syrian regime against its opponents since 2012, and the defeat of Isis in October 2017 are just a few of the most recent events that appear to justify the never-ending predictions of the failure of political Islam.

If we limit political Islam to Islamic parties and contrast them with secular ones, then, indeed, political Islam does not seem capable of efficient and distinctive governance, except maybe in the case of Iran. When in power, these parties tend to limit their religious agendas to identity politics (focusing on women and sexual minorities), and the claims to an Islamic state do not translate into major economic or social transformations. Even more so, parties with an Islamic agenda and an ambition to govern, from the Turkish Justice and Development Party (AKP) to the Tunisian Ennahda, have renounced the claim of an Islamic state. Scholars such as Asef Bayat have called this new phase, in which the hard reality of daily ruling takes precedence over Islamic claims, "post-Islamist."[1]

But if apprehended as a set of multiform and contradictory political identities, then political Islam is far from dissolving. As demonstrated in this book, political Islam is a foundational element of modern political identities framed by the nation-state. Distinguishing between political Islam as culture and as ideology can help solve the riddle. In analyses of the role of religion in politics, Rhys Williams has noted that it is investigated as either culture or ideology but rarely as both.[2]

Religion as culture refers to beliefs and norms shared by individuals. This provides clear guidelines about "'what is' as well as 'what ought to be.'" In this sense, religion is "less about beliefs" and more "about the meaning in the world." Williams notes that to embrace a religious worldview "is to absorb a set of taken-for-granted assumptions about one's duty to God and to society." Religion as culture works "'behind the backs' of participants." Its political presence and influence are "often effective without the active awareness of those experiencing it."[3] The national habitus that this book intends to reveal is this "hidden part of the iceberg." The coterminality of Islam territory and political power shape the modern political cosmology brought by the nation-state in ways unknown in premodern Muslim empires. It creates a connection between Islam and citizenship by establishing Islam as the parameter of public space for Muslims and non-Muslims, believers and nonbelievers alike. Not without humor, Nathan Brown notes the current absurd use in Egyptian political rhetoric of the term *Islamic sharia* by all protagonists from secular to Islamic, usually to discuss the part of state law that specifically deals with Islam. If the sharia has to be qualified as Islamic, then it is first secular state law or the law of the land.[4] Political Islam as culture is the bedrock on which political actors can ideologically compete through partisan divisions, including Islamic parties, which explains why these parties can lose (as we have seen in Indonesia, for example) without endangering political Islam as culture.

A majority of citizens across the secular/religious divide share the ingrained conviction that the nation and Islam are intertwined and that politics must follow some rules inspired by Islam. A study published by the Pew Research Center in 2013 reveals that 74 percent of Egyptians agree that sharia should be made the official law, with 74 percent also thinking that it should apply to both Muslims and non-Muslims.[5] In the same survey, 72 percent of Indonesians favor making sharia the official national law, and 50 percent believe that it should apply to both Muslims and non-Muslims. Meanwhile, 55 percent of Senegalese favor making sharia the law of the land. At the same time, the survey reveals that Muslims have different interpretations of sharia, "including whether divorce and family planning are morally acceptable."[6] That many Muslims actually feel uneasy about the application of punishments in criminal cases reveals the gap between Islam as political culture and Islam as ideology: the scope of "Islamic sharia" is at the core of contentious politics.

The same survey shows that views about instituting sharia in the domestic-civil sphere frequently mirror a country's existing legal system. In Egypt, 94 percent support giving religious judges the authority to decide family and property disputes. In Jordan, it is 93 percent, and in Indonesia, 66 percent. In Turkey, which has secular courts for family law, 14 percent of Muslims believe that religious judges should have the power to decide family and property disputes.[7]

Meanwhile, a Muslim Millennial Attitudes Survey by the Tabah Foundation in 2015 found 36 percent of surveyed Moroccans, 87 percent of surveyed Egyptians, and 33 percent of surveyed Jordanians believed that the state should be involved in "appointment of imams, administration of mosques, and arranging preparations for holy occasions."[8] Additionally, 34 percent of Moroccans, 62 percent of Egyptians, and 7 percent of Jordanians believe that religious leaders should have full authority to get involved in anything related to religion in society.[9] When asked whether "people who belong to different religions are probably just as moral as those who belong to mine," only 28.1 percent in Egypt and 18 percent in Jordan agreed strongly.

These surveys highlight the expectations of citizens vis-à-vis Islam envisioned as a set of public norms granted and regulated by the state. These norms outline the moral standard for society and are the defining features of political Islam.

Political Islam is also, particularly in the sense of the Rousseauian definition of civil religion, a resource for the state to shape and control the citizenry.[10] This book has shown that hegemonic Islam combines both shared values about the public role of Islam and state policies about right and wrong in religious matters.

Most Muslim states, to varying degrees, have utilized Islamic references to forge a public morality concerning what is right and wrong for the political community, along with who is a good or bad citizen. Interestingly, this political culture is not seen as incompatible with democracy. In the 2013 Pew polling already mentioned, in thirty-one of the thirty-seven countries where the question was asked, at least half of Muslims believed a democratic government, rather than a leader with a strong hand, is best able to address their country's problems. At least three-quarters of Muslims support democracy in Lebanon (81 percent) and Tunisia (75 percent). At least half in Egypt (55 percent), the Palestinian territories (55 percent), and Iraq (54 percent) do so as well. In Indonesia, 61 percent also prefer democracy.[11]

According to a 2012 World Values Survey in Egypt, 74.8 percent of 1,523 citizens surveyed selected at least 8 on the importance of living in a democratically governed country, with 1 meaning "not at all important" and 10 meaning "absolutely important." The same question was asked of 1,582 Turkish citizens in 2011, and the corresponding number was 76.9 percent. Meanwhile, 17.1 percent of Egyptians and 12 percent of Turks believe that ultimate interpretation of the laws by religious authorities is an essential characteristic of democracy.[12]

Islam and Public Space

The role of Islamic practices in the definition of public morality has been central to civic and national identity in postcolonial Muslim societies. This book has discussed how, from the eighteenth century onward, the modernization process in Muslim lands created renewed tensions between modern and religious individuals. The monitoring of the female body and the freedom of expression have become the major site of these tensions, triggering persistent discussion of alternative and sometimes conflicting models of correctness and rightness, of what is modern and what is Islamic, among religious authorities, politicians, and women's groups. This attentiveness has translated into state prescriptions that range from sexual rules to morals regarding modesty. Meanwhile, freedom of expression is continuously redefined and disputed for the sake of the national community's interests, as opposed to the rights of individuals.

The disciplinization of religion for political goals is hardly specific to Muslim-majority countries. The legislation against the hijab and niqab in European countries, for example, proceeds from the same logic. The conflation of the moral hierarchy of gender roles and the legitimacy of the political community, however, is specific to Muslim countries. We have seen how Islamic prescriptions can be used to redefine the good citizen, particularly during periods of political instability. The principles of family are evoked to mitigate social change, as greater social mobility for both men and women threatens the existing governmental structure and power. These principles of family feed into the dominant status of gender hierarchies, politicizing what had been strictly part of the social sphere in premodern Muslim societies. As conceptions of family become entangled with political consciousness and the formation of national identity, Islam gets construed in a way that permits gender inequality as a means of maintaining social harmony. The control of women and maintenance of gendered moral hierarchies provide a sense of national security and authority over conditions of social change that otherwise cannot be easily controlled.

Preeminence of the Community over the Religious Self

We have also seen in the previous chapters that ritual actions that take a public dimension shape the religious self. In all of the countries surveyed, a combination of culturally constructed values (*adab*) and Islamic law creates social customs, which emphasize the social over the individual being. In other words, daily interactions reinforce the idea that the self is subdued to social obligations. This standard extends to the very definition of equality. Whereas in the West uniform sets of individual rights define equality, in the countries studied, equality entails the equal obligation of individuals to promote communal welfare. This definition therefore has consequences for freedom of speech. Similarly, moral obligations to the family allow no room for the promotion of self above the interests of the community. Therefore, any conception of female emancipation beyond that allowed by religion is regarded as dissonant with the cultural values of the nation, often defined in religious terms.

A case in point is the controversy created by Turkish prime minister Recep Tayyip Erdoğan when he told a gathering of the women's branches of his Justice and Development Party that "each abortion is one Uludere"—a reference to air strikes on a village on the Iraqi border that killed thirty-four civilians in December 2011. Abortions, said the prime minister, were "a sneaky plan to wipe the country off the world stage."[13] It is worth noting that the same rhetoric is present in Western democracies, as shown by the political agenda of some Christian groups in the United States.

Generally speaking, gendered roles in the family reflect a hierarchy of social positions and purposes. These directly affect women's lives in both the private and the public spheres. At the core of the nationalist ideology of the Muslim countries surveyed lies an element of self-preservation in order to secure moral capital in a rapidly westernizing world. Globalization and consumerism pose threats to the social composition of Muslim communities, as they are viewed as contributing to moral depravity. Within this globalizing cultural setting, in which the terms and values of social relations are mutating, the reflex in most Muslim countries is to subordinate the rights of individuals, frequently women, to the preservation of social cohesion and political welfare. For this purpose, government officials have relied on the preestablished moral capital of religion and familial structure to control the social upheaval stirred by Western influences. Consequentially, women's behavior and sexuality often become restricted.

Presently, control of women's bodies and sexuality has guaranteed both continuity and stability in the public sphere. Likewise, securing a gendered moral hierarchy in the private sphere safeguards social harmony and political stability. Religious and political leaders alike reinforce the presumption of the women's role in family and society. The result is continuous tensions over the legitimate definition of women's rights. This sets advocates of self-empowerment against protectors of the political community, which is defined in Islamic terms.

It is important to note that the female body is a topic through which many Islamic religious authorities and institutions have critiqued postmodern society.[14] Islam serves as a countercultural voice that simultaneously rebukes Western cultural hegemony and serves political interests. Politicians and religious authorities in Middle Eastern countries critique the West by conveniently pitting Islam and secular values against the female body. The female body thus becomes a major site of cultural and political tension between the West and Islam, the past and present, and individual and collective rights.

Nonetheless, religious norms and references cannot be contained within national boundaries, especially at a time of global communication and expedited circulation of ideas that increase debate over Islamic orthodoxy. This means that circulation of ideas, along with transnational cultural agents who influence Islamic religiosity, increasingly challenge state policies, as attested by the rise of global radical Islamic movements.

Muslim Democracy: An Oxymoron?

The response to such a trite question is not a straight yes or no. First and foremost, the combination of religious prescriptions with secular principles of democracy is in and of itself a challenge for individual rights. Religious prescriptions translate into different duties according to the gender and age of the believer. Even in Western secular democracies, we can see that some of these religious prescriptions on abortion, contraception, and sexuality can for some citizens conflict with the indiscriminate tenets of secular law. In this respect, disputes over the role of Islamic parties and their legitimacy across countries stem from disagreements about how these principles can and should be implemented in secular laws and whether these rules should apply to all citizens, believers or not. I have discussed above when and how Islam can influence democratic governance and emphasized the role of Islamic prescriptions in the limitation of individual rights, especially when it comes to gender equality and freedom of speech. In these conditions, the question is no longer about the possibility of a Muslim democracy. It is instead about which dimension of political Islam influences which domain of democracy. Most scholars agree that there is no clear-cut distinction between democracy and nondemocracy and that most regimes today fall between these two opposites and can be described as hybrid.[15] As such, they lack one or more of the following features that define democracy:

1. Free and fair elections
2. Separation of powers
3. Rule of law and independence of the judiciary
4. Civil liberties

Since most Islamic movements operate within authoritarian regimes that do not respect most of these features, assessing the influence of Islamic groups or parties on each of these domains is not an easy task. Nevertheless, political experiences in Egypt, Morocco, Indonesia, Tunisia, Senegal, and Turkey show that most of the Islamic movements have come to terms with elections and operate within the framework of the nation-state. Rather, the separation of powers and judicial independence are more ambiguous. This is attested by the praetorian role of religious authority in the Islamic Republic of Iran, along with the turn to authoritarianism observed in the last five years in Turkey under AKP rule. The exception is Tunisia since the Jasmine Revolution, where the majority Islamic party has instituted the four major features of democratization mentioned above.

In the case of democracies such as Senegal and Indonesia, where elections and separation of powers do exist, the most controversial aspects concern the limits imposed on freedom of speech and sexual orientation by Islamic prescriptions. Some refer to this situation, for example in the case of Indonesia, as illiberal democracy.[16] Nonetheless, such qualifications are confusing because they imply that these limitations come primarily from Islamic actors, when in fact the so-called liberal or secular actors also implement them.

As noted above, although individual rights are acknowledged (e.g., vote, freedom of press), rights of the self are limited when it comes to blasphemy, sexual orientation, and gender relations, because they are seen as impinging on the morality of the political community. This tension between self and community is a challenge even in well-established democracies. Many analysts have pointed out that the polarization of the political debate in the 2016 American presidential elections reflects the social, economic, and cultural divides that plague the country. In other words, Donald Trump's voters tend to be middle Americans, left behind by the growth of a service economy, whose lifestyle is scorned (often called "white trash" or "redneck"). We can go one step further and argue that this political split also derives from the tension between the validation of the self and the interests of the community, especially when religion is at stake. Debates on abortion, contraception, and sexual minorities draw a line between, on one side, the partisans of the self's right to make choices regarding the body and, on the other side, the defenders of a moral order that defines the "good" American society. Evidently, the voters for Trump and Hillary Clinton did not fall neatly into these two camps. But the tension between self and community was a cultural and political dilemma that fueled the uneasiness of citizens vis-à-vis both candidates. It is also the predicament easiest to underestimate because it intersects with other, more obvious splits around class, education, consumption, and lifestyle.

In the case of Muslim states, not all countries are characterized by the same level of tension between self and community; nor do they address it the same way. Nonetheless, it is evident—from the states of women's rights, freedom of speech, and attitudes toward sexual orientation—that the self remains limited by the fate of the religious community and that the boundaries of this religious community overlap with those of the national and/or political community.

Could Islamic political cultures evolve toward more inclusive forms of civil religion in the future? Judging by the pollings mentioned above, a significant majority of Muslim citizens would think so. The biggest challenge to changing political Islam into civil religion is not only institutional but also cultural, as shown *a contrario* by the positive example of Senegal, where religious identities are embedded within a broader ethos of sociability revolving around ethnicity and territory. More generally, it seems that the more independent the religion is from the state, the higher the probability of a more inclusive, pluralist approach to civil society. Nonetheless, the current regional and international contexts, along with high concerns about security, tend to push all states and even citizens in the opposite direction: toward more control and regulation of religion.

Notes

1. Bayat, Asef. *Post-Islamism: The Many Faces of Political Islam.* Oxford: Oxford University Press, 2013.

2. Williams, Rhys H. "Religion as Political Resource: Culture or Ideology?" *Journal for the Scientific Study of Religion* 35, no. 4 (1996): 368–378.

3. Ibid., 370.

4. Brown, Nathan J. *Arguing Islam After the Revival of Arab Politics.* New York: Oxford University Press, 2017.

5. Wormald, Benjamin. "The World's Muslims: Religion, Politics and Society." Pew Research Center's Religion and Public Life Project. April 30, 2013. http://www.pewforum.org/2013/04/30/the-worlds-muslims-religion-politics -society-overview.

6. Ibid.

7. Ibid.

8. Tabah Foundation. "Muslim Millennial Attitudes on Religion and Religious Leadership." Futures Initiative at Tabah Foundation. 2016. http://mmgsurvey .tabahfoundation.org/downloads/mmgsurvey_full_En_web.pdf.

9. Ibid.

10. Cristi, Marcela. *From Civil to Political Religion: The Intersection of Culture, Religion and Politics.* Waterloo, ON: Wilfrid Laurier University Press, 2001.

11. Wormald, "The World's Muslims."

12. "World Values Survey Database." World Values Survey. Accessed January 7, 2017. http://www.worldvaluessurvey.org/WVSOnline.jsp.

13. Vela, Justin. "'Abortions Are like Air Strikes on Civilians': Turkish PM Recep Tayyip Erdogan's Rant Sparks Women's Rage." *Independent.* May 30, 2012. http://www.independent.co.uk/life-style/health-and-families/health-news/abortions -are-like-air-strikes-on-civilians-turkish-pm-recep-tayyip-erdogans-rant-sparks -womens-rage-7800939.html. It should be noted that abortions are currently legal in Turkey.

14. See, for example, the religious positions of Salafi groups that define moral positions through control of the body, in Meijer, Roel. *Global Salafism: Islam's New Religious Movement.* New York: Columbia University Press, 2009.

15. Levitsky, Steven, and Lucan Way. "The Rise of Competitive Authoritarianism." *Journal of Democracy* 13, no. 2 (2002): 51–65.

16. Menchik, Jeremy. *Islam and Democracy in Indonesia: Tolerance Without Liberalism.* New York: Cambridge University Press, 2016.

Glossary

adab   culturally constructed values
âdâb ijtimâ'îya   good social behavior
Ahl al-Kitab   People of the Book, that is, Jews and Christians
akhlaqul karimah   good morals
al-Ka'bah   Allah's house
al-mahakim al-ahliyyah   Native Courts
al-mahakim al-wataniyyah   National Courts
al-mahkim al-mukhtaltah   Mixed Courts system
al-maslahah al-mursalah   public interest
al-qanun   nonreligiously based set of laws
al-walâya wa al-barâ'a   loyalty and enmity
aql   man's capacity to understand, comprehend, think about, and appreciate
   Allah's creatures
Ashab al-Feel   People of the Elephant
awqaf   religious endowments
batil   void
confréries   religious orders
dahiras   community groups
dar al-harb   abode of war
dar al-Islam   abode of Islam
dawah   proselytization or preaching
dhimmīs   religious minorities under the caliphates
faqih (**pl.** *fuqaha)*   jurisconsult(s)
fatwa   religious ruling
fiqh   Islamic jurisprudence
gammus   ceremonies
halal   permitted
halqa   a circle of study around a shaikh
haram   forbidden
hashiya   supercommentary
hifdz al-'aql   the intellect
hifdz al-din   the religion
hifdz al-mal   the property

201

hifdz al-nafs the body
hifdz al-nasl the lineage
hijra migration
hudud criminal punishments in Islamic jurisprudence
ijma juristic consensus
ijtihad interpretation
ikhtilaf disagreement between schools of jurisprudence
infitah economic liberalization
istihsan juristic preference
jahiliyyah state of ignorance, barbarity, and idolatry pervading the Muslim world
  before the revelation of the Prophet Muhammad
jizya tax required from non-Muslims who lived under the caliphates
jus ad bellum modes of initiating war
jus in bello modes of conducting war
kafir infidel, heretic
kalante kinship joke
khalife caliph
laïcité French version of secularism
langues nationales national languages
madhahib traditional Sunni schools of jurisprudence
madrasah diniyah mandatory after-school religious education
maggals celebrations
Mahdi messianic figure who will reestablish the true religion and rule for seven,
  eight, or nine years before the end of the world
maleki the school of jurisprudence founded by Malik ibn Anas in the eighth
  century
maqasid al-Shari'a foundational goals of Islam
maslaha common good
mawdui topics
mektebs Quran schools
millet religious communities in the Ottoman Empire
mujaddid renewer
mujahidat female fighters against the French in Algeria
mujahidin combatants
mujtahidin interpreters
mukhtasar summaries
mukhtasarat compendium of legal rules
musta'mins non-Muslim foreigners living temporarily in the abode of Islam
mu'tamad official opinion within the schools of jurisprudence
nas people
ndigels vote instructions
peraturan daerah or *perda* regional regulation
perda injil regional regulation inspired by biblical values
perda syariah Islamically based regulations
qadi judge
qiyas analogical deduction used in the production of legal interpretations in
  the four schools of jurisprudence
risala message
rwh al-Shari'a the spirit of the law
sabb blasphemy
Salaf early Companions of the Prophet Muhammad

Salafiyya reformist religious thought

şeyhülislam mufti at the head of the Ottoman
religious hierarchy

shafi'i one of the four schools of Islamic law in Sunni Islam, founded by the
Arab scholar Al-Shafi'i, a pupil of Malik, in the early ninth century

sharh commentary

shura consultation

siyaare communal visits by disciples to their marabouts

siyasa shariyya governmental implementation of Muslim law

syar laws that apply to non-Muslims living under caliphate rule or to the relations between the caliphate and non-Muslims at the international level

tafriq one of the forms of divorce recognized by Islamic law. It relies on the
court to order the divorce in the case of absence of the husband, or upon his
refusal to consider the wife's petition

takfiri Muslim who accuses another Muslim (or an adherent of another Abra-
hamic faith) of apostasy

takhayyur practice of choosing which rules to follow from various schools of
Islamic Law

talaq divorce procedure initiated by the husband

talfiq legal term describing the derivation of rules from material of various
schools of Islamic law

talibes students or followers

tammadun progress

taqlid tradition

tariqa Sufi order

tawassut middle way

ta'zir punishment for offenses at the discretion of the judge or the sultan

teranga hospitality

ulama Islamic scholars

ummah community

ummah muslimah Muslim community

ummah wahida one community

wasa'il means

wasiat wajibah obligatory bequest

watan nation

zakat almsgiving

Bibliography

Abdelmassih, Mary. "Coptic Christian Woman Unwittingly Becomes Focal Point of Islamic Clash with Christianity." *Assyrian International News Agency.* November 12, 2010. http://www.aina.org/news/20101111233506.htm.

Abouharb, M. Rodwan., and David L. Cingranelli. *Human Rights and Structural Adjustment.* Cambridge: Cambridge University Press, 2007.

Akyol, Mustafa. "Why Is Turkey Reviving an Ottoman Sultan?" *Al-Monitor.* September 29, 2016. http://www.al-monitor.com/pulse/originals/2016/09/turkey-reviving-sultan-abdulhamid-ii.html.

al-Afghani, Jamal al-Din. "Wa-I'tasimu Bi-habl Allah Jami'an Wala Tafarraqu." *Al-Manar* (Cairo) 24 (1923).

Al-Baghdadi, Abu Bakr. "A Message to the Mujahidin and the Muslim Ummah in the Month of Ramadan." Al-Hayat Media Center. 2014. https://www.gatestoneinstitute.org/documents/baghdadi-caliph.pdf.

Al-Banna, Hasan. *Bayn al-ams wa'l-yawm* (Between yesterday and today). Beirut: Ar-Risalah, n.d.

Aldeeb, Sami. "Religious Teaching in Egypt and Switzerland." Text sent to the symposium organized by the Movement for Human Rights. Beirut, Lebanon, 2000.

Algar, Hamid. *Wahhabism: A Critical Essay.* North Aledon, NJ: Islamic Publications International, 2002.

al-Ghannouchi, Rachi. "Enahda Program Does Not Include Shari'a." *Al-Majalla.* October 3, 2011. http://arb.majalla.com/2011/10/article55227372/ تطبي-النهضة-برنامج-في-ليس-الغنوشي-راشد.

Al-Muhairi, Butti Sultan Butti Ali. "The Incompatibility of the Penal Code with Shari'a." *Arab Law Quarterly* 12, no. 3 (1997): 307–329.

"Al-Qaradawi's Statement on Shiites." Islamopedia Online. April 22, 2010. http://www.islamopediaonline.org/fatwa/al-qaradawis-statement-shiites.

al-Sibai, Mustafa. "Islamic Socialism." In *Arab Socialism*, edited by Sami A. Hanna and George H. Gardner, 66–79. Leiden: Brill, 1969.

al-Ṭahṭāwī, Rifāʿah. *al-Qawl al-Sadid Fi al-Ijtihad Wa al-Tajdid.* Cairo: Matbaʿat wadi al-neel, 1867.

al-Ṭahṭāwī, Rifāʿah, and Daniel L. Newman. *An Imam in Paris: Account of a Stay in France by an Egyptian Cleric, 1826–1831.* London: Saqi, 2004.

Altikriti, Anas. "Hamas Is Not al-Qaida." *Guardian.* September 21, 2009. http://www.guardian.co.uk/commentisfree/2009/sep/21/hamas-al-qaida.

Amal, T. A. *Politik syariat Islam: Dari Indonesia hingga Nigeria.* Ciputat, Jakarta: Pustaka Alvabet, 2004.

Amarah, Muhammed. *Risalat al-tawhid lil Imam Muhammad Abduh.* Cairo, Egypt: Dar al-Shoruq, 1994.

American Center for Law and Justice. "Religious Freedom and Persecution in Egypt." 2009. http://media.aclj.org/pdf/egypt_memo.pdf.

Archer, Toby. "Welcome to the Ummah: The British State and Its Muslim Citizens Since 9/11." *Cooperation and Conflict* 44, no. 3 (2009): 327–349.

Asad, Talal. *Formations of the Secular: Christianity, Islam, Modernity.* Stanford, CA: Stanford University Press, 2003.

Assyaukanie, Luthfi. *Islam and the Secular State in Indonesia.* Singapore: Institute of Southeast Asian Studies, 2009.

Awad, Lewis. "Bahth jari can Jamal al-Dyn al-Afghani; al-Irani al-ghamid ft Misr." *Al-Tadamon* no. 1:1–no. 1:22 (April 16–September 10, 1983).

Ayalon, Ami. *Language and Change in the Arab Middle East: The Evolution of Modern Political Discourse.* New York: Oxford University Press, 1987.

Babou, Cheikh Anta. "Brotherhood Solidarity, Education, and Migration: The Role of the *Dahiras* Among the Murid Muslim Community of New York." *African Affairs* 101, no. 403 (2002): 151–170.

Barro, Robert J., and Rachel M. McCleary. *International Determinants of Religiosity.* Cambridge, MA: National Bureau of Economic Research, 2003.

Başkanlığı, Diyanet İşleri. *Kuruluşundan günümüze Diyanet işleri başkanlığı: Tarihçe-teşkilat-hizmet ve faaliyetler (1924–1997).* Ankara: Türkiye Diyanet Vakfı, 1999.

Bayat, Asef. *Post-Islamism: The Many Faces of Political Islam.* Oxford: Oxford University Press, 2013.

Beaman, Lori G. "The Myth of Pluralism, Diversity, and Vigor: The Constitutional Privilege of Protestantism in the United States and Canada." *Journal for the Scientific Study of Religion* 42, no. 3 (2003): 311–325.

Beaumont, Peter. "Hamas Destroys al-Qaida in Violent Gaza Battle." *Guardian.* August 16, 2009. http://www.guardian.co.uk/world/2009/aug/15/hamas-battle-gaza-islamists-al-qaida.

Beck, Colin J. "State Building as a Source of Islamic Political Organization." *Sociological Forum* 24, no. 2 (June 2009): 337–356.

"Being LGBT in Indonesia: Country Report." UNDP in Asia and the Pacific. 2014. http://www.asia-pacific.undp.org/content/dam/rbap/docs/Research%20&%20Publications/hiv_aids/rbap-hhd-2014-blia-indonesia-country-report-english.pdf.

Bellah, Robert N. "Civil Religion in America." *Daedalus* 134, no. 4 (2005): 40–55.

———. "Islamic Tradition and the Problem of Modernization." *Beyond Belief: Essays on Religion in a Post-traditional World.* New York: Harper & Row, 1991.

Berger, Maurits. "Apostasy and Public Policy in Contemporary Egypt: An Evaluation of Recent Cases from Egypt's Highest Courts." *Human Rights Quarterly* 25, no. 3 (2003): 720–740.

bin Laden, Osama. "Declaration of Jihad Against Americans Occupying the Land of the Two Holy Mosques." August 1996. http://college.cengage.com/history/primary_sources/world/two_holy_mosques.htm.

Bostom, Andrew G. *The Legacy of Jihad: Islamic Holy War and the Fate of Non-Muslims.* Amherst, NY: Prometheus Books, 2005.

Brown, Nathan J. *Arguing Islam After the Revival of Arab Politics.* New York: Oxford University Press, 2017.

Brown, Nathan J., and Adel Omar Sherif. "Inscribing the Islamic Shari'a in Arab Constitutional Law." In *Islamic Law and the Challenges of Modernity*, edited by Yvonne Yazbeck Haddad and Barbara Freyer Stowasser, 53–80. Walnut Creek, CA: Altamira: 2004.

Bruinessen, Martin Van. "Islamic State or State Islam? Fifty Years of State-Islam Relations in Indonesia." In *Indonesien am Ende des 20*, edited by Ingrid Jahrhunderts. Hamburg: Abera-Verlag, 1996.

Bryson, Jennifer S. "Egyptian Parliament Attempts to Repeal Blasphemy Law." *Arc of the Universe*. May 12, 2016. http://arcoftheuniverse.info/egyptian-parliament-attempts-to-repeal-blasphemy-law.

Buku guru: SMP/KTs kelas 08 pendidikan agama Islam dan budi pekerti. Jakarta: Kementerian Pendidikan dan Kebudayaan, 2013.

Buku guru: SMP/MTs kelas 09 pendidikan agama Islam dan budi pekerti. Jakarta: Kementerian Pendidikan dan Kebudayaan, 2015.

Buku guru kementerian kelas 11–12 pendidikan agama Islam dan budi pekerti. Jakarta: Kementerian Pendidikan dan Kebudayaan, 2015.

Bulliet, Richard W. "The Shaikh Al-Islām and the Evolution of Islamic Society." *Studia Islamica* 35 (1972): 53–67.

Burgis, Michelle. "Faith in the State? Traditions of Territoriality, International Law and the Emergence of Modern Arab Statehood." *Journal of the History of International Law* 11, no. 1 (2009): 37–79.

Butt, Simon. "Asia-Pacific: Illegitimate Children and Inheritance in Indonesia." *Alternative Law Journal* 37, no. 3 (2012): 196–198.

———. "Polygamy and Mixed Marriage in Indonesia: Islam and the Marriage Law in the Courts." In *Indonesia: Law and Society*, edited by Tim Lindsey. Sydney: Federation Press, 1999.

Calhoun, Craig. *Nationalism*. Concepts Social Thought. Minneapolis: University of Minnesota Press, 1998.

Camara, Samba. "Political Islam and the Negotiation of Political Roles Among Peripheral Sufi Leaders in Senegal." *International Journal of Political Science and Development* 2, no. 6 (2014): 105–116.

Cammack, Mark. "Indonesia's 1989 Religious Judicature Act: Islamization of Indonesia or Indonesianization of Islam?" *Indonesia* 63 (1997): 143–168.

Cammack, Mark, and Michael Feener. "The Islamic Legal System in Indonesia." *Pacific Rim Law & Policy Journal* 21, no. 1 (2012): 13–42.

Cammett, Melani Claire. *Compassionate Communalism: Welfare and Sectarianism in Lebanon*. Ithaca, NY: Cornell University Press, 2014.

Candraningrum, Dwei. *The Challenge of Teaching English in Indonesian's Muhammadiyah Universities (1958–2005): Mainstreaming Gender Through Postcolonial Muslim Women Writers*. Berlin: Lit, 2008.

Cardinal, Monique. "Islamic Legal Theory Curriculum: Are the Classics Taught Today?" *Islamic Law and Society* 12, no. 2 (2005): 224–272.

Carre, Olivier. "L'Ideologie politico-religieuse nasserienne a la lumiere des manuels scolaires." *Politique Etrangere* 37 (1972): 535–553.

Castle, Chris, Moustapha Diagne, Dominique Gomis, Amadou Mody Moreau, Cheikh Ibrahima Niang, Karim Seck, Placide Tapsoba, Ellen Weiss, and Abdoulaye Sidbé Wade. "'It's Raining Stones': Stigma, Violence and HIV Vulnerability Among Men Who Have Sex with Men in Dakar, Senegal." *Culture, Health & Sexuality* 5, no. 6 (2003): 499–512.

Cesari, Jocelyne. *The Awakening of Muslim Democracy: Religion, Modernity, and the State*. New York: Cambridge University Press, 2014.

———. "Disciplining Religion: The Role of the State and Its Consequences on Democracy." *Journal of Religious and Political Practice* 2, no. 2 (2016): 134–154.

————. *Why the West Fears Islam: Exploration of Muslims in Western Liberal Democracies.* New York: Palgrave Macmillan, 2013.

Cesari, Jocelyne, and Jonathan Fox. "Institutional Relations Rather Than Clash of Civilizations? When and How Is Religion Compatible with Democracy?" *International Political Sociology* 10, no. 3 (2016): 241–257.

"The Chair for Human Rights' Suggestion Does Not Correspond to the Moroccan Identity." *Jadid Presse.* November 1, 2015. http://www.jadidpresse .com/ الوطني-المجلس-أطروحة-زعزاع-المالك-عبد.

Chaumont, E. "Al-S̲h̲aybānī, Abū ʿAbd Allāh Muḥammad b. al-Ḥasan b. Farḳad." In *Encyclopaedia of Islam,* edited by P. Bearman, T. Bianquis, C. E. Bosworth, E. van Donzel, and W. P. Heinrichs. Leiden: Brill Publishers, 2008.

Chaves, Mark, Peter J. Schraeder, and Mario Sprindys. "State Regulation of Religion and Muslim Religious Vitality in the Industrialized West." *Journal of Politics* 56, no. 4 (1994): 1087–1097.

Clark, Janine A. *Islam, Charity, and Activism: Middle-Class Networks and Social Welfare in Egypt, Jordan, and Yemen.* Bloomington: Indiana University Press, 2004.

"Coast-to-Coast Anti-Islam Movement Results in Protests, Attacks Against Mosques." Real Courage. July 22, 2010. http://www.realcourage.org/2010 /07/coast-to-coast.

Cochrane, Joe. "'Beef-Gate' Transfixes Scandal-Prone Indonesia." *New York Times.* May 16, 2013. http://www.nytimes.com/2013/05/17/world/asia/beefgate -transfixes-scandal-prone-indonesia.html.

"Compulsory Religious Education an Abuse of Human Rights, Says European Court." National Secular Society. October 12, 2007. www.secularism.org .uk/compulsoryreligiouseducationanab.html.

"Constitution de la République du Senegal." Government of Senegal. 2001. http://www.constitutionnet.org/vl/item/constitution-de-la-republique-du -senegal-du-22-janvier-2001. Translation by author.

"A Conversation with El Hadji Baye Lamine Niass, Niassene Family of the Tijaniyya Confrérie in Senegal." Berkley Center for Religion, Peace, and World Affairs. November 17, 2014. https://berkleycenter.georgetown.edu /interviews/a-conversation-with-el-hadji-baye-lamine-niass-niassene-family -of-the-tijaniyya-confrérie-in-senegal.

Cornell, Svante E. "The Islamization of Turkey: Erdoğan's Education Reforms." *Turkey Analyst.* September 2, 2015. http://www.turkeyanalyst.org/publications /turkey-analyst-articles/item/437-the-Islamization-of-turkey-erdoğan's-education -reforms.html.

Cristi, Marcela. *From Civil to Political Religion: The Intersection of Culture, Religion and Politics.* Waterloo, ON, Canada: Wilfrid Laurier University Press, 2001.

Croft-Cusworth, Catriona. "Why Islamic Parties Don't Win Indonesian Elections." Lowy Institute. March 31, 2014. https://www.lowyinstitute.org/the -interpreter/why-islamic-parties-dont-win-indonesian-elections.

Cuno, Kenneth M. "Reorganization of the Sharia Courts of Egypt: How Legal Modernization Set Back Women's Rights in the Nineteenth Century." *Journal of the Ottoman and Turkish Studies Association* 2, no. 1 (2015): 85–99.

Dakroub, Hussein. "Beheading Condemned by Hamas and Hizbollah." *Independent.* May 14, 2004. http://www.independent.co.uk/news/world/middle -east/beheading-condemned-by-hamas-and-hizbollah-563351.html.

Daslani, Pitan. "Commentary: Rhoma's Idaman Party Promotes Islam as Religion of Peace." *Jakarta Globe.* December 2, 2016. http://jakartaglobe.id /opinion/commentary-rhomas-idaman-party-promotes-islam-religion-peace.

Dawisha, Adeed. "'Identity' and Political Survival in Saddam's Iraq." *Middle East Journal* 53, no. 4 (1999): 553–567.

Debs, Richard A., Frank E. Vogel, and Al-Sayyid Ridwan. "The Development of a National Legal System." In *Islamic Law and Civil Code: The Law of Property in Egypt*, 98–115. New York: Columbia University Press, 2010.

Denny, Frederick Mathewson. *Islam and the Muslim Community*. San Francisco: Harper & Row, 1987.

Dessouki, Ali. "Official Islam and Political Legitimation in the Arab Countries." In *Islamic Impulse*, edited by Barbara Freyer Stowasser, 135–141. London: Croom Helm, 1987.

Devereux, Robert. *The First Ottoman Constitutional Period: A Study of the Midhat Constitution and Parliament*. Baltimore: Johns Hopkins University Press, 1964.

Diallo, El Hadji Samba, and Catherine Lena Kelly. "Sufi Turuq and the Politics of Democratization in Senegal." *Journal of Religious and Political Practice* 2, no. 2 (2016): 193–211.

Diouf, Mamadou. "The Senegalese Murid Trade Diaspora and the Making of a Vernacular Cosmopolitanism." Translated by Steven Rendall. *Public Culture* 12 (2000): 679–702.

"A Discussion with Cheikh Djibril Diop Laye, Imam and Member of the Layene Order of Senegal." Berkley Center for Religion, Peace, and World Affairs. November 17, 2014. https://berkleycenter.georgetown.edu/interviews/a -discussion-with-cheikh-djibril-diop-laye-imam-and-member-of-the-layene -order-of-senegal.

"A Discussion with Sheikh Saliou Mbacke, Continental Coordinator of IFAPA." Berkley Center for Religion, Peace, and World Affairs. July 3, 2014. https:// berkleycenter.georgetown.edu/interviews/a-discussion-with-sheikh-saliou -mbacke-continental-coordinator-of-ifapa.

"Diversity and Tolerance in the Islam of West Africa." Africa Online Digital Library. Accessed December 23, 2016. http://aodl.org/islamictolerance.

"A Divine Law and a Nation Supported by Divine Victory, These Are the Two Pillars of the Building of a Just State." شريعة ربانية وأمة مؤيدة بالنصر الإلهي، هذان هما الركنان الأساسيان في بناء الدولة العادل. Al 'Adl Wa Al Ihsane. January 20, 2012. http://www.aljamaa.net/ar/document /51883.shtml.

Dixon, Valerie. "Land of the Free, Home of the Mosque near Ground Zero." *On Faith* (blog), *Washington Post*. July 21, 2010. http://newsweek.washingtonpost .com/onfaith/panelists/valerie_elverton_dixon/2010/07/the_mosque_a_fitting _response.html.

"Document—The Unreleased Interview with Usamah bin Laden—21st October 2001." Terrorisme.net. August 19, 2016. http://www.terrorisme.net/2002/08 /19/obl-interview.

Doumato, Eleanor Abdella, and Gregory Starrett. *Teaching Islam: Textbooks and Religion in the Middle East*. London: Lynne Rienner Publishers, 2007.

Duara, Prasenjit. *Rescuing History from the Nation: Questioning Narratives of Modern China*. Chicago: University of Chicago Press, 1997.

Earle, Edward Mead. "The New Constitution of Turkey." *Political Science Quarterly* 40, no. 1 (1925): 73.

El-Affendi, Abdelwahab. *Who Needs an Islamic State?* London: Grey Seal, 1991.

Eliade, Mircea. *Myths, Dreams, and Mysteries: The Encounter Between Contemporary Faiths and Archaic Realities*. New York: Harper, 1961.

Eltahawy, Mona. "Eygpt's War on Atheism." *New York Times*. January 27, 2015. http://www.nytimes.com/2015/01/28/opinion/mona-eltahawy-egypts-war-on -atheism.html.

Emon, Anver M. "Codification and Islamic Law: The Ideology Behind a Tragic Narrative." *Middle East Law and Governance* 8 (2016): 275–309.

Esposito, John, and John Voll. *Makers of Contemporary Islam.* Oxford: Oxford University Press, 2011.

Fadl, Khaled Abou El. *The Great Theft: Wrestling Islam from the Extremists.* New York: HarperSanFrancisco, 2007.

Fahlesa Munarabi. "Islamic Activism: The Socio-political Dynamics of the Indonesian Forum of Islamic Society (FUI)." PhD diss., University of New South Wales, 2016.

Faisal, Devji. *Landscapes of Jihad: Militancy, Morality, Modernity.* Ithaca, NY: Cornell University Press, 2005.

Fakhry, Majid. "The Theocratic Idea of the Islamic State in Recent Controversie." *International Affairs* (Royal Institute of International Affairs 1944–) 30, no. 4 (October 1954): 450–462.

Feldman, Noah. "A Lesson for Newt Gingrich: What Shari'a Is (and Isn't)." *New York Times.* July 17, 2016. https://www.nytimes.com/2016/07/17/opinion/sunday/a-lesson-for-newt-gingrich-what-shariah-is-and-isnt.html.

Findley, Carter Vaughn. "The Advent of Ideology in the Islamic Middle East (Part II)." *Studia Islamica* 56 (1982): 147–180.

———. *Turkey, Islam, Nationalism, and Modernity: A History, 1789–2007.* New Haven, CT: Yale University Press, 2010.

Finkel, Andrew. "What's 4+4+4?" *Latitude* (blog), *New York Times.* March 23, 2012. http://latitude.blogs.nytimes.com/2012/03/23/turkeys-education-reform-bill-is-about-playing-politics-with-pedagogy.

Fortna, Benjamin C. "Education and Autobiography at the End of the Ottoman Empire." *Die Welt Des Islams,* n.s., 41, no. 1 (2001): 1–31.

Foucault, Michel. *The Government of Self and Others: Lectures at the Collège de France, 1982–1983.* Edited by Arnold I. Davidson. Translated by Graham Burchell. Houndmills, Basingstoke, Hampshire, UK: Palgrave Macmillan, 2010.

Fox, Jonathan. *Political Secularism, Religion, and the State: A Time Series Analysis of Worldwide Data.* Cambridge: Cambridge University Press, 2015.

Fox, Jonathan, and Shmuel Sandler. *Bringing Religion into International Relations.* New York: Palgrave Macmillan, 2004.

Friedland, Roger. "Money, Sex, and God: The Erotic Logic of Religious Nationalism." *Sociological Theory* 20, no. 3 (2002): 381–425.

Fulton, Lauren. "A Muted Controversy: Freedom of Speech in Turkey." *Harvard International Review* 30 (2008): 26–29.

Galal, Rami. "Sisi's Call for Religious Tolerance Divides Muslims." *Al-Monitor.* May 25, 2015. http://www.al-monitor.com/pulse/originals/2015/05/egypt-salafist-sufi-religion-extremism-azhar-quran-sheikh.html.

Gardella, Rich. "Insurgent Groups Condemn al-Qaida Tactics." *NBC News.* October 16, 2007. http://www.msnbc.msn.com/id/21267335.

Gelling, Peter. "Indonesia Bans Sects It Deems Blasphemous." *New York Times.* November 16, 2007. http://www.nytimes.com/2007/11/16/world/asia/16indo.html.

Gerges, Fawaz A. *Why Jihad Went Global.* Cambridge: Cambridge University Press, 2005.

Gesink, Indira. *Islamic Reform and Conservatism: Al-Azhar and the Evolution of Modern Sunni Islam.* New York: I. B. Tauris, 2014.

Ghosh, Ranjan. *Making Sense of the Secular: Critical Perspectives from Europe to Asia.* New York: Routledge, 2013.

Glover, John. "The Prophet Muhammad Reincarnated and His Son, Jesus: Re-centering Islam Among the Layenne of Senegal." *Journal of Historical Geography* 42 (2013): 24–35.

———. *Sufism and Jihad in Modern Senegal: The Murid Order.* Rochester, NY: University of Rochester Press, 2007.

Gözaydın, İştar. *Diyanet, Türkiye Cumhuriyeti'nde Dinin Tanzimi.* Istanbul: Iletisim Yayinlari, 2009.

Graham, William A. "Traditionalism in Islam: An Essay in Interpretation." *Journal of Interdisciplinary History* 23, no. 3 (1993): 495–522.

Gramsci, Antonio, and David Forgacs. *The Gramsci Reader: Selected Writings, 1916–1935.* London: Lawrence and Wishart, 1999.

"Grand Ayatollah al-Baghdadi of Iraq Discourages the Participation of Muslims in International Policy Organizations." Islamopaedia Online. April 22, 2010. http://www.islamopediaonline.org/fatwa/grand-ayatollah-al-baghdadi-iraq -discourages-participation-muslims-international-policy-organi.

Greenfeld, Liah, ed. *Globalization of Nationalism: The Motive-Force Behind Twenty-First Century Politics.* Colchester, UK: ECPR Press, 2016.

Greenslade, Roy. "Egyptian Student Jailed for Proclaiming That He Is an Atheist." *Guardian.* January 13, 2015. https://www.theguardian.com/media /greenslade/2015/jan/13/egyptian-student-jailed-for-proclaiming-that-he-is -an-atheist.

Grim, Brian J., and Roger Finke. *The Price of Freedom Denied: Religious Persecution and Conflict in the 21st Century.* New York: Cambridge University Press, 2011.

Guèye, Cheikh. *Touba: La capitale des mourides.* Paris: Karthala Editions, 2002.

Gueye, Mame Safiétou Djamil. "Genre et gouvernance urbaine au Sénégal: La participation des femmes à la gestion urbaine." In *Thèses de la Faculté des sciences économiques, sociales, politiques et de communication.* Louvain-la-Neuve, Belgium: Presses Universitaires de Louvain, 2009.

Hafez, Mohammed M. *Why Muslims Rebel: Repression and Resistance in the Islamic World.* Boulder, CO: Lynne Rienner Publishers, 2003.

Haim, Sylvia G. *Arab Nationalism: An Anthology.* Berkeley: University of California Press, 1962.

Hallaq, Wael B. *The Impossible State: Islam, Politics, and Modernity's Moral Predicament.* New York: Columbia University Press, 2012.

———. *An Introduction to Islamic Law.* New York: Cambridge University Press, 2009.

Halliday, Fred. "The Politics of the Umma: States and Communities in Islamic Movements." *Mediterranean Politics* 7, no. 3 (2002): 20–41.

Hamoudi, Haider Ala. "'Lone Wolf' Terrorism and the Classical Jihad: On the Contingencies of Violent Islamic Extremism." *Florida International University Law Review* 11, no. 1 (2015): 19–38.

Hanioğlu, M. Şükrü *A Brief History of the Late Ottoman Empire.* Princeton, NJ: Princeton University Press, 2010.

Harrod, Andrew. "Turkey PM Pushes International Blasphemy Laws." *Frontpage Mag.* September 18, 2012. http://www.frontpagemag.com/fpm/144562 /turkey-pm-pushes-international-blasphemy-laws-andrew-harrod.

Hashemi, Kamran. *Religious Legal Traditions, International Human Rights Law and Muslim States.* Boston: Martinus Nijhoff Publishers, 2008.

Hashemi, Nader, and Danny Postel. *Sectarianization: Mapping the New Politics of the Middle East.* New York: Oxford University Press, 2017.

Hassan, Riaz. *Faithlines: Muslim Conceptions of Islam and Society.* Karachi: Oxford University Press, 2002.

Hefner, Robert W. *Civil Islam: Muslims and Democratization in Indonesia.* Princeton, NJ: Princeton University Press, 2000.

———. *Shari'a Politics: Islamic Law and Society in the Modern World.* Bloomington: Indiana University Press, 2011.

Hourani, Albert Habib. *Arabic Thought in the Liberal Age: 1798–1939*. London: Oxford University Press, 1983.

Houtsma, M. T. *E. J. Brill's First Encyclopaedia of Islam, 1913–1936*. Leiden: E. J. Brill, 1987.

Hudson, Charles. *The Southeastern Indians*. Knoxville: University of Tennessee Press, 1976.

Human Rights Watch. "Policing Morality: Abuses in the Application of Shari'a in Aceh, Indonesia." Human Rights Watch. 2010. https://www.hrw.org/sites/default/files/reports/indonesia1210WebVersionToPost.pdf.

Huntingon, Samuel P. *The Clash of Civilizations and the Remaking of the World Order.* New York: Simon & Schuster, 1998.

Husry, Khaldun Sati. *Origins of Modern Arab Political Thought*. Delmar, NY: Caravan Books, 1980.

Hussein, Walaa. "Al-Azhar Rewrites Curricula." *Al-Monitor*. June 29, 2015. http://www.al-monitor.com/pulse/originals/2015/06/egypt-azhar-curriculim-revise-religious-discourse-extremism.html.

Ibrahim, Ayman S. "So ISIS Is Not Infidel—Are Christians?" *First Things*. December 16, 2014. https://www.firstthings.com/web-exclusives/2014/12/so-isis-is-not-infidelare-christians.

Ichwan, M. N. "Official Ulema and the Politics of Re-Islamization: The Majelis Permusyawaratan Ulama, Sharilhringatization and Contested Authority in Post–New Order Aceh." *Journal of Islamic Studies* 22, no. 2 (2011): 183–214.

"Ikhtilaf." *Encyclopaedia Britannica*. July 20, 1998. https://www.britannica.com/topic/ikhtilaf.

Imara, Muhammad. *Jamal al-Din al-Afghani: al-Amal al-Kamila*. 2nd ed. 2 vols. Beirut: al-Mu'assasa al-'Arabiyya lil-Dirasat wal-Nashr, 1972.

'Ināyat, Ḥamīd. *Modern Islamic Political Thought*. Austin: University of Texas Press, 1982.

"Indonesia: Controversial Education Bill Is Passed." EA Foundation. June 2003. http://www.ea.org.au/ea-family/Religious-Liberty/Indonesia-Controversial-education-bill-is-passed-1.

"Indonesia: Inter-religious Marriage." Law Library of Congress. July 2015. https://www.loc.gov/law/help/inter-religious-marriage/indonesia-inter-relgious-marriage.pdf.

"Indonesia 2014 International Religious Freedom Report." United States Department of State. Accessed December 22, 2016. http://www.state.gov/documents/organization/238510.pdf.

Isaac, Jeffrey C. "Analyzing Democracy." *Perspectives on Politics* 9, no. 2 (2011): 241–245.

Islamic State. "The Islamic State Is a True Imamah." In *The Return of Khilafah. Dabiq* 1 (Ramadan 1435): 26.

———. "Remaining and Expanding." *Dabiq* 5 (Muharram 1436): 8.

———. "Shari'ah Alone Will Rule Africa," *Dabiq* 8 (Jumada Al-Akhirah 1436): 20.

"Issa Rohou LAHI fils de l'imam de tous les imams, imam des deux lieux saints." Layene. Accessed January 5, 2017. http://www.layene.sn/new/l_francais/rohoulaye.php.

Jaffrelot, Christophe. "Refining the Moderation Thesis: Two Religious Parties and Indian Democracy: The Jana Sangh and the BJP Between Hindutva Radicalism and Coalition Politics." *Democratization* 20, no. 5 (2013): 876–894.

Jaggers, Keith, and Ted Robert Gurr. "Tracking Democracy's Third Wave with the Polity III Data." *Journal of Peace Research* 32, no. 4 (1995): 469–482.

Johansen, Baber. "Apostasy as Objective and Depersonalized Fact: Two Recent Egyptian Court Judgments." *Social Research* 70, no. 3 (2003): 687–710.

Johnston, David L. "Hassan al-Hudaybi and the Muslim Brotherhood: Can Islamic Fundamentalism Eschew the Islamic State?" *Comparative Islamic Studies* 3, no. 1 (2007): 39–56.

Joseph, Richard. "Prebendalism and Dysfunctionality in Nigeria." Brookings Institution. July 26, 2013. https://www.brookings.edu/opinions/prebendalism -and-dysfunctionality-in-nigeria.

Kaplan, Michael. "ISIS Not Islamic? John Kerry Calls Terror Group 'Apostates.'" *International Business Times.* February 3, 2016. http://www.ibtimes .com/isis-not-islamic-john-kerry-calls-terror-group-apostates-2291791.

Karpat, Kemal H. *The Politicization of Islam: Reconstructing Identity, State, Faith, and Community in the Late Ottoman State.* New York: Oxford University Press, 2001.

Kaymakcan, Recep, and Oddbjørn Leirvik. *Teaching for Tolerance in Muslim Majority Societies.* Istanbul: Centre for Values Education (DEM) Press, 2007.

Keddie, N. R. *Sayyid Jamāl ad-Dīn "al-Afghānī": A Political Biography.* Berkeley: University of California Press, 1972.

Kelas 10 bahasa Indonesia wahana pengetahuan. Jakarta: Kementerian Pendidikan dan Kebudayaan, 2013.

Kelas 10 pendidikan agama Islam dan budi pekerti. Jakarta: Kementerian Pendidikan dan Kebudayaan, 2014.

Kelas 12 buku siswa pendidikan agama Islam dan budi pekerti. Jakarta: Kementerian Pendidikan dan Kebudayaan, 2015.

Khalafallah, Haifaa G. *Rethinking Islamic Law: The Genesis and Evolution in the Islamic Legal Method and Structures.* Ann Arbor, MI: ProQuest, Inc., 1999.

Korkut, Senol. "The Diyanet of Turkey and Its Activities in Eurasia After the Cold War." *Acta Slavica Iaponica* 28 (2010): 117–139.

Kringelbach, H. N. "'Marrying Out' for Love: Women's Narratives of Polygyny and Alternative Marriage Choices in Contemporary Senegal." *African Studies Review* 59, no. 1 (2016): 155–174.

Kudsi-Zadeh, Albert. "Jamal al-Din al-Afghani: A Select List of Articles." *Middle Eastern Studies* 2, no. 1 (October 1965): 66–72.

Kutlu, Sönmez. "Avrasya coğrafyasında Kadim dini bilginin kaynakları ve yeniden üretilmesi sorunu." Paper presented at the Seventh European Innovation Council, Ankara, Turkey, 2008.

Laborde, Cécile. *La Confrérie layenne et les Lébou du Sénégal.* Bordeaux: Centre d'Étude d'Afrique Noire, Institut d'Études Politiques de Bordeaux, Universite Montesquieu-Bordeaux IV, 1995.

Laccino, Ludovica. "Egypt Writer Karam Saber Sentenced to Five Years in Jail for Atheist Book." *International Business Times.* June 5, 2014. http://www .ibtimes.co.uk/egypt-writer-karam-saber-sentenced-five-years-jail-atheist -book-1451453.

Laia, Kennial Caroline. "Rights Activists Lash Out at MUI's Anti-LGBT Fatwa." *Jakarta Globe.* March 15, 2015. http://jakartaglobe.beritasatu.com/news /rights-activists-lash-muis-anti-lgbt-fatwa.

Landau, Jacob M. *Parliaments and Parties in Egypt.* Tel-Aviv: Israel Publishing House, 1953.

Lapidus, Ira M. *A History of Islamic Societies.* Cambridge: Cambridge University Press, 1988.

Lauzière, Henri. *The Making of Salafism: Islamic Reform in the Twentieth Century.* New York: Columbia University Press, 2016.

Lee, Dwight E. "The Origins of Pan-Islamism." *American Historical Review* 47, no. 2 (1942): 278–287.

Leichtman, Mara A. "Revolution, Modernity and (Trans)National Shi'i Islam: Rethinking Religious Conversion in Senegal." *Journal of Religion in Africa* 39, no. 3 (2009): 319–351.

Levitsky, Steven, and Lucan Way. "The Rise of Competitive Authoritarianism." *Journal of Democracy* 13, no. 2 (2002): 51–65.

Lijphart, Arend. "Constitutional Design for Divided Societies." *Journal of Democracy* 15, no. 2 (2004): 96–109.

Lliteras, Susana Molins. "A Path to Integration: Senegalese Tijanis in Cape Town." *African Studies* 68, no. 2 (2009): 215–233.

l-Tarbiyah al-waṭanīyah: Miṣr wa-Dawruhā al-Haḍārī lil-ṣaff al-Awwal al-Thānawī. Cairo: Jumhūrīyat Miṣr al-'Arabīyah, Wizārat al-Tarbiyah wa-al-Ta'līm, Qiṭā' al-Kutub, 2002–2003.

Luciani, Giacomo. *The Arab State.* Berkeley: University of California Press, 1990.

MacIntyre, Alasdair C. *After Virtue: A Study in Moral Theory.* Notre Dame, IN: University of Notre Dame Press, 1984.

Mahmood, Saba. *Politics of Piety: The Islamic Revival and the Feminist Subject.* Princeton, NJ: Princeton University Press, 2005.

———. *Religious Difference in a Secular Age: A Minority Report.* Princeton, NJ: Princeton University Press, 2016.

Mané, Mamadou. "Les valeurs culturelles des Confréries musulmanes au Senegal." UNESCO. 2012. http://www.unesco.org/new/fileadmin/MULTIMEDIA /FIELD/Dakar/pdf/EtudeconfrériesSenegal4Dec2012.pdf.

Martin, Richard C., ed. *Encyclopedia of Islam and the Muslim World.* Farmington Hills: Gale, Cengage Learning, 2016.

Mashhour, Amira. "Islamic Law and Gender Equality: Could There Be a Common Ground? A Study of Divorce and Polygamy in Sharia Law and Contemporary Legislation in Tunisia and Egypt." *Human Rights Quarterly* 27, no. 2 (2005): 562–596.

Masud, Muhammad Khalid. *Shari'a Today: Essays on Contemporary Issues and Debates in Muslim Societies.* Islamabad: National Book Foundation, Iqbal International Institute for Research and Dialogue, 2013.

Matthee, Rudi. "Jamal al-Din al-Afghani and the Egyptian National Debate." *International Journal of Middle East Studies* 21, no. 2 (May 1989): 151–169.

Matthiesen, Toby. *The Other Saudis: Shiism, Dissent and Sectarianism.* Cambridge: Cambridge University Press, 2014.

M'Baye, Babacar. "The Origins of Senegalese Homophobia: Discourses on Homosexuals and Transgender People in Colonial and Postcolonial Senegal." *African Studies Review* 56, no. 2 (2013): 109–128.

Mecham, Quinn, and Julie Chernov-Hwang. *Islamist Parties and Political Normalization in the Muslim World.* Philadelphia: University of Pennsylvania Press, 2014.

Meijer, Roel. *Global Salafism: Islam's New Religious Movement.* New York: Columbia University Press, 2009.

Menchik, Jeremy. *Islam and Democracy in Indonesia: Tolerance Without Liberalism.* New York: Cambridge University Press, 2016.

Metcalf, Barbara Daly. *Islamic Revival in British India: Deoband, 1860–1900.* Princeton, NJ: Princeton University Press, 1982.

"Millet." *Encyclopaedia Britannica.* July 20, 1998. https://www.britannica.com /topic/millet-religious-group.

Mir, Mustansir. "Elephants, Birds of Prey, and Heaps of Pebbles: Farāhī's Interpretation of Sūrat al-Fïl." *Journal of Qur'anic Studies* 7, no. 1 (2005): 33–47.

Mirsepassi, Ali, and Tadd Fernee. *Islam, Democracy and Cosmopolitanism: At Home and in the World.* New York: Cambridge University Press, 2016.

Mitchell, Richard P. *The Society of the Muslim Brothers.* New York: Oxford University Press, 1993.

"MK: Laki-Laki." Hukumonline.com. February 17, 2012. http://www.hukumonline.com/berita/baca/lt4f3e288a2589c/mk-lakilaki-buaya-darat-wajib-bertanggung-jawab.

Moaddel, Mansoor. *Jordanian Exceptionalism: A Comparative Analysis of State-Religion Relationships in Egypt, Iran, Jordan, and Syria.* New York: Palgrave MacMillan, 2002.

Mourad, Mahmoud. "Egyptian Poet Goes on Trial Accused of Contempt of Islam." Reuters. January 28, 2015. http://www.reuters.com/article/us-egypt-courts-poet-idUSKBN0L121M20150128.

Moustafa, Tamir. "Conflict and Cooperation Between the State and Religious Institutions in Contemporary Egypt." *International Journal of Middle East Studies* 32, no. 1 (2000): 3–22.

———. "The Islamist Trend in Egyptian Law." Simons Papers in Security and Development 2, School for International Studies, Simon Fraser University, Vancouver, May 2010.

Mufti, Malik. *Sovereign Creations: Pan-Arabism and Political Order in Syria and Iraq.* Ithaca, NY: Cornell University Press, 1996.

Muhammed, Abu al-Saud, and Muhammed Kamel. "Parliamentarian Country and Shar'ia Is the Base of Legislation." *Al-Masry al-Youm.* December 3, 2012. http://www.almasryalyoum.com/news/details/166153.

Naji, Abu Bakr. *The Management of Savagery: The Most Critical Stage Through Which the Umma Will Pass.* Translated by William McCants. Cambridge, MA: John M. Olin Institute for Strategic Studies at Harvard University, 2006.

Nasr, Vali Reza. *Islamic Leviathan: Islam and the Making of State Power.* Oxford: Oxford University Press, 2001.

"National Profiles: Indonesia. Public Opinion." Association of Religious Data Archives. Accessed January 7, 2017. http://www.thearda.com/internationalData/countries/Country_109_5.asp.

"A New Bin Laden Speech." Middle East Media Research Institute. July 18, 2003. https://www.memri.org/reports/new-bin-laden-speech.

"The 1945 Constitution of the Republic of Indonesia." World Intellectual Property Organization (WIPO). Accessed December 23, 2016. http://www.wipo.int/edocs/lexdocs/laws/en/id/id048en.pdf.

O'Kane, Joseph P. "Islam in the New Egyptian Constitution: Some Discussions in *al-Ahram.*" *Middle East Journal* 26 (spring 1972): 137–148.

Otto, Ben, and Sara Schonhardt. "Islamic Political Parties Make a Comeback in Indonesian Election." *Wall Street Journal.* April 10, 2014. http://www.wsj.com/articles/SB10001424052702303873604579493311138076926.

Ozlem, Altan. "Turkey: Sanctifying a Secular State." In *Textbooks and Religion in the Middle East,* edited by Eleanor Abdella Doumato and Gregory Starret, 197–214. Boulder, CO: Lynne Rienner Publishers, 2007.

Parker, Ron. "The Senegal-Mauritania Conflict of 1989: A Fragile Equilibrium." *Journal of Modern African Studies* 21 (1991): 155–171.

Parlina, Ina. "Constitutional Court Rejects Blasphemy Review Request." *Jakarta Post.* September 20, 2013. http://www.thejakartapost.com/news/2013/09/20/constitutional-court-rejects-blasphemy-review-request.html.

"Partai Kebangkitan Bangsa (PKB)." Pemilu Indonesia. Accessed December 23, 2016. http://www.pemilu.com/pkb.

Pasha, Mustapha Kamal. "Nihilism and the Otherness of Islam." *Millennium: Journal of International Studies* 42, no. 1 (2013): 177–197.

"Personal Status Laws in Egypt: FAQ." Promotion of Women's Rights Project. Accessed January 3, 2017. http://www2.gtz.de/dokumente/bib-2010/gtz2010 -0139en-faq-personal-status-law-egypt.pdf.

Peters, Rudolph. *Jihad in Classical and Modern Islam: A Reader.* Princeton, NJ: Markus Wiener, 1996.

Pew Research Center. "Indonesia." Global Indicators Database. Accessed January 7, 2017. http://www.pewglobal.org/database/indicator/38/country/101.

———. "Senegal." Global Indicators Database. Accessed January 7, 2017. http://www.pewglobal.org/database/indicator/43/country/194.

Pink, Johana. "Nationalism, Religion and the Muslim-Christian Relationship: Teaching Ethics and Values in Egyptian Schools." Center for Studies on New Religions. 2004. www.cesnur.org/2003/vil2003_pink.html.

Piscatori, James P. *Islam in a World of Nation-States.* Cambridge: Cambridge University Press, 1986.

Polat, Necati. "Regime Change in Turkey." *International Politics* 50, no. 3 (2013): 435–454.

"Presentation de l'Association Nurul Mahdi." Layene. Accessed January 5, 2017. http://www.layene.sn/new/nurul_mahdi.php.

"The Principles of the Muslim Brotherhood." Ikhwan Web. February 1, 2010. http://www.ikhwanweb.com/article.php?id=813.

"Prinsip Dasar." Partai Amanat Nasional. Accessed December 23, 2016. http://www.pan.or.id/prinsip-dasar.

Qutb, Sayyid. *Ma'alim fi al-Tariq.* Cairo: Kazi Publications, Egypt, 1964.

———. *Milestones.* Translated by S. Badrul Hasan. Karachi: International Islamic Publishers, 1981.

Raghavan, Sudarsan. "In New Egyptian Textbooks, It's like the Revolution Didn't Happen." *Washington Post.* April 23, 2016. https://www.washington post.com/world/middle_east/in-new-egyptian-textbooks-its-like-the-revolution -didnt-happen/2016/04/23/846ab2f0-f82e-11e5–958d-d038dac6e718_story .html.

Ramadan, Rajab. "Saint Mark's Coptic Orthodox Cathedral Supports the Civil State and the Islamic Shar'ia." *Al-Masry al-Youm.* July 4, 2012. http://www .almasryalyoum.com/news/details/193451.

Reiser, Stewart. "Pan-Arabism Revisited." *Middle East Journal* 37, no. 2 (1983): 218–233.

"Religious Freedom and Apostasy." Islamopedia Online. Accessed August 10, 2016. http://www.Islamopediaonline.org/country-profile/egypt/religious-minorities -and-freedom-religion/religious-freedom-and-apostasy?page=253.

Riedler, Florian. *Opposition and Legitimacy in the Ottoman Empire: Conspiracies and Political Cultures.* Abingdon, UK: Routledge, 2011.

Rizvi, Sayyid Muhammad. *Muhibb al-Din al-Khatib: A Portrait of a Salafi-Arabist (1886–1969).* Master's thesis, Simon Fraser University, 1991.

Rokkan, Stein. "Dimensions of State Formation and Nation-Building: A Possible Paradigm for Research on Variations Within Europe." In *The Formation of National States in Western Europe,* edited by Charles Tilly, 562–600. Princeton, NJ: Princeton University Press, 1975.

Sadaqah, Hussam, Muhammed Ghareeb, and Mahmoud Ramzi. "Egypt Is a Civil Country and the Higher Constitutional Court Interprets the Shar'ia." *Al-Masry al-Youm.* November 21, 2013. http://www.almasryalyoum.com/news /details/344590.

Saddam 17 Jul Revolution Anniversary Speech. Daily Report. Near East & South Asia, FBIS-NES-94-137, July 18, 1994, 34–40.

Saddam Address Ba'th Party Congress 5 October. Daily Report. Near East & South Asia, FBIS-NES-92-195, October 7, 1992, 20–32.

Saddam Husayn Anniversary Speech. Daily Report. Near East & South Asia, FBIS-NES-93-011, January 19, 1993, 32–40.

Saddam Speaks on Allies' Ground Attack 24 Feb. Daily Report. Near East & South Asia, FBIS-NES-91037, February 25, 1991, 33–34.

Saddam Speech 20 Jan (After Aerial Bombardment on 1991-01-17). Daily Report. Near East & South Asia, FBIS-NES-91-014, January 1–22, 1991.

Saeed, Javaid. *Islam and Modernization: A Comparative Analysis of Pakistan, Egypt, and Turkey.* Westport, CT: Praeger Publishers, 1994.

Salamon, Ahmad. *Reform of Al-Azhar in the 20th Century.* PhD diss. History department, New York University, 1980.

Sayyid, Bobby. *Islamism as Philosophy: Decolonial Horizons.* London: Bloomsbury Academic, 2017.

"Sayyid Quṭb." *Encyclopaedia Britannica.* April 2014. https://www.britannica.com/biography/Sayyid-Qutb.

"School's In." *Economist.* December 13, 2014. http://www.economist.com/news/asia/21636098-indonesias-schools-are-lousy-new-administration-wants-fix-them-schools.

Schwedler, Jillian. *Faith in Moderation: Islamist Parties in Jordan and Yemen.* Cambridge: Cambridge University Press, 2007.

"Senegal: Growing Intolerance Towards Gay Men." *HIV AIDS Policy Law Review* 14, no. 1 (2009): 31.

Seventh Year, Second Semester Islamic Education Textbook, 2002–2003 school year.

Sfeir, George N. "The Abolition of Confessional Jurisdiction in Egypt: The Non-Muslim Courts." *Middle East Journal* 10, no. 3 (1956): 248–256.

Shavit, Uriya. *Scientific and Political Freedom in Islam.* London: Routledge, 2017.

Shaw, Stanford J., and Ezel Kural. *History of the Ottoman Empire and Modern Turkey.* Cambridge: Cambridge University Press, 1976.

Simanjuntak, Hotli. "'Qanun Jinayat' Becomes Official for All People in Aceh." *Jakarta Post.* October 23, 2015. http://www.thejakartapost.com/news/2015/10/23/qanun-jinayat-becomes-official-all-people-aceh.html.

"Sisi Calls for 'Religious Revolution' at Cairo's Islamic University." *Jerusalem Post.* May 31, 2015. http://www.jpost.com/Middle-East/Sisi-calls-for-religious-revolution-at-Cairos-Islamic-University-404583.

Skovgaard-Petersen, Jakob. *Defining Islam for the Egyptian State: Muftis and Fatwas of the Dār al-Iftāʾ.* Leiden: Brill, 1997.

SMA/MA/SMK/MAKs kelas 10 semester 2 sejarah Indonesia. Jakarta: Kementerian Pendidikan dan Kebudayaan, 2014.

SMA/MA/SMK/MAKs kelas 11 pendidikan agama Islam dan budi pekerti. Jakarta: Kementerian Pendidikan dan Kebudayaan, 2013.

SMA/MA/SMK/MAKs kelas 12 pendidikan agama Islam dan budi pekerti. Jakarta: Kementerian Pendidikan dan Kebudayaan, 2014.

Smith, Etienne. "Religious and Cultural Pluralism in Senegal: Accommodation Through 'Proportional Equidistance'?" In *Tolerance, Democracy, and Sufis in Senegal,* edited by Diouf Mamadou, 147–179. New York: Columbia University Press, 2013.

Smith, Roger M., and Clark D. Neher. *Southeast Asia: Documents of Political Development and Change.* Ithaca, NY: Cornell University Press, 1974.

SMP/KTs kelas 07 pendidikan agama Islam dan budi pekerti. Jakarta: Kementerian Pendidikan dan Kebudayaan, 2014.

SMP/KTs kelas 08 pendidikan agama Islam dan budi pekerti. Jakarta: Kementerian Pendidikan dan Kebudayaan, 2013.

SMP/KTs kelas 09 pendidikan agama Islam dan budi pekerti. Jakarta: Kementerian Pendidikan dan Kebudayaan, 2015.

Snow, David A., and Scott C. Byrd. "Ideology, Framing Processes, and Islamic Terrorist Movements." *Mobilization* 12, no. 2 (2007): 119–136.

Somer, Murat. "Conquering Versus Democratizing the State: Political Islamists and Fourth Wave Democratization in Turkey and Tunisia." *Democratization* 24, no. 6 (2017): 1–19.

Starrett, Gregory. *Putting Islam to Work: Education, Politics, and Religious Transformation in Egypt.* Berkeley: University of California Press, 1998.

Stepan, Alfred. "Stateness, Democracy, and Respect: Senegal in Comparative Perspective." In *Tolerance, Democracy, and Sufis in Senegal,* edited by Mamadou Diouf, 216. New York: Columbia University Press, 2013.

Stepan, Alfred C., Juan J. Linz, and Yogendra Yadav. *Crafting State-Nations: India and Other Multinational Democracies.* Baltimore: Johns Hopkins University Press, 2011.

Sutton, Phillip, and Stephen Vertigans. "Islamic 'New Social Movements'? Radical Islam, al-Qa'ida and Social Movement Theory." *Mobilization* 11, no. 1 (2006): 101–115.

Swanson, Guy. *Religion and Regime: A Sociological Account of the Reformation.* Ann Arbor: University of Michigan Press, 1967.

Syadzali, Munawir. *Islam and the Governmental System: Teachings, History, and Reflections.* Jakarta: University of Indonesia Press, 1990.

Tabah Foundation. "Muslim Millennial Attitudes on Religion and Religious Leadership." Futures Initiative at Tabah Foundation. 2016. http://mmgsurvey .tabahfoundation.org/downloads/mmgsurvey_full_En_web.pdf.

Taizir, Aswita. *Muhammad Abduh and the Reformation of Islamic Law.* PhD diss., McGill University, 1994.

Tambiah, Stanley Jeyaraja. *Buddhism Betrayed? Religion, Politics, and Violence in Sri Lanka.* Chicago: University of Chicago Press, 1992.

Tamimi, Azzam S. "Democracy in Islamic Political Thought." Ireland On-line. Accessed January 4, 2017. http://ireland.iol.ie/~afifi/Articles/democracy .htm.

Tanuwidjaja, Sunny. "Political Islam and Islamic Parties in Indonesia: Critically Assessing the Evidence of Islam's Political Decline." *Contemporary Southeast Asia* 32, no. 1 (2010): 29–49.

Taylor, Charles. *The Secular Age.* Cambridge, MA: Harvard University Press, 2007.

"Tentang Pan." Partai Amanat Nasional. Accessed December 23, 2016. http:// www.pan.or.id/tentang-pan.

Tenth Year, Second Semester Islamic Education Textbook, 2002–2003 school year.

Text of Saddam Husayn 27 Apr Al-Anba Interview. Daily Report. Middle East & Africa, FBIS-MEA-83-085, May 2, 1983.

Tharoor, Ishaan. "Why Turkey's President Wants to Revive the Language of the Ottoman Empire." *Washington Post.* December 12, 2014. https://www .washingtonpost.com/news/worldviews/wp/2014/12/12/why-turkeys-president -wants-to-revive-the-language-of-the-ottoman-empire.

Thiam, Rokhaya. "Étude sur les associations et réseaux de femmes religieuses au Sénégal." Internal Report, *World Faiths Development Dialogue.* 2014.

Toronto, James A., and Muhammad S. Eissa. "Egypt: Promoting Tolerance, Defending Against Islamism." In *Teaching Islam: Textbooks and Religion in the Middle East,* edited by Eleanor Abdella Doumato and Gregory Starrett. London: Lynne Rienner Publishers, 2007.

Toth, James. *Sayyid Qutb: The Life and Legacy of a Radical Islamic Intellectual.* Oxford: Oxford University Press, 2013.

Tremblay, Pinar. "How Erdogan Used the Power of the Mosques Against Coup Attempt." *Al-Monitor.* July 25, 2016. http://www.al-monitor.com/pulse /originals/2016/07/turkey-coup-attempt-erdogan-mosques.html.

———. "Turkish Alevis Refuse 'Sunnification." *Al-Monitor.* September 11, 2013. http://www.al-monitor.com/pulse/originals/2013/09/turkey-shiites-alevis -sunnification-gulen-mosque-cemevi.html.

"Turkey." End Blasphemy Laws. Accessed January 3, 2017. http://end -blasphemy-laws.org/countries/europe/turkey.

"Turkish-Armenian Scribe Sentenced to Thirteen Months for Blasphemy in Blog Post." *Hurriyet News Daily.* May 22, 2013. http://www.hurriyetdailynews .com/turkish-armenian-scribe-sentenced-to-13-months-for-blasphemy-in -blog-post-.aspx?pageID=238&nID=47371&NewsCatID=341.

United States Commission on International Religious Freedom (USCIRF). "USCIRF 2013 Annual Report: Indonesia." USCIRF. 2013. http://www .uscirf.gov/sites/default/files/resources/Indonesia%202013.pdf.

Van der Veer, Peter, and Hartmut Lehmann. *Nation and Religion: Perspectives on Europe and Asia.* Princeton, NJ: Princeton University Press, 1999.

Vela, Justin. "'Abortions Are like Air Strikes on Civilians': Turkish PM Recep Tayyip Erdogan's Rant Sparks Women's Rage." *Independent.* May 30, 2012. http://www.independent.co.uk/life-style/health-and-families/health -news/abortions-are-like-air-strikes-on-civilians-turkish-pm-recep-tayyip -erdogans-rant-sparks-womens-rage-7800939.html.

Villalón, Leonardo A. "Generational Changes, Political Stagnation, and the Evolving Dynamics of Religion and Politics in Senegal." *Africa Today* 46, no. 3/4 (1999): 129–147.

———. *Islamic Society and State Power in Senegal: Disciples and Citizens in Fatick.* Cambridge: Cambridge University Press, 2006.

Vince, Natalya. "Colonial and Post-colonial Identities: Women Veterans of the 'Battle of Algiers.'" *French History and Civilization* 2 (2009): 153–168.

"Visi dan Misi PPP." Partai Persatuan Pembangunan. September 20, 2016. http://ppp.or.id/page/visi-dan-misi-ppp.html.

Walsh, Declan. "Egypt's President Turns to Religion to Bolster His Authority." *New York Times.* January 9, 2016. https://www.nytimes.com/2016/01/10 /world/middleeast/egypt-abdel-fattah-el-sisi-islam.html.

Weiss, Max. *In the Shadow of Sectarianism: Law, Shi'ism and the Making of Modern Lebanon.* Cambridge, MA: Harvard University Press, 2010.

White, Ben. *The Emergence of Minorities in the Middle East: The Politics of Community in French Mandate Syria.* Edinburgh: Edinburgh University Press, 2012.

Wickham, Carrie Rosefsky. *The Muslim Brotherhood: Evolution of an Islamist Movement.* Princeton, NJ: Princeton University Press, 2015.

Wiktorowicz, Quintan. "Civil Society as Social Control: State Power in Jordan." *Comparative Politics* 33, no. 1 (2000): 43–61.

Williams, Rhys H. "Religion as Political Resource: Culture or Ideology?" *Journal for the Scientific Study of Religion* 35, no. 4 (1996): 368–378.

Woischnik, Jan, and Philipp Muller. "Islamic Parties and Democracy in Indonesia." Konrad Adenauer Stiftung. 2013. http://www.kas.de/wf/doc/kas_35685 -544-2-30.pdf?131015120646.

Wood, Graeme. "What ISIS Really Wants." *Atlantic.* March 2015. http:// www.theatlantic.com/features/archive/2015/02/what-isis-really-wants /384980.

Wood, Leonard G. H. *Reception of European Law, Origins of Islamic Legal Revivalism, and Foundations of Transformations in Islamic Legal Thought in Egypt, 1875–1960.* PhD diss., Harvard University, 2011.

"World Islamic Front Statement Urging Jihad Against Jews and Crusaders." Federation of American Scientists. Accessed January 9, 2017. https://fas.org/irp/world/para/docs/980223-fatwa.htm.

"World Values Survey Database." World Values Survey. Accessed January 7, 2017. http://www.worldvaluessurvey.org/WVSOnline.jsp.

Wormald, Benjamin. "The World's Muslims: Religion, Politics and Society." Pew Research Center's Religion and Public Life Project. April 30, 2013. http://www.pewforum.org/2013/04/30/the-worlds-muslims-religion-politics-society-overview.

Wright, Robin. "Inside the Mind of Hezbollah." *Washington Post*. July 16, 2006. http://www.washingtonpost.com/wp-dyn/content/article/2006/07/14/AR2006071401401.html.

Wright, Zakariya. "Al-Hajj Malik Sy." Tariqa Tijaniyya. 2016. http://www.tijani.org/al-hajj-malik-sy.

Yavuz, M. Hakan. *Islamic Political Identity in Turkey*. Oxford: Oxford University Press, 2003.

Yili idare faaliyet raporu. Ankara: Başbakanlık Aile ve Sosyal Araştırmalar Genel Müdürlüğü, 2009.

Yosephine, Liza. "Komnas HAM Slams Vilification of LGBT by Officials." *Jakarta Post*. February 5, 2016. http://www.thejakartapost.com/news/2016/02/05/komnas-ham-slams-vilification-lgbt-officials.html.

Zaman, Muhammad Qasim. "Religious Education and the Rhetoric of Reform: The Madrasa in British India and Pakistan." *Comparative Studies in Society and History* 41, no. 2 (1999): 294–323.

Zollner, Barbara H. E. *The Muslim Brotherhood: Hasan al-Hudaybi and Ideology*. London: Routledge, 2009.

Zubaida, Sami. "Islam and Nationalism: Continuities and Contradictions." *Nations and Nationalism* 10, no. 4 (2004): 407–420.

Index

Muslim Millennial Attitudes Survey, 193–194

Nahdlatul Ulama (NU; Indonesia), 112, 115, 129, 140, 147(n15)
Naji, Abu Bakr, 176–177, 185
Naoot, Fatima, 83
Napoleonic code, 42–43
Nasrallah, Hassan, 177
Nasser, Gamal Abdel, 68, 162–163
nation building: inculcating radical transnational movements, 8–9; Ottoman constitution as model for, 79–80, 105(n81); society-state-religion nexus, 63–64; Young Turk Movement, 55(n13)
National Awakening Party (PKB; Indonesia), 140–141
National Courts (Egypt), 43–44
National Mandate Party (PAN; Indonesia), 140
nationalism, 68–71, 86; civil Muslim nationalism in Senegal and Indonesia, 110; convergence of individual and national identities, 15–16; global reach of Islam, 161–162; Islam as defining feature of national uniqueness, 75–78; Islam as political culture, 64–65; Islam as religious nationalism, 2; linking political Islam with, 6–7; religion in nationhood, 13–21; Senegal's laïcité and neutrality, 120–125
nation-state: absorption of Islam into state institutions, 68–71; adapting Islamic concepts to the state system, 46–48; changing nature of religious communities within a secular state, 5; compatibility with Islamic tradition, 2; consequences of state-Islam fusion, 86–96; defining civil religion, 109–110; homogenization of culture and religion after the Ottoman Empire, 64–65; national identities in Muslim countries, 16–18; nationalization of religion, 67–79; objectives and founding principles of the Muslim Brotherhood, 162–163; political power and, 16; sharia as state law by Islamists and Ulemas, 48–54; state-centered analysis of religious mobilization, 5–6; territorialization of Islamic belonging, 14–15;

transfer of religious authority over legal matters, 45–46; *ummah* as nation of Muslims, 166–172. *See also* democracy
Native Courts (Egypt), 42–44
Natsir, Mohammad, 111
neo-Sufis, 167
Netherlands: religion in nationhood, 13
New Order (Indonesia), 33–34, 110–111, 129
news media: Abduh's advocacy for educational reform, 30; Abduh's journalism, 57(n53); al-Afghani's Protestant-type reform and, 25–26
Niassènes (Senegal), 122–123
Nisanyan, Sevan, 85
nizammiyyah courts, 43, 60(n137)
non-Muslims. *See* Christianity and Christian populations; Coptic Christians (Egypt)

Omarien community (Senegal), 122
On Education (Spencer), 30
organic ideology, 166–167
orientalization of Islamic thinking: Abduh's reforms, 26–32; al-Afghani and the Protestant reform model, 25–26; *taqlid* and progressiveness, 22–24
Ottoman Empire: Abdulhamid II's reforms, 105(n72); as constitutional model for emergent states, 79–80, 105(n81); disintegration and restructuring of social order, 14; *mekteb* education practices, 34–35; *millet* system, 5, 10(n17); Muhammad Ali's modernization, 59(n103); Native Courts, 43; political and religious reforms following, 16–17; politicization of *ummah,* 166, 169; revivalist movements, 166–167; Turkey's religious and historical curricula, 77–78

Pakistan: civil punishments under sharia law, 81
pan-Arabism: Islam as defining feature of national uniqueness in Egypt, 75; nationalist discourse, 65; objectives of, 18
Pancasila Agreement, 110, 139, 147(n16)

About the Book

The debate continues unabated: Is political Islam decipherable through the tenets of the Islamic tradition—or is it a tool of secular actors who shrewdly misuse religious references? Is it an expression of modernity, or a return to the past? Eschewing these dichotomies, Jocelyne Cesari demystifies the continuous process of interaction between secular and religious actors and institutions that is at the core of political mobilization in the name of Islam.

Cesari traces the origins of political Islam to the inception of the modern nation-state, revealing the decisive role of secular nationalist rulers in its creation. In the process, she puts to rest the myth that there has been a lack of modernization in the Muslim world—and shows how that myth has proven dangerous. Ranging from Senegal to Egypt, from Indonesia to Iraq, her analysis provides a much needed corrective to the "conventional wisdom."

Jocelyne Cesari is professor of religion and politics at the University of Birmingham; senior research fellow at Georgetown University's Berkley Center for Religion, Peace, and World Affairs; and professorial fellow at the Australian Catholic University.